Reconstructing Aesthetics

Reconstructing Aesthetics

Writings of the Budapest School

EDITED BY

Agnes Heller
and
Ferenc Fehér

Basil Blackwell

BH
41
R26
1986
cop. 2

First published 1986

Basil Blackwell Ltd
108 Cowley Road, Oxford OX4 1JF, UK

Basil Blackwell Inc.
432 Park Avenue South, Suite 1505,
New York, NY 10016, USA

British Library Cataloguing in Publication Data

Reconstructing aesthetics : writings of the Budapest school.
  1. Aesthetics   2. Communist aesthetics
  I. Heller, Agnes   II. Fehér, Ferenc
  700'.1   BH39
  ISBN 0-631-14658-X

Library of Congress Cataloging in Publication Data
Main entry under title:

Reconstructing aesthetics.

  Includes index.
  1. Communist aesthetics—Addresses, essays, lectures.
2. Lukács, György, 1885-1971—Addresses, essays,
lectures. I. Heller, Agnes.   II. Fehér, Ferenc,
1933—   .
BH41.R26 1986   700'.1   85—22894
ISBN 0-631-14658-X

Typeset by Pioneer, Perthshire
Printed in Great Britain by TJ Press Ltd, Padstow, Cornwall

Contents

Acknowledgements   vii

1   The Necessity and the Irreformability of Aesthetics
FERENC FEHÉR and AGNES HELLER   1

2   Is the Novel Problematic? A Contribution to the Theory
of the Novel
FERENC FEHÉR   23

3   What is Beyond Art? On the Theories of Post-Modernity
FERENC FEHÉR   60

4   Mass Culture
SÁNDOR RADNÓTI
(translated by Ferenc Fehér and John Fekete)   77

5   On the Drama of Euripides
G. M. TAMÁS
(translated by Ferenc Fehér)   103

6   Aesthetic Judgement and the World View in Painting
MIHÁLY VAJDA
(translated by John Fekete)   119

7   Don Giovanni
GÉZA FODOR
(translated by Thomas Sail)   150

List of Contributors   248

Index   251

Acknowledgements

The editors and the publishers are grateful to the following for permission to reproduce articles as chapters of this book: the editors of the journal *Philosophical Forum*, for chapter 1 'The Necessity and the Irreformability of Aesthetics' by Ferenc Fehér and Agnes Heller; Telos Press Ltd, St Louis, Missouri, USA, publishers of the journal *Telos*, for chapter 2 'Is the Novel Problematic? A Contribution to the Theory of the Novel' by Ferenc Fehér, and chapter 4 'Mass Culture' by Sándor Radnóti; the editorial board of the journal *Thesis Eleven*, Phillip Institute of Technology, Bundoora, Australia, for chapter 3 'What is Beyond Art? On the Theories of Post-Modernity' by Ferenc Fehér.

The editors wish to express their special appreciation to Professor John Fekete for his contribution to the volume.

1

The Necessity and the Irreformability of Aesthetics

FERENC FEHÉR AND AGNES HELLER

I

Aesthetics as an independent philosophical discipline is the product of bourgeois society. This sentence does not maintain either the nonsensical thesis that philosophers prior to bourgeois society did not meditate upon the existence and nature of art, of the 'aesthetic', of the 'aesthetic sphere', nor does it deny that from Plotinus to the various Christian ontologies there existed systems of thought which, departing from different premises, characterized the world after the fashion of the aesthetic, which created a quasi-aesthetics out of ontology and thereby, we may say, produced a philosophical aesthetics as well. Aesthetics, however, as a relatively separate part of a philosophical system, which is unimaginable without the whole (the system) is a child of bourgeois society, and at the same time its existence is tied to the recognition that bourgeois society *in statu nascendi* is essentially problematic. Thus we have circumscribed the period of its birth. It is the fermenting crisis of the mid-eighteenth century that brings forth its first representative *oeuvres*; while the age of the revolution, its conclusion and the subsequent process of intellectual summarization complete the formula.

The first among the factors which 'provoked' the unfolding of 'separate' aesthetics as a specialized discipline of philosophy, was the emergence of a particular activity oriented towards beauty, and its objectification. This activity has an independent function, that is, it is not a by-product of other types of activities, not a mediating vehicle of various ideologies, not a maid-servant of theology and religious belief, and not an articulation of communal self-consciousness, but independent of all these (though perhaps expressive of some of them), it is a self-reliant activity.

Here, of course, two periods have to be distinguished. In the first, and, chronologically earlier period the detachment of all 'high cultures' from all types of everyday and productive activities, and the separation of the artist, the 'specialized artisan' (even if a highly respected one) from the other social strata is simultaneous with or, more precisely, is a part of, the general development of civilization.

The second is actually the period of the problem under discussion here and it involves the universalization of bourgeois activities based on the predominance of purposive rationality. In a certain sense this age is the result of a development in which 'production according to the measure of beauty' — in Marx's opinion a fundamental potentiality inherently possessed by productive man — not only becomes obsolete, but becomes definitely hostile to the spirit of the age, to the rational spirit of computable effectivity. This is the age of bourgeois society *sensu stricto* when from within high culture a special 'branch of production' must be yielded in order to compensate for beauty vanished from the world.

This functional independence of aesthetics can be evaluated negatively as it was done by Rousseau in *La Nouvelle Héloïse*, in an entirely utopian manner, intended to recapture the independence of aesthetics and to dissolve objectified aesthetics into the spontaneous homogeneity of popular life void of all mediations. The functionally independent activity may be defined through its connection with other activity functions and then directly inserted into a system, as was done by Kant, when he placed judgement, the 'organ' of aesthetical activity, as a mediator between cognitive and practical reason. Finally, a role of eminence may be bestowed upon aesthetics (more precisely, upon the historical period most adequate for human activities giving rise to the aesthetic sphere) within a general philosophy of history, as was the case with Hegel who conceived of Greek antiquity as the aesthetical epoch *sui generis*. In all these and many other cases the entry of aesthetics, and of aesthetic activity into the philosophical system (regardless whether the latter is elaborated with the strictest systematicality or is coherent only by 'being-in-itself') and its relative functional independence within the system is, in any case, the acknowledgment of the status quo; namely the manifestation of the fact that the objectification of beauty is in one way or the other a *separate type of activity*, which, exactly because of its being separated within the general system of activities, is in need of an explanation.

The second factor is the lack of the *sensus communis* based on 'organic communities' developing 'organically' in bourgeois society. We need not demonstrate in detail the existence of *sensus communis* with regard to the past as we could not do it within the given limits anyway. Suffice it to mention its antithesis; the modern bourgeois epoch that was boundlessly individualized and emancipated from the fetters of all canons and prescriptions, but which in this emancipation became the world-historical epoch of a reckless and supercilious subjective taste directly provoking by its 'vices' the appearance of philosophical aesthetics, as the arbiter in chaos.

The detachment of art from everyday life is the third factor in the emergence of philosophical aesthetics as a specialized branch. This means that the life-evidence of art vanishes and its specific social function has to be given a foundation; that is, the greatest paradox has to be provided with rational foundation. This paradox can be formulated in the following way. On the one hand, art and beauty are accepted with increasingly less tolerance in the system of needs of an atomized and specialized everyday life void of communities and of public activity. Art is *ipso facto* non-atomistic, but intersubjective, non-specialized and approachable without special skill or knowledge; and common since communicable. Through its communicability, art creates human contact; it constitutes an ideal community and a kind of public life. Yet, on the other hand, the need for art does exist, and exactly as a need for a 'counter-image' of a given everyday life, as the need for forlorn totality, for the forlorn public and collective character of life, and as the need for the cathartic experience: the 'elevation' above alienated everyday life. The attempts to solve this paradox constitute the recurrent fundamental motive of the philosophical aesthetics of the last two centuries.

In the theoretical foundation of the life-evidence of art, the main preoccupation of philosophical aesthetics, the attempt at the solution of the 'fundamental paradox' assumed new dimensions. The first of them is this. The circumstance has to be explained also theoretically, why the work of art, the activity oriented towards the objectification of beauty, assumes amidst the ever-increasing alienation of life-relations a specifically new function: that of the conservation of the 'species values' (*gattungsmässige Werte*). Of course, art as a depository of the 'species values' instead of life, a life becoming increasingly void of values is a highly problematic achievement of a new period of world history which has to justify even the *raison d'être* of such depositories by the help of philosophical aesthetics. This can be done only by multiplying the fundamental artistic paradox, as the conservation of the 'species values' is a very ambiguous function. On the one hand, depository is, *per definitionem*, a value preserver, on the other, a substitute for life. Hence the often cited Rilke postulate: *Du mußt dein Leben ändern*. The work of art, however, conserves (or at least it may conserve) the atomization of life just as well. The work itself is nothing but a 'beautiful appearance' which, with the passing of the effects, may just as well reintroduce us into life, feeding into the recipient the false feeling of assurance of having fulfilled his duty in the intermezzi of reception, as, according to the general postulate, it may guide him out of it, in the direction of a real transformation. That is why works of art (and the complementary philosophical-aesthetic theories) that radically negate modern bourgeois society declare war upon this claim of totality — again in an ambiguous way and reproducing the paradox. As a rule, the appearance of totality (the appearance-totality) can be denied only together with the *claim* of totality, more precisely in a way that this claim is transformed into a bare *ought*, with which the existing is pinned to the wall.

The second dimension of the multiplication of the fundamental paradox is the dilemma of the historicity versus validity of the work of art, so clearly exposed by the famous remark by Marx about the paragon-like character of the Homeric epic poems that it needs no more details.[1] Only one additional remark is necessary here: the *work of art* as one of the most important battlefields of the interpretation of the validity of values demonstrates in itself why it is precisely philosophical aesthetics that is developed by bourgeois society.

Finally, the universalization of commodity production creates a new situation for the work of art. The artistic reception obeys the regularities of the commodity realization, that is it is realized in terms of supply and demand, accidental to the structure of the work of art, and the fact or even the widespread character of the reception betrays but very little about its quality (its profundity, cathartic impact, its positive function or the function of a 'substitute-for-life', etc.). This circumstance requires in any case the philosophical interpretation of the impact of the work of art, as an act constituting the work of art.

II

Another paradox: just because the task of aesthetics is the foundation of the specific function of the aesthetical activity (creation) and reception, it has never been — from the mid-eighteenth century onwards continuously — 'pure' aesthetics any more (in the sense as the line leading from the *Poetics* of Aristotle to Boileau's catalogue of canonic regulations was constituted by 'pure' aesthetics, 'pure' ones, which articulated and systematized aesthetical judgements free of all kinds of sociological elements). Aesthetics has been from this time on a kind of general philosophy which evaluates and interprets the 'aesthetic sphere', the 'aesthetics', the 'objectified beauty', arts within this framework on the basis of general ideological and general theoretical preferences inferred from its own system. The answer to the question, 'What is the place of the aesthetic (of the objectified beauty, of art, of arts) in life, in history?' is inseparably connected with the response given to the second question: 'What is the place of the aesthetical in the philosophical system?'

With the exception of Kant, who took the standpoint that beauty — as opposed to knowledge and morality — has no metaphysics, only a critique (as a consequence, he formulated the complex of aesthetics exclusively from the viewpoint of reception), every significant aesthetics is at the same time a type of philosophy of history as well, from Hegel through Schelling to Kierkegaard and Lukács. Historiosophical foundation is no 'alien body' in the organism of these aesthetical systems, no 'prolegomena', which will be followed by proper explication. The historiosophical character, that is the recognition of the problematical character of the bourgeois present — to put the minimum formulation of the critical attitude — lays a foundation for the two constituents which were mentioned previously as the indispensable substantial-functional characteristics of modern aesthetical systems and those of modern works of art: historicity and the task of the defence of the species values.

It ensues from the above train of thought that aesthetics always 'locates' art (or the arts) and activity oriented towards their creation in the hierarchy of the type of activities and of objectifications, and this 'location' is the function of the relation of the thinker in question to bourgeois society. Does he consider it to be the untranscendable, even if deeply problematic, climax of human development, or is he striving for its real or mystical transcendence? The decision of the young Schelling — placing the aesthetical on the summit of philosophical hierarchy — was in close connection with his idea regarded by Marx as 'the sincere thought of his youth', which borrowed its power and panorganic ontological vehemence in the case of the philosopher, not at all committed politically, from the great experiment having taken place 'outside his philosophy' oriented to the transcendence of the bourgeois hierarchy, to establish an organic-collectivistic society. The decision of the aged Hegel, however, which places the realm of the aesthetic in his *Aesthetics* — in spite of his admiration felt for the work of art — at a very low level on the pilgrimage of the Absolute Spirit, is no simple repetition of the verdict of early Enlightenment, namely, that aesthetical perception is nothing but a *perception confuse*. This is the formulation of the lessons of a world-historical crisis situation: the age of Greek Antiquity, the proper period of the aesthetic, has irrevocably been passed, simultaneously its place in the hierarchy of the type of activities has been reduced to a lower rank. This 'degradation' of the aesthetic does not at all mean a lack of 'the aesthetical sense' with a gigantic thinker, but a decision of historiosophical character.

Here, however, a restriction and a distinction seem to be necessary. Every aesthetical theory of an historiosophical character locates the arts in the system of human activities, but not each of them creates a hierarchy within the system. The hierarchic or non-hierarchic character depends on the historiosophical perspective. In the present, a perspective which adopts the standpoint of the *Entzauberung der Welt*, of depriving the world, either in a bitter or in an affirmative manner, of its aesthetic magic, which takes sides — either in a disillusioned or in a technocratically self-complacent way — with the degradation of the aesthetic, is just as much imaginable (such a position has actually been formulated) as the opposite one, for which the choice, the hierarchy in itself, is a scandal. Hierarchy is, however, unavoidable for aesthetics within its own world. To its most general question: What is art, and what is it good for? various responses are given by the works of art as 'individuals' and as groups — that is, as genres. There is the obligation to choose among them, to create a hierarchy of the answers.

Therefore if aesthetics, as an historiosophical discipline, is faithful to its own principles, then it has to order the various arts into a kind of hierarchy according to its ever-given conception, consequently the aesthetical value of various arts, although not always in an explicit form, will depend on the philosophical system. Aesthetics of an historiosophical origin and character implies, then, not only the value-free and sociologistic statement and interpretation according to which certain periods are capable of creating works representing historically valid species values in certain branches of art for some reason or other, while other periods are — again because of pertinent concrete causes — incapable of creating such in the given branches of art. Nor does it merely catalogue the 'rival' branches these periods may develop. Genuinely historiosophically-spirited aesthetics is haughty enough, that is it is convinced enough of the value of its general ordering principles to create a hierarchy of arts and branches of arts only by creating a hierarchy of historical epochs. Lyric poetry occupied in Hegel's system the first rank of the hierarchy exactly because it is the infant of developed subjectivity, completed inwardness, namely, bourgeois society. And Hegel is — in spite of all the critical accents, despite his clear and bitter insight into this world — an evolutionist, who considers bourgeois society to be the proper place for the homecoming of the Absolute Spirit. Lukács, on the other hand, is indifferent towards lyric poetry — just as much in his youth as in his maturity and old age. He places higher the so-called objective genres: epic and drama, precisely because epic and drama are the manifestations of the crisis of a world situation, at the same time its victims as well, and they testify by their own fate the thesis which is one of the most important purposes of the philosophers: capitalism is a mortal enemy of the objectivations of culture. The same statement cannot be proclaimed — at least not so unambiguously, with not such an explicit evidence — in regard to lyric poetry and music. On the other hand, that is why Adorno proves to be so 'music-centred', so susceptible to lyric poetry, and so silent before the great 'objective' genres. He, who hated capitalism, did not acknowledge a cultural period worthy of developed individuality prior to it, and considered the attempts at surpassing the given world, 'the transcendence of bourgeois coolness', to be partly an elevated, partly a futile and dangerous illusion. Thus, he could find in these great genres of inwardness the intellectual and sensuous gratification rendered by this world just as much as the world's passionate critique. The elevated hierarchical position of lyric poetry and music was an historiosophical judgement of 'negative dialectics'.

Let us follow historiosophical aesthetics *ad absurdum*, up to the final point of its judgements and prejudices. Its hierarchic decision 'places' not only the various arts and branches of arts according to the premises of the philosophy of history: it is the given historiosophical principle that decides among artists and the turns of the philosophy of history often mean a change in the assessment of the concrete work of art. The negative example, Lessing's flat refusal of the *tragédie classique*, originates obviously from theoretical preconceptions. But the positive instance, that of the warmest predilection is of an historiosophical origin to a no lesser degree: Kierkegaard's verdict that anoints *Don Giovanni* the prince and paragon of all music is tied to the historiosophical — in his case it is more precise to say quasi-historiosophical — decision by which he 'locates' the aesthetic state in the hierarchy of life (giving thereby incidentally a radically reverse value accent to the conception of sensuality borrowed from Feuerbach) which was going to be the inspiring muse of the Wagnerian music. It is similarly an historiosophical preconception that drives Novalis to injustice in his critique of *Wilhelm Meister* (although injustice paired with an extraordinarily deep insight), it is the change of the historiosophical conception again that moves Friedrich Schlegel to change his previous assessment of this work. Finally, Lukács draws with a calm daring the final and untenably intolerant conclusion of a very ancient principle of historiosophically-spirited aesthetics. In his correspondence with Béla Balázs, the Hungarian poet and aesthetician of film, Lukács argues in the following manner: Since my philosophy of history has changed, Tolstoy has taken the place of Dostoyevsky, Fielding that of Sterne, Balzac that of Flaubert, in my assessment of art.

III

The theory of art of bourgeois society, philosophical aesthetics, can only be grasped in its *differentia specifica*, if it is compared with the theory of art of pre-capitalist periods. The first result of the comparison is the following: the theories of art of epochs antecedent to bourgeois society (which are not aesthetics in the above sense) mostly regarded artistic ability as a *special* capacity, but did not regard art (the 'aesthetical', the 'objectified beauty', etc.) as a domain or sphere of life to which special functions are assigned. Suffice it to mention the notion of *kalokagathia*: beauty is inherent in life, accordingly undifferentiated (and often undifferentiable) from greatness, from morality, from regulation of behaviour, from religious ideas, etc. As a consequence of this undifferentiated mixture there was no theoretical need to lay a philosophical foundation for art. This was just as much superfluous with regard to aesthetic judgement: aesthetic judgement was founded empirically by a generally existent and generally acknowledged *sensus communis*. Another paradox: the value judgements of an empirical *sensus communis*, unconscious of its own philosophical foundation and not needing it, were more profoundly based than the aesthetical choices of the modern age, made, as a rule, the more developed, the more 'organized' a society is, increasingly by 'connoisseurs'.

This statement, of course, cannot hold true without certain qualifications. First of all, today we generally do not accept the argumentation with which the art theory of a given age (most certainly expressing a *sensus communis*) laid the foundation for its judgements. Who would accept now as the cause of the difference in artistic quality the factor mentioned by Aristotle, namely, that superior people represent superior deeds, while inferior people represent inferior deeds? Second, the present recipient chooses and forms his hierarchy according to his own preferences of a *Weltanschauung*, namely the preferences of the *Weltanschauung* of his own age. Consequently he does not accept necessarily the value hierarchy of a once-existing *sensus communis*. To mention only the best-known counter-example: while admiration for Raphael reached its highest point of exaltation with such connoisseurs as Winckelmann and Goethe, the whole post-Romantic period is pre-Raphaelite, irrespective of how in fact Raphael's works were appreciated at this time. Finally, not even the very few available data demonstrate a monolithic uniformity within the once existing *sensus communis*. Euripides — so highly appreciated by Aristotle — was, for instance, very rarely awarded a first prize by the audience of the theatrical festivities in Athens. In the final analysis, that epoch approved (since it did not reject) the high opinion of Sophocles, who on the occasion of the death of his younger fellow playwright let the Chorus appear on stage in the veil of mourning. Later on, it accepted the judgement of Aristotle, but not even the most homogeneous *sensus communis* was exempt from certain inner conflicts, preparing thereby the 'dispersion', that is the infinite variety of the judgement of taste.

The decisive argument, however, with which we can argue for the infallibility, or rather for the durability of the judgements of the once-existing *sensus communis* is the circumstance, not to be underestimated, that in a very great number of instances even the hierarchy was accepted by posterity. The decisive argument here is the following: the value hierarchy formulated by the once-existing *sensus communis* may have been changed, but the domain of values never changed. All the painters who played a part in the hierarchy drawn up in Vasari's book, may be rearranged on the value scale, but *they* will be put on the list, no others. This statement is valid both in a positive and negative sense: everyone who had been taken into account by the *sensus communis* known to us finds adherents in an ever-given posterity; and no one, of whom we know that had been unanimously refused by his own age, has ever returned into the circulation of aesthetical experiences. (Vasari is therefore a unique source, since from him we can hear about the refusals too.) Of course, for the sake of logical completeness, the annihilation of works of art and that of documents recording artistic judgements, our fragmentary knowledge in regard to them should also be taken into account. Thus it is always conceivable that we may discover a work of art which was not appreciated by its own epoch, but which becomes highly esteemed in the present. Practically, however, all such discoveries verified at least the dominant canon in those cases when we have been left no recorded judgement about the concrete work of art in question.

The status of the concrete judgements incorporated in the aesthetics of the bourgeois age is entirely different. First of all, they are not the most superior, most 'refined' expressions of a universally dominant *sensus communis*, but the results of an individual ideological decision and of the postulates of a particular philosophical system. Second, as a consequence of the previously mentioned situation — and not because of the lack of capacities of the modern critic of art — modern philosophical aesthetics contains at least just as much 'fallacy' as 'truth', in the simple sense that during the process in which 'object content' became antiquated and 'reality content' emerged, a major part of their judgements have been refuted. The two concepts were invented and distinguished by Walter Benjamin. 'Object content' (*Sachgehalt*) is the dimension of meaning of the work of art, which adheres most closely to the present, grows out of it, 'tells' something to it. 'Reality content' (*Wahrheitsgehalt*) is more continuous, it is conceivable — at least in principle — in any given later epoch, independently of the concrete environment, it is connected with the general evolution of the human species. Of course, this evolution has a 'quasi-natural' being-in-itself only for a naturalistic epistemology. This is a *constructed* continuity created from the standpoint of the present. Therefore every judgement which discovers a certain 'reality content' beyond the 'object content' which is discovered in the work and which is bound up to the present of the genesis of the work, runs a general risk: there is no guarantee that the constructed continuity will be a continuity possessing real existence, that its discovered 'reality content' will enter the unbroken concatenation of artistic pleasure and will not simply remain the recipient's subjective and transitory judgement of taste.

Moreover, it is an exception if modern aesthetic judgement meets *universal acknowledgement*, if it is not a direct sign of opportunism. (Whoever would have thought anything like this in the case of Aristotle?) The second, more remarkable, more betraying circumstance is that the judgements — the positive judgements just as much as the negative ones — have to be explicated by the modern aesthetician. While either in its own age or in the present it would have been senseless to demand an explanation of why Vasari regarded Michelangelo as the greatest artist, why he appreciated Giorgione, later, however, regardless of whether we accept or refuse them, we can understand certain standpoints (to mention the negative ones first) only with an explanation. This is so, for example, in the case of Lessing's rejecting attitude towards Racine, Rousseau's annihilating opinion of the French garden or the *Misanthrope*, Lukács's negative criticism of Kafka. And the situation is similar with the positive examples: the rediscovery of certain extremists of mannerism, such as in the case of Arcimboldi and Gorgonzola, was the outcome of the intellectual reproduction of a world-historical experience, in which experience and interpretation are inseparable.

No doubt, ideological, religious, ethical and other preferences played a significant role in the theory of art of pre-capitalist periods transformed into aesthetical standpoints, or 'decisions'. In this respect it would appear that the situation does not differ from the historiosophical primacy over aesthetics of the bourgeois period. Apart from the fact, however, that the term 'historiosophical primacy' is hardly interpretable in the whole pre-capitalist era which had been characterized by a lack of historicity, the ideological, ethical, religious, etc. preferences were not 'philosophical postulates', but themselves parts of the *sensus communis* and in no way individual preferences. The refusal and the prohibition of the pictorial representation of the deity in the whole world of the Old Testament (just as much as in the case of the Mohammedan prohibition stemming from different roots) was a real religious preference and prescription as against the aesthetical sphere. But it was partly a collective preference and prohibition, partly one which did not lay claim to the right of a 'purely aesthetical value judgement.' The Bible did not intend to demonstrate aesthetically that all sculptural representations of Baal were 'ugly'. And when in exceptional cases aesthetical value judgements of general philosophical origin contradicted *sensus communis*, as in the case of Plato's negative evaluation of Homer, the judgement rested on generally accepted ideological-ethical premises, namely on ones that bore the character of *sensus communis*. In the given case the premise of the judgement was, 'art should instruct to the good'. So at least the judgement itself needed no further interpretation.

It would be, however, a misconception of the situation and an utter act of discrimination against philosophically dominated aesthetics if we left out of consideration the following contradiction. The frequency of 'misjudgements' or of such value judgements which are entirely unacceptable for the later recipient of any ideology (or for that matter, for a contemporary recipient with a different *Weltanschauung*) is only characteristic of philosophical aesthetics in so far as it is forming a judgement about contemporary art or about a work of art which is being linked directly to its own period. At the same time only this aesthetics is capable of conceiving (even if it sometimes misconceives) the art of antecedent periods, since this is the only aesthetics capable of grasping the 'reality content', once the 'object content' has already become antiquated. The reason is obvious. The vision of art of pre-capitalistic ages, lacking any kind of a historical conception, appreciated the works of past epochs, if it was confronted with them at all, on the basis of its own *sensus communis*. It could by no means differentiate between the 'object content', which faded out with the period that generated it, and the 'reality content' emerging from behind the veil of this antiquation.

For the periods in question and their art theory only that art was meaningful which belonged to their life, or only those works of the past which corresponded to their *sensus communis*. Greek gods had to be assimilated so that the Homeric epic poetry and the sculpture of Athens could become an interpretable art and a model for Rome to follow. The most direct 'object content', the religious prescriptions and norms regulating the system of customs had to be present so that art as a complex of experience could function. This circumstance displays the reason for the superiority of modern aesthetical theories, in spite of their frequent 'errors': they recognized the 'message' of 'reality content' behind the faded-out 'object content' of past ages, while conceptions of art of pre-capitalistic ages, which identified their own 'object content' with the 'reality content' (or, more precisely, were never able to distinguish between them) could discover nothing in other 'object contents'; or could do so only where this 'object content' became part and parcel of their own world through some special adaptation. For the aesthetical theories of the bourgeois historical period — as a consequence of the ineradicable mediating role of the individual-ideological standpoint — 'reality content' does not appear 'organically' in 'object content'. This means primarily that the separately appearing 'object content' may evoke such attractions or repulsions in the interpreting recipient, in the philosophically oriented aesthetician, on the basis of which (and as a result of certain preferences regarding the 'object content') he accepts elements which have a lesser significance as far as 'reality content' — the manifestation of the continuity of the human species — is concerned. And on the contrary, he refuses values closely connected with this continuity, because of ideologically repulsive elements of the 'object content'. The example of the first tendency is perhaps placing *Kalevala* side by side with the Homeric epic poems, on the ground of national motifs. An example of the second tendency is the rejection of African plastic art in the Victorian period, because of the overtly erotic character of this art. But even if all these sources of error are included, it is only the aesthetics of the bourgeois epoch, which draws a sharp line of demarcation between 'object content' and 'reality content', that is capable of being receptive to the aesthetical, in the cases where 'object content' is not only blurred and antiquated, but because of its inconceivable distance becomes an obstacle to the reception of the art work. The greatest achievement of this aesthetics was of course the rediscovery of Homer by Vico, as against the favourite of the Renaissance, Virgil.

IV

The dominant impression regarding modern philosophical aesthetics is the still high 'percentage of error' of their concrete judgements, which provoked a complete wave of opposition against the 'abstract aesthetical view'. The principal source of 'error' lies (so goes the usual characterization) in the 'deductive procedure', in the method according to which the aesthetician deduces his value judgement of single arts, branches of arts, works of art, from his conception of history, from the negative or positive evaluation of single historical epochs, from their higher or lower rank on the hierarchy of periods of world history. All this is also inseparable from ascribing a predetermined place to the aesthetic in the system of human objectivations and that of philosophy. That is why, from the end of the nineteenth century onwards, the tendency appeared and gradually grew into a movement dominating whole national cultures (especially French culture) and permeated by the spirit of rejecting philosophical aesthetics as such. The 'revolts' against the tyrannically systematizing authority departed from different premises and expressed not only the spontaneous resistance of practising artists. Konrad Fiedler's counter-argument was the opposition of the *theoretician*; there is no art, he wrote, there are only arts. The concept of art is an arbitrary abstraction, a myth of rationalism attempting forcefully to unify everything into a system, and the judgements of the unitary aesthetics originating from this myth are non-valid and irrelevant as far as living, concretely existing arts are concerned. The chief slogan of another counter-movement, more widespread and stemming from various directions is, philosophical aesthetics has to be substituted for *art criticism*, which is of an *inductive* character and which does not seek to include a single work within any tyrannical system. The principal methodological postulate of the 'art critical opposition' is that the artistic analysis should be centred on the concrete being and character of concrete works independent of all philosophical 'presuppositions' — this is the fuel that feeds impressionist art criticism from Théophile Gautier up to the present average criticism — or at least independent of the appreciation of the *whole* function of art. The greatest representative of this 'bifurcation in evaluation' is Theodore Adorno, who furnished in his musico-sociological writings a deep-going and magnificent characterization of the 'rootlessness' of New Music, comprehensive in spite of some unjust evaluations, simultaneously with the perfect separation of the evaluation of the works themselves. The postulate of the 'inductive' conception of art, 'relying solely on the work', breaking with 'lifeless abstraction', has meanwhile become a commonplace demand. But in spite of its widespread character, no solution was gained thereby. In our opinion, the 'errors' of philosophical aesthetics and criticism arise not from its deductive character. Therefore, 'error' is not the proper word to describe the situation. The so-called 'inductive' conception of art is not exempt from philosophical presuppositions either. In overtly impressionist criticism these presuppositions are also present, even if not in an *explicit form*. This means, however, that in the majority of cases there is no 'freedom from abstractions' but only a confusion of ideas. There is always unavoidably present a 'precipitation' of philosophical thought, in a simplified form catering to the needs of everyday life. Even if we mention a critic mostly hostile to, or at least on very problematic terms with, the 'deductive conception of art', but completely in possession of philosophical culture (we are speaking of Adorno) it is clear also with him how deeply his predilections (e.g. for the 'deductive' structure which characterizes the rationalism of the New Music) and his antipathies (for instance, against the populist character of Bartók's compositions) were rooted in philosophical value premises — in the latter case in the sociological-ontological conviction that the concept 'people' in modern society is a mere romantic mystification.

Impressionist criticism lays claim to the right of pure judgement of taste, not, to be sure, with the claim of a particular judgement of taste. 'I am pleased with it, *period*!' — this is the merely personal judgement of the subject of an interview picked at random, so it has hardly any reference to the evaluated work of art. This judgement will only characterize the subject as such, rather than the work of art. Kant was perfectly right in saying that in so far as the judgement of taste is an aesthetical judgement (and every proper critical judgement, also the impressionist, is an aesthetical one in this sense, since it has the intention to say something about a work of art, not about itself), it implies an element of the general, consequently the *sensus communis*, not as empirically existent, but as a postulate. Every judgement of taste laying claim to aesthetic validity, just because it is a taste of judgement claiming aesthetic validity, undermines, to a certain degree, its own subjectivity, and has become widened into a norm. The most irrefutable evidence of its being widened into a norm is the fact that it has to give an account of itself, it has to explain itself, its decisions, its reasons for the decisions. The dissection of the work of art into content and form is practically identical with this self-explanation: 'I am pleased with it, since it expresses this content in one way or another, because the content appears in such a way', etc. This tendency dividing the conception of art into two irreconcilably hostile camps, namely sociological and formalistic, is an irresistible movement characteristic only of the age of philosophical aesthetics, one which was unknown for the pre-capitalist vision of art, since the latter had not been obliged to lay a philosophical foundation for itself, for its choices and judgements. Then it was sufficient to point to the great artistic personality and to add: from such personalities such deeds are born. Inductive criticism, based on subjective judgement of taste gets into a state of self-deception as a result of being widened into a norm. It becomes unavoidable that its judgements of taste, since they are widened into norms, and therefore explained either from the point of view of content or of form, react in a deductive way upon its new judgements.

V

In what way, however, on what ground, can a judgement of taste be widened at all into a norm-giving one in the modern age? If there is no longer a homogeneous community, together with the adequate, empirically-given *sensus communis*, then the 'refined individual' no longer articulates and shapes the collective judgement of taste. But if his judgement of taste is necessarily something more than bare subjectivity, whence does its generality originate? If the idea does not hang above the world as a kind of deity, whence its inter-subjective generality?

Max Weber says correctly of the spirit of the modern age that it is no longer monotheistic. Its mythology involves no god, but gods, according to the general pluralism of the age, of dynamic society. In the wake of Weber's metaphor, we may say that every judgement of taste, becoming aesthetically norm-giving (i.e. becoming widened into a norm, into something conceptual during the process of self-explanation) expresses the existing community of taste of an existing social stratum or group, that is one from among many. This is the limit of its generality, its being a *sensus communis*. At the same time, however, it is the sufficient ground of its existence, as the existence of one *given* community of taste. Of course, a merely extensional description would only be sufficient for an historical relativist. We want, however, to state only two facts. First, every aesthetic judgement representing some community of taste, being widened into a norm in this sense, 'has bought its ticket' for the modern Olympus and become one of the fighting deities of the Weberian mythology of modern aesthetics. Second, though there are numerous deities of this type (with their adequate hierarchy) they are not innumerable. The number of the potential combinations of judgements of taste which come to be widened into a norm, and that of existing communities of taste can, of course, only be computed within the framework of concretely given media.

Here we have to point out only one, deeply problematic aspect of this situation. The *sensus communis* of the ancient sort was a spontaneous totality. With Aristotle (and he serves here only by way of illustration) *sensus communis* had an aesthetical aspect just as much as an ethical and a legal one, if the latter two could have been at all distinguished from each other at that time. The judgement of taste, however, that generates a norm, widens its purely subjective character up to the borderline of a group. In this sense it creates or expresses a certain kind of *sensus communis*, but it does not intend to have anything in common with a 'deductive' conception of art, striving to grasp somehow the whole field of aesthetic experience. Thereby it is at the mercy of the ever-given particular attitudes, of modes, which are 'the eternal rotation of the new'. At least in one respect, therefore, it does not transcend the limitation of philosophical aesthetics. All the errors of philosophical aesthetics 'happen' with respect to judgements of greatness. Either it underestimates great phenomena, according to its philosophical preferences, since they 'do not fit in' its preformed hierarchy; or, on the contrary, it analyses as great works of art those which are artistically poorly constructed, and significant only from the point of view of the theoretical abstraction. Impressionist, inductive criticism, however, moves in the sphere of the daily, of the voguish and its category, homologous with greatness, stems from the sphere of the vogue, too: this is sensation, or sheer novelty. The two types of 'errors' are a necessary consequence of structures. Through the contradiction between these inductive and deductive approaches, we have arrived at the antinomic structure of the aesthetics of the bourgeois age.

VI

Our analysis does not analyse in detail the decisive cause of the antinomy, the fact that there are no communities in bourgeois society and that the artist can meet the public only in the market-place (i.e. only indirectly). These causes are just as obvious as they are fundamental. Here we shall only mention their consequences.

Kant writes that the artist creates a new idea in every significant work of art. This creation of the idea is precisely the work of genius. The new idea as idea in general is, however, conceptually indefinable, that is it cannot be brought under a concept, or deduced from one. Formulating the fundamental dilemma of bourgeois art Kant adds: there is a type of work of art which represents the idea without taste; and another type which represents taste without the idea. The latter is, of course, no work of a genius.

In pre-capitalist epochs such a contradiction did not exist. Genius created *per definitionem* new ideas in those periods as well. But new ideas themselves were also slumbering, in the form of a potentiality, in the taste of the community, in ideas in which men could 'recognize themselves'. What was new in the creations of a genius, in such a context met general acknowledgement and pleasure, even if not everybody was pleased with it (since agreement among all members of a community is not a condition of the *sensus communis*). On the other hand, not only can ideas not exist without communal taste but, on the contrary, communal taste cannot exist without ideas in the pre-capitalist world either, since community — with its systems of ideas, its institutions not separated from the 'body' of the community — is idea incarnate in a certain sense. To express it once more in Kantian terminology — even the artist who is no genius reproduces nothing but the idea of the genius, according to the judgement of taste.

The isolated individual of bourgeois society, in so far as he is a 'genius', creates the idea in his capacity of an isolated individual obviously not out of nothing. The problems of the age determine his 'object contents' as well. But the duty of the genius, the creation of the idea, cannot rely on anything existing collectively. The genius thereby runs the risk of 'the lack of taste' simultaneously with the creating of the idea. That is, the creation of a work of art, which may either evoke universal esteem or remain without the slightest echo, *independently* of its aesthetically valuable or valueless character. The emergence of taste without idea and works of art embodying this type of taste, their becoming general, is such an obvious process in bourgeois society that we need not analyse it in detail.

Duo si faciunt idem, non est idem: the artist, the genius, may run the risk of 'the lack of taste' of his idea (his artistic thought), without endangering the 'meaning', the 'mission' of his objectivation; the evaluating recipient (the critic) would not respond then, to its notion, as a critic. The author of the non-generalizable judgement, as we have seen, creates a purely subjective judgement of taste, one of no aesthetical character. Criticism as a genre, however, belongs to bourgeois public life, it is one of its manifestations. Prior to this epoch, no systematic art criticism existed. The critic's function, his social assignment, is the formation of public opinion, as a minimal mission: the influencing of other recipients through the attempt to reveal his own processes of reception, his own experiences, through the attempt to generalize his own judgement. The solution of an antinomic situation is, of course, antinomic too: either one judges the idea departing from taste or taste departing from the idea. The first is the way of all inductive art criticism, especially that of its emphatically impressionist form; the latter is the way of philosophical (historiosophical) aesthetics.

VII

To be able to interpret this antimony, we have to make another categorical excursion. Every great work of art creates a new idea. This is what was called 'form' by the young Lukács. But when we said that the indispensable basis of this idea, of this form, of this 'reality content' — we may call it whatever we want — was a *sensus communis* in the pre-capitalist world, either existent or at least sporadically present and in this sense potential, we may just as well say that it grew out of a collective 'object content' which served at the same time as the collective standpoint of various communities. Collective 'object content' is subject-matter and *Weltanschauung* at the same time, in which the former is subordinated to the latter, and becomes an element of it. In this sense the young Lukács was perfectly right when he wrote in *The History of Modern Drama*: it is the *Weltanschauung* that constitutes the form of the work of art. If the work of art grows out of a collective 'object content' organically, i.e. in a generally conceivable way, without the need of 'interpretation' and 'commentaries', as a form, as an idea, as 'reality content', then 'object content' may easily be bracketed in the evaluation of the work of art. Or at least it poses no problem, as it is no problem for the artist either to 'find' the adequate 'object content', from which a new idea may originate. The art of pre-capitalist epochs, of 'ancient times' might correspond so adequately to the Kantian criterion ('artistic pleasure without concept') since it was superfluous to grasp at all what was to be grasped in it only conceptually, namely its object content. It was evident, it was given. Ancient or Christian myths as common cultural possessions never became questionable as a 'subject-matter', and the standpoint in terms of which the meaning of mythical subject underwent various changes was either the collective *Weltanschauung* of an entire community or at least that of social strata fulfilling a communal function, and the work of art was born as their 'assignment'.

This 'natural' or 'organic' connection between 'object content' and 'reality content' has become disrupted in bourgeois art. 'Object content' itself — out of which reality content grew — became a problem, partly because of its much too 'individualized' character, which demanded commentaries so that the Other, the recipient, could grasp it. It required incessant intellectual efforts both on the part of the creating artist and of the recipient, so that the subjective theme, bearing the mark of the creating personality, could become inter-subjective. Partly it always remained questionable whether the chosen subject-matter was aesthetically valuable or not. Therefore the 'discovery' of subject and *Weltanschauung*, or standpoint (a natural point of departure for ancient art) became a very risky procedure and especially favourable conditions were needed for artistic success. We have already mentioned that the origin of the whole aesthetical mythology of a separate 'content' and a separate 'form' (and not only in its vulgar versions, but also on the level of a Lessing, a Goethe, a Schiller) is due to this specific situation. Such too historiosophical, too sociological, too conceptual questions like the following: Why exactly this subject? and Why exactly this *Weltanschauung?* do not simply mean that philosophy of history or sociology have intruded into the sphere of the purely aesthetical. Rather, such questions grow out of the actual structure of bourgeois art. It is not the work of art as an individual formation that makes these conceptual and only conceptually conceivable questions necessary, but rather the individual character of the 'object content' which creates the basis of the concrete quality and which is often not transformable into an inter-subjective complex. And since, as a consequence of the general situation, in evaluating 'reality content' we always evaluate the *Weltanschauung* as well which constitutes it, that is why the philosophy of history, the *Weltanschauung*, the standpoint of the evaluating person, of the recipient, plays such a decisive role in evaluating concrete works of art.

According to the young Lukács, *Weltanschauung*, constituting the form, vanishes, becomes 'absorbed' in the form. In the case of outstanding works of art this is, indeed, the end-result which would make it possible to form pure aesthetical judgements. This is, however, an end-result in fact, and Walter Benjamin is probably right in emphasizing the fact that 'object content' becomes obsolete only during an extraordinarily slow process. Contemporaries are confronted, however — *volens-nolens*, consciously or non-consciously — with this 'object content', with this subject-matter subordinated to *Weltanschauung*, with this standpoint, which constitutes in its unique character the unique and inimitable 'individuality of work of art'. Thus for the art reception of the modern age, purely aesthetical judgement is no 'rarity', no 'borderline case' which 'needs time to be realized', but is actually impossible. Even in the case of the works of past ages, which fitted in a once-existing *sensus communis* unproblematically with their 'object content', this 'object content' became a concrete quality to be interpreted from the viewpoint of the present. The antimony of deductive and inductive judgements became an unavoidable world-historical situation of the modern age.

The greatest achievement of deductive or philosophical aesthetics is that it chooses the human species for its own point of departure, for the basis of its generalization, raising these questions: What is art 'in general'? What is the task of art in general? and What is its place in the system of human activities? and so on. We remind the reader again of what has been said about the distinction between 'object content' and 'reality content'. This is why the claim of totality raised by philosophical aesthetics is a coherent community possessing solid existence is now at best a postulate. This is why the claim of totality raised by pholosophical aesthetics is a mere postulate. But its postulate is the claim of totality, and would its claim for generality prove to be unfounded ever so many times, philosophical aesthetics still creates a distance thereby between its own standpoint and the particularity of a stratum or the particularity of 'the individuality of a work of art'. The reverse of this attitude is that represented by Walter Benjamin, the most vehement opponent of aesthetic 'systematicity', who regarded philosophical systems themselves as the representatives of the hierarchic alienation of the world. He saw such systems as forcefully subjecting the living individuals, or works of art, to the requirements of the system. Deductive aesthetics must have the self-awareness (and make others be aware of it as well) that its ideological preferences are indispensable for the deep insight into modern art on the part of the modern recipient. On the other hand, it must accept the situation with a clear self-consciousness that it cannot form pure aesthetical judgements. The preconditions of the latter are missing from life, *sensus communis* and a collective *Weltanschauung* or standpoint.

Inductive art criticism faces two dangers. The first is that it is also based on subjective ideological preferences. These interfere with its analyses just as much as with the judgements of deductive aesthetics, only — not being rendered conscious — these preferences are not clear and distinct, but operate in a form which confuses the clarity of the analysis. Further, the identification of inductive art criticism with the particularity of some of the taste groups (and this is, as we have mentioned, inevitable, if it is about an aesthetical judgement and not one being confined within the limits of mere subjectivity) hides in itself the danger of becoming quickly dated. The self-identification of the ephemeral *sensus communis* of taste groups (even if critical ones) transforms pure aesthetical judgement, promised by inductive criticism, into a highly unstable equilibrium. At the other pole of the antimony, inductive art criticism possesses two remarkable assets. First, the 'individuality of the work of art' as an 'individual', as a lively, concrete cosmos, in the majority of the cases stands forth as a better concrete expression of human totality, embodies the latter to a much greater degree than does a 'totalized' system which is often of an alienated-hierarchical character. Second (and as a consequence of what has been said above), the modern work of art is a kind of 'individual' which can hardly be subjected to general rules, for instance, to those of a genre. Nearly every significant individual creates a new species. But the question of what species will unfold from which individual can only be answered by inductive art criticism. It is not by chance, then, that inductive art criticism did more for the acceptance of modern art (in regard to both its individuality and its species characteristics) than the most significant philosophical aesthetics.

Aesthetics is, consequently, irreformable, in the sense that its antinomic character is untranscendable. Therefore, its 'sources of error' are ineliminable as well. On the other hand, it is indispensable. At both poles (i.e. of inductive art criticism and philosophical aesthetics) efforts need to be made to avoid, or at least to minimize, the inherent dangers of the respective standpoints. Deductive criticism has to question the process of validation of its value judgements with respect to the individuality and distinctiveness of works of art. Similarly, inductive criticism has to question the validity of its particular judgements with respect to their value beyond the present moment. *It is a postulate of art that the value of the artwork and the validity of the aesthetic judgement concerning it should be in unison.*

NOTES

1 See Karl Marx, *Grundrisse*, tr. M. Nicolaus (Harmondsworth: Penguin Books, 1973), p. 110.

2

Is the Novel Problematic?
A Contribution to the Theory of the Novel

FERENC FEHÉR

The nineteenth century is the period of the triumph of the novel: 'the bourgeois epic' leaves behind all of its ageing competitors. Not only are there tireless efforts to revive epic poetry, a non-novelistic genre, but artistic judgement (often even that of the *great novelists* themselves) is full of doubts with respect to the triumphant new genre. In the midst of the modern world there is an unremitting search for epic materials. Thus, Frank Norris is convinced that he has found them in the American wild west. Criticism typically evaluates Tolstoy's novels by comparing them with the epic; and the Russian novelist finds this all the more flattering as he, like Hegel, loves, of all epic works, the stories of Homer and of the Old Testament.

Lukács's *The Theory of the Novel*, which appeared during the 'real ending' of the nineteenth century amid the catastrophes of the Great War, solves the enigma of this period. It is *The Theory of the Novel* that most clearly draws all the philosophical and aesthetic consequences of Goethe's, Schiller's, and Hegel's period. The study begins by contraposing the epic and the novel, the age of the epic and modern bourgeois society, and Lukács unambiguously decides in favour of the former. In this, of course, it goes beyond the classical period in a more than problematical sense: it transforms the defence of progress through contradictions into an overtly romantic anti-capitalism that nevertheless also contains a specifically revolutionary viewpoint.

The Theory of the Novel rediscovers the idea of alienation and reintegrates it into European philosophy, after it had been forgotten for almost three-quarters of a century. The basic thesis of *The Theory of the*

Novel (both on the level of aesthetics and of the philosophy of history) is that the age of the epic and its artistic production are of a higher order and greater value than capitalism and its epic, the novel. The standard of evaluation, the referential base, is an entirely unique philosophical mixture. Built on Hegel and *Lebensphilosophie*, it gropes towards what Marx, 70 years earlier, had called 'human essence' in a text Lukács himself read only two decades after writing this theory of the novel. The age of the epic is characterized by its 'self-certainty'; *life and essence are identical notions.*[1] Similarly, the epic universe is homogeneous in the sense that the relations and creations of man are just as substantial as his personality.[2] On the other hand, the form of the novel is the expression of a transcendental homelessness.[3] The novel is the epic of a time for which totality (and, therefore, the dominant homogeneity of the world, as well as human substantiality, and the substantial relation between man and his products) has become only a problem and an aspiration.[4] The novel is thus problematic in a double sense: first, it expresses the problematic character of both the structures and the man of its age; secondly, and as a result, its mode of expression, its whole construction is full of unaccomplished (unaccomplishable, according to Lukács) tasks or problems. The outlook of the intransigent judge who, from *Don Quixote* to *L'Éducation Sentimentale*, finds almost no canonical solutions, is not that of critical rigour but the logical consequence of his philosophy of history. It is precisely because of these relentlessly drawn conclusions that *The Theory of the Novel* is a classic. Posterity may call into question not only its fundamental conception, but also its value judgements and classifications. Yet, it is undeniable that this essay is the only one to have gone to the heart of the matter. It made explicit bourgeois civilization's latent bad faith concerning an artistic phenomenon which is itself the fruit of bourgeois society.

The position taken here, however, is entirely different from Lukács's own. This leads to a paradoxical situation. According to the Lukácsian theory, the novel is a problematic genre because the world that has created it is 'problematic' in all of its structures. This viewpoint completely corresponds to that early nineteenth-century opposition that viewed emerging capitalist existence and its cultural forms with resignation or hatred without, nevertheless, being able to break out of the bourgeois way of posing questions. To argue against the 'problematic' character of bourgeois existence and its cultural forms from a Marxist viewpoint would indeed be paradoxical. However, the point is obviously not to discover harmony and 'substantiality' where Lukács's investigations have revealed a whole series of significant dilemmas. Rather, we must modify the *criterion*.

To claim that the novel is problematic implies that we have a criterion of what is non-problematic and that even in the case of utopian aspirations, it somehow comes down to us from the past. Although it is impossible to place Goethe, Schiller, Hegel and Lukács in the same category as the Romantics, we do find a *common model* among all sceptical observers and all hostile critics of the novel: the idealization of the unmediated communal organic and homogeneous world as the source of the 'perfect' genre, the epic. Like the judgements on the spatio-temporal location of the epic world, the positions associated with this model may be fundamentally different. None of the great figures of German classicism believed in the possibility of its revival and Lukács's work is also an elegy to its definitive disappearance. Although different periods thought that the roots of epic perfection could be found in the ancient *polis* or in the German, Oriental or French heroic age, the basis of the artistic canon is always a comparison of societies. The old problem is posed over and over again: the affirmation of the supremacy of the organic community over non-communal society.

This is not foreign to Marx himself. His famous pronouncement[5] alludes precisely to the Homeric epic and has a distinctly normative character since it refers to an 'unsurpassable model', the human basis of which he describes as the age of the 'normal' childhood of mankind. In Marx's philosophy of history this model is concretized. On the one hand, he rationally interprets this exemplary 'normalcy' in terms of the category of 'human essence', conceived as dynamic historical potentiality given from the beginnings of human society (even though its full unfolding can only come with the liquidation of alienation when each constitutive element of this whole historical movement can be — in principle — appropriated by each and every individual). Thus, the human and artistic canon will no longer float above history as a model created by reason, but will become an integral product of history. On the other hand, while maintaining the existence of alternative possibilities in history, Marx is an 'evolutionist' to the extent that he considers every evolutionary sequence that develops the powers of the species as the foundation of values. Thus, the realized domain of human essence is enriched even if it be through the liquidation of earlier harmonious spheres and objectifications which could rightfully have been considered as prefigurations of realized human essence (realized at least *within* a limited sphere). Thus, for Marx, the evolution of Ancient Greece, along with the epic and tragedy which it produced, remain unsurpassable models since they realized 'substantiality' for the free individuals of the 'limited sphere', that is they show that it was possible for these individuals to assimilate the historically elaborated 'human essence' of their time. Yet, he would regard as methodologically unacceptable any attempt to place the *polis* and its cultural forms above subsequent human development in the *hierarchy* of values, on the grounds that they were not problematic.

In the following, we shall elaborate on the novel as a genre from this twofold viewpoint. This will provide us with the basis for the rejection of the scale of values in *The Theory of the Novel*. With all its 'formlessness', 'prosaic' nature and lack of fixed rules, the novel does not occupy an inferior place in a normative hierarchy of artistic forms established in relation to human substantiality. If it were only that the novel is an 'adequate' expression of its time, functioning as the self-expression of bourgeois society with means that the old-style epic did not have yet at its disposal, we would be limited to the sort of answers that could be expected from sociological relativism. Ranke is obviously wrong: all epochs are *not* equally close to God. On the other hand, the specific perfection of the novel — this original artistic genre produced by bourgeois society — is that its essential structure contains all the categories derived from capitalism: the first society based on *'purely social' and no longer 'natural' life-forms.*

The novel's 'formlessness' and 'prosaic' character corresponds structurally to the formless and chaotic progress through which bourgeois society annihilated the first islands of realized human substance, while also generating a major development of the powers of the species. Thus, the novel expresses a stage in human emancipation not only in its 'content', in the notions of collectivity structured by its categories, but also in its form. The form of the novel could not have come into being without the appearance of the categories of 'purely social' society, and the birth of this society is an enrichment, even if we take into account the unequal evolution it produces.

The novel is not problematic: it is ambivalent. Its whole structure includes characteristics that come from the mimesis of the specific structure of a concrete 'social society' (capitalism, in which it has its roots), as well as features that characterize all types of social societies. Originally, this ambivalence had no special meaning. As long as 'purely social' society was struggling against quasi-natural feudal estates and patriarchal 'natural' communities, and there was no possibility for a different type of purely social society to come about, nascent capitalist categories did not hinder the new, triumphantly emerging form. When the establishment and consolidation of capitalism made it clear that this society was not the ultimate stage in human emancipation, a new conflict broke out between civil (*bürgerliche*) and 'human' society. This confrontation allowed for the first time an examination of certain formal characteristics of the novel as unbefitting the dignity of man 'properly speaking', and to refer to them with increasing distrust. The naive self-confidence with which the bastard genre, coming in the wake of the epic, took possession of the universe, was finally understood: it was the confidence of civil (*bürgerliche*) emancipation which, liberated from the pressure of its adversaries, was transformed into the self-sufficiency of the well-established bourgeois. The average novelistic production of the actualized bourgeois society testifies adequately to this metamorphosis. The phrase 'transcendental homelessness' is quite relevant to the novel. With the universalization of the social movement which engendered its formal structures and imposed them to the detriment of older and more traditional cultural forms, it becomes less and less possible for the novel to achieve higher and richer levels. The writer's loss of faith in the validity of the given form-structure is the beginning of the crisis of the novel. The changes in subjective artistic attitudes are by no means the causes of the crisis. When Marx notes that capitalism is hostile to certain branches of intellectual production (particularly to poetry) he is alluding both to the ever-increasing fetishism that renders the artist's apprehension of the totality more and more difficult, as well as to the human void that characterizes the majority of the reified public. But the opposite idea is equally true: all real art aspiring to human substance must be hostile to capitalism. In the case of the novel this means that the previously mentioned ambivalence is raised to consciousness (always in the context of the author's particular world-view). The result is an effort to destroy the original artistic form which emerges along with the dynamics of capitalism, and to replace it by another form, better suited to the presumed or real aspects of human emancipation. In most cases, the crisis led to an impasse and to a totally amorphous transformation of the original form. In other cases, it initiated both a specific recreation of the vast possibilities inherent in the old form and innovations that went beyond the epic genre of the first 'social society'. Methodologically, all of this forces the general analysis of the novel as a new epic genre equal to the classical epic, to develop 'on two fronts'. First, in a detailed confrontation with the classical epic, it must prove that the novel entails an *increase in emancipation*, in spite of the loss of the specificity and the formal symmetry of the epic. Secondly, it must show the ambivalence and the striving for autonomy of those elements that within the framework of the bourgeois social phenomenon can no longer achieve high artistic fulfilment. We can thus prove the purely bourgeois origin of the novel but also that its dynamic leads beyond civil (*bürgerliche*) society.

The novel is born in a society without community; the structure of its world is not communal. The world of the novel is not substantial (to use the term of *The Theory of the Novel*). It is dominated by *the duality of the self and the external world*. This duality means that the individual is neither the direct personification of the prevalent forces in the described sphere of existence, nor are the self-objectifications of the hero immediately given, in forms that can be appropriated and used. This is the source of dilemmas, but is not in principle 'problematic'. On the contrary, as the beginnings of reification in general, the reified situation expressed in the novel provides an impetus that cannot be compared with epic portrayal. It reveals possibilities unknown to the epic. First of all, the 'natural' tendency of the hero — the drive to construct his own universe, whether it be an illusory or a real one — is unimaginable in the epic. Lukács rightly insists on the fact that the inner assurance of epic heroes comes from the fact that, while they are one with their world and are in a homogeneous unity with the latter, they are nevertheless 'guided' on a path that has been laid out for them. This guidance, this divine providence, vitalizes (in the Hegelian sense of the term) all the actions of these heroes, but excludes in principle the possibility of transgressing, transforming, or recreating the boundaries of their world. The *Gottverlassenheit* of the hero of the novel, an idea presented with desperate insistence in *The Theory of the Novel*, was not at first tainted with the least trace of despair. The heroes of early novels share the self-confidence with which bourgeois production begins the cell-by-cell construction of its world on the picturesque ruins of the past. Even if, as is the case in Cervantes, the world to be built is *a priori* an illusory one, initially it will not bring about a disillusionment. *Don Quixote* is the first novel, because its hero possesses a freedom which is in principle unthinkable in the epic: the ability to revolt in the very midst of real experience and to oppose to it a different, merely possible experience. (There is thus no question here of escape to the magical islands of the imagination.) If God has abandoned the hero of the novel, he has also given him freedom. This structural element, which fundamentally determines the form, is the deeper expression of the fact that the epic genre of the 'purely social' society contains a higher level of emancipation than the classical epic. In the second place, and as a result of the above, the epic's world-historical orientation changes under the impact of the dynamic of emerging bourgeois praxis. As opposed to all preceding formations which were oriented towards the past, capitalism is oriented towards the future as a result of the 'infinite process' of capitalist production. This orientation towards the future is the initial tendency of the novel, and it is matched by the activity in which the hero constitutes his own world. In the epic, not only is the universe's general framework determined from the outset by the will of the Olympians, but so is action: the hero will only accomplish the task that has been assigned him. Although we have no knowledge of the way the public in Antiquity experienced the epic, it seems obvious that it could not have evoked the same emotional tension of its listeners, and later readers, as the novel. It was clear, for example, that the fate of a Hector, like that of his conqueror, was predestined. With the exception of mediocre and extremely fetishistic literature, the hero of the novel does not act according to dictates from above, but according to his own teleological determinations. Thus, he constitutes his own universe, or rather, he tries to constitute it according to its own presumed teleology. The result of this teleological positing is the causal series that forms the architecture of the novel. Early in the history of the novel, this individual teleology attempts with naive and self-assured illusionism to construct a total world (in conformity with bourgeois philosophy, based on the concept of the universal individual), out of a single teleological presupposition. Defoe's *Robinson Crusoe* is the greatest example of this. Later, the ontological vision will deepen. Balzac's *La Comédie Humaine* is already marked by the Hegelian cunning of Reason: the efforts of different individuals conflict and invalidate each other, resulting in a universe that none of the heroes could have imagined or wanted.

Then, in direct proportion to the increasing reification of the bourgeois world, the duality of the Self and its environment increasingly becomes the dominant element of the structure of the novel — a disturbing and destructive element which will finally seem insurmountable. *The Theory of the Novel* rightly stresses that the empirical subject, the man of the novel, contains less and less of the dominant forces of the universe (in himself, in his positing, in his acts) while the outside world becomes a convention, a second nature that is much more difficult to conquer than the first one. As a result, the emancipatory conquests of the novel share the same fate as bourgeois emancipation in general: the representational sphere of the novel contracts as increasing reification degrades the proud product of civil society, the free bourgeois individual, into the subject of a semblance of liberty, deprived of 'normal' relations with the objectifications of his own world.

This is particularly clear in the representation of *production* and of the *economy*. Hegel's description of the vitality of the creation and consumption of tools in the epic is so eloquent that we have only to confront it with the sphere of objectification in any modern novel in order to see immediately the disparities between these two ages of epic literature. However, it would be wrong to believe that the novel is inferior to the epic in the representation of the most elementary material sphere of life. We must correct a rather general error here. The idea that, unlike the novel, the epic can represent production, is not accurate. Indeed, material exchange with nature in its immediacy never played a decisive role in the classical epic any more than in the novel.[6] The epic was the art of free men, *liberated from work*, much more so than the deliberately and universally democratic novel. However, the epic poetry of the heroic era was based on an ingenious thematic invention: its predominant theme was *war* or the *struggle with nature* — the latter also manifesting itself usually as a type of war. Neither theme meant the contraction of the realm of epic expression. In the *Grundrisse* Marx states that in the age of organic communities, war was one of the fundamental activities which constituted the collectivity, while their immediate struggle with nature represented the most elementary and striking activity of self-preservation. On the other hand, campaigns as well as travel, organized epic communities into 'autonomous units' which had to resupply through their own means everything that had been lost, destroyed or consumed. Thus, some representative productive capacities, if not the actual production of the age, can be apprehended in the epic.

But it is striking that at its beginnings the novel had not less, but more opportunities to represent human productive capacity — the most fundamental force of production. Defoe's *Robinson Crusoe* is a characteristic bourgeois odyssey that in this respect proves the superiority of the novel over the epic rather than its weakness. Hegel gives us a beautiful analysis of epic poetry and the stages of its development, from the cosmogonies to the epics centred on a single hero. In this sense, Defoe's novel is the cosmogony of bourgeois productive capacities and at the same time an epic poem with a single hero. And, its emancipatory superiority over the original model manifests itself in the positive characteristic of abandonment by God. Here, man has recourse only to himself, he carries out his project of self-creation in terms of his own forces. One could laugh at Defoe's narrowmindedness, characteristic of the English bourgeoisie, when he recreates the prejudices of his own country on a desert island. But, in fact, the path from *Robinson Crusoe* to *The Phenomenology of Mind* is a direct one, even if the model of the 'Robinsonade' is gradually eliminated. It is precisely this ideal of self-creation that gives Defoe's novel — and in principle all novels — their purely artistic superiority over its Ancient counterpart. There, the material reproduction of life was but a secondary, although indispensable, element of heroic existence. In the novel, this re-creation demands the maximum of energy and, more than once, of heroism. What the representation loses in sublimity is recovered because of the general humanization of the sphere of existence. Moreover, this is not one exceptional episode in the course of three centuries of history of the novelistic genre. Balzac's cycle is also a special kind of odyssey, although its heroes pilot their ship only between the Scylla and the Charybdis of second nature. While most of the characters in this cycle have only remote ties with the direct process of material exchange with nature, it is still from Balzac that we can most clearly learn the direction taken by human productive capacities in the firmly established empire of the bourgeoisie, as well as the human faculties necessary for the universal realization of the values of the Robinsonian epic.

We have just indicated the point up to which the bourgeois novel was capable of exploiting the fruit of its own 'increase' in emancipation. Generally, after Balzac, and even before him, a new tendency develops in the novelistic genre. On the artistic level, the new epic abandons the most fundamental and elementary dimension of life and knowingly excludes it from its representational sphere. The institutions and the processes of human production have become so reified that they seem henceforth incompatible with the principle of living presentation and the individuals linked to them who become entirely 'without substance'. Although less and less frequently, immediate needs and their satisfaction still appear in the novel. But they are increasingly expressed solely in terms of the transmission of money as the reward of a specific profession. The sphere of production and economic regulation is increasingly depicted exclusively in the moral reflexes of objective activity. *The Theory of the Novel* sadly notes that the theme of the great novel is the failure to adapt. This not only means that the novel has lost a 'thematic sphere' and that the boundaries of representation have narrowed, but also that the hero no longer stands on firm ground. The following dilemma appears: either the novel must depict men who in fact no longer have any relation to the fundamental spheres of activity, or it must render its characters more and more ethereal by showing them only in those functions isolated from material production and reproduction. This inevitably leads to the creation of an artificial milieu. Such an artificial milieu did not exist in the epic: travel and war were forms of action oriented towards self-preservation. Especially in the ancient epic the 'fantastic' milieu was entirely 'natural' to the man of that time, in the same way that myth was part of his code of ethics and renewed his sense of justice and state regulation. In the epic, therefore, the difference between the fantastic and the empirically real had no value dimension. (The problem appears in a somewhat different light in the medieval epic.) In the realm of the novel, the divergence between the artificial and the empirical—'natural' milieu takes on a pronounced evaluative connotation. It brings to life the gap between average bourgeois existence and the islands of possible realization of human values. This obviously causes tremendous artistic difficulties, since an unusual artistic imagination is required to create a humanly believable atmosphere for such an exceptional milieu. In this respect, too, the novel becomes ambivalent. To the extent that it moves away from the realm of activities immediately related to survival, it anticipates — at least in so far as possibility is concerned and, only very rarely, realization — the atmosphere of a social situation in which survival activities are already relegated to the background and work has become an end in itself.

We can find a similar trend in the relationship between the representation of institutions and the novel. Initially, in the novel we find the same higher stage of emancipation that we found in our review of the economy and production. Hegel quite correctly denies the existence of epic institutions representing the universal as separate from man and opposed to his particularity. To the extent that we can speak of 'institutions' in the epic, they can only be an *a priori*, predestined and unchangeable 'order', as is clear from their analogues on Olympus. As Lukács points out in *The Theory of the Novel*, this is the other side of the 'vitality' of the heroic age, which for Hegel underlines the other side of the happy 'guided existence' of the heroes of the epic. The fact that man has his natural place in a natural community gives him practically integral dimensions: as

Hector dies, the silent phalanx closes again, and the structure of existence remains unchanged. The novel, on the other hand, rejects in its very essence the authority of every Olympus and considers human institutions, for better or for worse, as human creations.

Thus, the bourgeois 'epic' triumphantly broadens its possibilities of representation into a universe of quasi-epic dimensions. It is not only able to understand and authoritatively reject the structure of feudal institutions, but also to document in the historical novel the major dimension of its own institutions — the dimension of being created by men. Lukács is right when he refuses to consider the historical novel as a special genre. As far as representation is concerned, however, we can see here a different dimension which gives us a panorama of the genesis of human institutions that was still impossible in the epic. This initially appears as a natural process in Walter Scott. The importance of the historical novel does not lie in the conquest of a new 'thematic sphere', nor in a more penetrating description of man's character as an individual. Balzac had already noted how Walter Scott's heroines were undefined and lifeless. We can speak in Scott of an undeniable contraction of man's inner world without anachronistically projecting some modern psychologism. The historical novel provides aesthetic pleasure in an entirely different way. Every time we see human institutions disintegrate or come into being as an apparent result of exclusively individual passions and actions, we relive the liberating experience that man himself creates his own institutions, independent of what these institutions become in his hands and of what we feel about the author's judgement of these institutions. The humanization of human space and the transformation of natural society into purely social society shaped the dominant atmosphere of the historical novel. This is the source of the real improvement of this form over that of the epic. However, as soon as Fabrizio del Dongo comes back from Waterloo, as soon as Balzac is forced to transpose Scott's method into the private battles of his heroes, the immense process of the novel's extension is brought to a halt and the movement is gradually reversed. Obviously, this is no more accidental than what happened in the representation of the sphere of production. The increasingly fetishizing and reifying character of bourgeois production is itself perceivable as a universal trait to the extent that bourgeois society itself becomes universal. The split between the Self and the external world appears most clearly in that representational dimension which, in its beginnings, manifested most forcefully the supremacy of the new epic genre over the old one. The man of the novel no longer knows what to do with the institutions of his world and experiences them as increasingly transcendent with respect to his own empirical existence (hence the profoundly felt truth of a Kafka). He ends up by simply forgetting institutions or at least attempting to forget them.

The third dimension of representation in which we can observe the growing hostility between the Self and the external world is a result of the fact that the *public sphere is excluded from the novel*. In this respect, oversimplification has characterized the comparison between the two great periods of the epic genre. The best analysts could take their starting point in an indisputable dimension of civil (*bürgerliche*) society, a dimension that could be unambiguously attacked by the Jacobins as well as by Marx's great analysis (*Zur Judenfrage*): the destruction of the public character of the ancient community, the separation of bourgeois and citizen. The conclusion was always that the epic expresses the spirit of a people while the novel only deals with a private anecdote. This is undeniable. Yet, Jürgen Habermas's magnificent work has put an end to this oversimplified interpretation.[7] He contrasts the representative character of the public sphere in the feudal and courtly period with its substitute in the first centuries of the rise of the bourgeoisie: public opinion based on the family as the foundation of the intimate sphere. This public opinion aimed at the generalization of its collective and humanitarian ideals in the constitution of an ideal, humanistic and public sphere. Of course, what was at issue was an illusory public sphere. The bourgeois individual at its basis was a 'private person engaged in commodity production' in bitter and irreconcilable opposition to all other men in the market, precisely because he could only create his own private sphere at the expense of others. On the other hand, up to the universalization of civil society, this illusory public sphere was real to the extent that only by creating a public opinion which accepted the human values of the intimate sphere was it possible to oppose the bourgeoisie as a class to the world of the representative public sphere of the feudal period. In relation to the early novel, Habermas draws very interesting conclusions from the public character of the intimate sphere. For our purposes, the main elements of his analysis can be summarized as follows.

The 'self-evident' public sphere of the epic had undoubtedly been destroyed and, as we shall see later, this made the creation of the novel very difficult. Considering its starting point, the most generalized danger confronting the novel was that it faced the danger of becoming submerged in banality. Even the most insipid epic is the product of the collective spirit, and a whole human group can recognize in it its own problems, experiences and destinies. But the novel always risks becoming a purely private story, in the most pejorative sense of the term. However, as can be seen in the novels of Richardson, Goldsmith, the young Goethe and Rousseau, the small community of the intimate sphere, with its universalizing tendency, heralded not only a modification of structures, but a turning-point in universal history.

The field of force that arises out of the conflicts and interactions of small communities is of a higher order because it is a mechanism which stimulates the variety of human individuality better than the homogeneity of an organic collectivity. Obviously, civil (*bürgerliche*) society (and thus also the bourgeois epic) could not realize its own dynamism. On the one hand, the intimate sphere based on the isolated subject of commodity production could only generalize its ideal of humanity in an illusory way. On the other hand, precisely because of its intimate quality, it was in an ambivalent relation to the world of objectifications. However, this is not the problematic of all societies, but only of one type which has become social.

Yet, in the background of the intimate sphere constituting the universe of the novel, there were many latent contradictions that were to lead to the definitive split between the Self and the external world. It was not in principle inevitable that the family be the exclusive framework of the intimate sphere. Nevertheless, the 'empirical' nature of civil society prescribed that this be so.

Within capitalism, the family was first and foremost an economic unit of distribution and not of production. Similarly, it never became a political unit: a political microcollective model of the new society. (Obviously, we make an exception of the semi-patriarchal peasant forms of life that continue to vegetate outside the periphery of the interest of the novel.) This intensified the definitive detachment of the hero in the novel from the domain of activity in the sphere of objectifications. This resulted in the *a priori* limitation of the intimate sphere's values, and in their inherent inappropriateness for generalization into the ideal of humanity demanded by the bourgeois public sphere. Every time the novel tried to represent these layers of existence, whose main human values lay in productive activity, it became lost in a hopeless parochialism, as is the case, for example, in most so-called peasant novels, or else it had to abandon its own 'natural' atmosphere and correlated methods. Secondly, the illusory collective and public character of the family was mostly founded on the protection it offered in the face of a hostile external world. During the rise of the bourgeoisie such protection could be taken literally. In a Richardson or a Goldsmith the family was a haven for the victims of aristocratic tyranny and cynicism. Later on, protection acquired a wider meaning. At the end of the nineteenth century and the beginning of ours, the so-called genealogical novels showed the acceptance of carefully cultivated family traditions as the adoption of the bourgeois community and as the only form in which the bourgeoisie appeared as a community. However, the gradual disintegration of the monogamous bourgeois family is one of the most striking and most analysed phenomena of the last century — even if its consequences are only now becoming obvious. This process first became apparent in the gradual disappearance, or at least decrease, of the family's economic function, to the point where the family could no longer ensure solid life-long bonds.[8] The value of the family was even more deeply shaken. In eighteenth-century English novels, familial intrigues were already the driving force of the action and this motif was to become the dominant one in the nineteenth-century novels. It is clear that the intimate familial sphere was capable of protecting the ideal of humanity against aristocratic values, but not of warding off the increasing competition in the external world. Hegel has distinctly designated the modern individual, the hero of the novel, as a product of civil (*bürgerliche*) society and not of the family. His remark originally held more self-confidence than resignation: he believed the small community of the family to be narrow and insufficient compared with the educational and humanizing force of the whole integration. After Hegel, however, this aphorism took on an entirely different meaning. The hero of the novel was increasingly forced to destroy the values of the intimate sphere in order to become a prototype of his time. When Dickens makes a great attempt to restore the intimate familial sphere as the refuge of humanity, he must pay the price of peculiarity and of the grotesque exception, for his experiment.

Here too, we are able to detect the ambivalence of the novel: the rupture of family ties is at the same time one of the stages in the emancipation of man. Marx considered the destruction of the power of blood-ties by expanding bourgeois society to be a generally positive accomplishment. Only thus could the consciousness of the human species be created 'from the zoology of the species of human animals'. However, the monogamous bourgeois family itself had become a similar network of pseudo-consanguineous ties, and hence an obstacle to human emancipation.

It had to be overcome for there to be progress in human development. This progress was made willy-nilly. The departure from the traditional ways of living and from the system of inheritance was but rarely followed by the creation of freely chosen, small human communities. Most of the time there ensued a process that might be called the increasing anonymity of the hero of the novel. We know less and less about the origin, the family and the past of this hero. It is striking that names, which at the beginnings of the novel had such a characterizing force, lose this force and no longer have much to do with the characters they designate. When finally a character is called K. or A. G. this is but the end of a long development. This anonymity, which renders the identity of K. or of 'the Stranger' uncertain, signifies the total disintegration of the novel's public dimension rooted in the intimate sphere. In this sense there is certainly a regression with respect to the public character of the epic: it is indeed only afterwards — and most often with a negative result — that one can see whether the actions of the anonymous hero bear a wider human meaning or not. On the other hand, we have arrived at the terminal point of a process of 'disintegration' with a positive value-content: the novel has freed itself from all its natural or quasi-natural links. It has torn away the semblance of freedom and now the question becomes concerned with the creation of real freedom.

The epic's public sphere and its disintegration inevitably affect another sphere of representation: the novel's description of everyday life and of the non-everyday. The epic never encountered this dilemma. Since everyday life in the organic community was organized around communal principles, it is *a priori* clear that the separation between these two aspects of life was a very relative one. Hence, as far as its homogeneity is concerned, it does not matter in the epic whether it portrays a council of military chiefs or a feast in the tent of one of its heroes. The means of the epic are equally adequate to both of these descriptions. In the epic the atmosphere, the rhythm, the system of customs and collective events are all regulated in the same way, whether the setting is the home or a (metaphorical) public square. For the hero of the novel, on the other hand, the house, and later the apartment, is really a fortress that isolates him from his neighbour. Therefore, other techniques are needed to represent this setting than the so-called public scenes. It would obviously be a crude simplification to suggest that in the novel everyday life is identical to the non-public sphere and non-everyday life to the public one. We have just seen how the intimate bourgeois sphere tries to constitute a new kind of public sphere by attempting to generalize its values so that the daily activities of the home are important elements of the intimate sphere. However, a double difficulty arises here which the novel can never solve without ambiguity. The birth of industrial civilization objectively enlarged the circle of daily life. There came into being numerous forms of action unimaginable for men in the organic community. Since no social principle or convention was attached to them, an infinite variety of individual habits were established. In terms of epic descriptions, the two domains represented a heavy task formerly unknown to the epic. Not only did everyday functions that were by no means self-evident have to be shown but, more importantly, the complex network of individual relations that were their corollaries. The novel rarely had at its disposal such a convenient milieu as that of *Robinson Crusoe*, where daily life itself had to be produced in a daily confrontation with nature, where, because of the unusual situation, philogenesis, the development of all forms of daily activity and their dramatic character, took on universal human significance. Generally, there were two ways of solving the dilemma: either the author tried to encompass the infintely expanding life-circle (including the description of infinitely varied habits) and in that case details proliferated in uneventful descriptions which could not be digested by the reader; or he abandoned all attempts at representation, which posed the problem of the verisimilitude of what was portrayed. When they contained moral and human significance, all the elements of the poetic medley of the old epic seemed equally likely to the listener or the reader. But readers and critics constantly levelled the superficial accusation of 'unreality' against the novel and when we look closer at these complaints we find that their criteria were the stereotypes of everyday life. The naturalist movement even made the programmatic demand, that the novel give a complete and scientifically authentic catalogue of the forms of daily activity to replace 'unreal' and 'romantic' flights of the imagination. This contrast implied the conviction that 'scientific' description evokes the essence of human life more faithfully than attempts to attain 'unlikely' heights. Supposing that it could even be raised, this question could not be resolved in the world of the ancient epic. In the bourgeois epic, on the other hand, the polarization of everyday and non-everyday life had as its consequence that these two spheres in the end reproduced the antagonism between the public and the private realm, independently of the question as to which sphere more faithfully reflected human essence. The authors who opted for everyday life or for 'verisimilitude', gave a more detailed image of the circle of daily life, but reduced the human universality of the work: the paradigmatic and public character of the actions portrayed. Those who preferred the other solution, could create a public atmosphere, could give a public and hence universally valid character to actions and habits only by abstracting from the realm of activities involved in survival and reproduction.

Undoubtedly, the objective articulations of the structure of modern society provoked the dichotomy of bad materialism and bad spiritualism in the bourgeois epic. In this sense the manifestation of the phenomenon was 'necessary'. But the dilemma that is raised is not therefore insoluble. The successful representation of daily life, the solution to the dichotomy, was fundamentally linked to the destiny of the intimate sphere. If the original hopes of the bourgeoisie had been realized, if the human values of the intimate sphere had been generalized in the realm of reason, the principles of the organization of the activities of daily life possessing social generality would have emerged from the customs and habits of everyday life itself. There are important indications of this in the episodes representing scenes dealing with pure 'everydayness' in the novels of a Fielding, a Goldsmith, a Goethe, a Jane Austen, or a Tolstoy. This solution became impossible because of the infinite, value-neutral variability of the system of daily habits and actions that was the result of the failure of the attempt to universalize the values of the intimate sphere. At most, only the atmosphere of a series of adventures or of historical acts could produce a temporary solution. However, here too, the novel shows itself to be ambivalent. An idea that was to play a crucial role in the struggle to overcome alienation had been formed, namely the idea that one of the essential meanings of the forms of non-daily activities is to enable us to organize our daily lives in a humanized framework, once we return to 'normal' life. The best, although not unique, example in this context is the epilogue to *War and Peace*. A glance at the family life of the Bezukhovs after the great historical tempest indicates human enrichment (together with all the problems that this notion implies in Tolstoy) and also preparation for a new phase of non-daily activity. The other side of the ambivalence is that alluded to by Lucien Goldmann: the bourgeois novel is more and more dominated by the dualism of the values of 'authentic' and 'inauthentic' life (*eigentliches und uneigentliches Dasein*), and within this split, the 'prose' of daily life is always to be found in the sphere of inauthenticity.

Goldmann has also brought to the fore a second network of problems:

the status of values in the novel. His theory is based on the following considerations: the novel as such is a universe dominated by values ignored by society. It implicitly expresses 'authentic' values that do not exist in it as manifest realities.[9] This is in connection with the fact that the form of the novel is clearly homologous to the structure of exchange in the system of the market economy.[10] Finally, according to Goldmann, the following process takes place: as soon as exchange-value relegates use-value to the background and renders it implicit, authentic values are also relegated to the background of the novel. All this establishes the exceptional importance of mediation in bourgeois existence and in the form homologous to it.[11]

Many objections can be made to this train of thought. First of all we could note that Goldmann uncritically adopts Heidegger's category of 'authenticity'.[12] More important, though, is the methodology which he uses to enlarge Marx's notion of economic value into that of value in general. Only by disregarding the fact that there is no basis in Marx for such an operation can Goldmann claim that use-value becomes authentic and exchange-value inauthentic. The notion of the implicit dimension of use-value in Goldmann is also problematic. Marx has indeed shown that in the act of exchange the concrete and specific quality (hence, use-value) of what is exchanged disappears and that only its quantitative aspect, rendered homogeneous by the general measure of value is taken into consideration. In spite of this, the use of the term 'implicit' with respect to use-value is awkward because, unless the commodity manifested its characteristic use-value, it could not take part in the exchange process. Finally, what homology can be shown to exist between use-value and the manifestation of human 'authenticity'?

Nevertheless, Goldmann's way of posing the question is important in two ways. Although the theory of the 'homology with the market' is exaggerated, it points to a number of structural peculiarities in the form of the novel that make possible a new theoretical interpretation. On the other hand, this schema is the first to have brought out the problem of the relation between axiology and the theory of genres. We could briefly formulate this relation as follows: every specific artistic form is universal or episodical, is connected to world history or to a specific period, and one of the criteria of its historical character is precisely its capacity to reproduce the hierarchy of dominant values of its time in relation to the value development of the human species. This criterion can be represented even more precisely by the part of this hierarchy that the form is capable of reproducing and by the values that play the predominant role in it.[13]

From this perspective one can simultaneously see the world-historical and universal character of the epic and of the novel, and their total opposition. In the ancient epic, in conformity with the internal structure of organic communities, a firm and fixed hierarchy of values is dominant. It is communal ethical convention (*Sittlichkeit*) that bears values in this unalterable form: thus, Alexander the Great ordered his hierarchy of values on the model of Achilles. There are exceptional moments when the individual can modify customs (Homer, for instance, shows us how cannibalism disappears from the list of heroic values and becomes a sign of barbarism), but even here it is the past before the given *Sittlichkeit* that is evoked in the present of the narration. The consequence of a rigid value hierarchy for the construction of the work is that in the epic only a small, well-defined number of human types can play the role of organizing centre, a role that Hegel demanded of this genre: the most heroic, the most handsome, and the wisest alone can fulfil this task. The order of the characters, the architectonic order of the epic, is given once and for all on the basis of the hierarchy of values. The novel radically breaks with this tradition, but it keeps the universality of the representation of values. This is expressed first and foremost in the fact that the novel, already in its formal changes (and hence not solely in its contents), incorporates a great conquest of the bourgeois era: the flexible and dynamically changing character of the system of values. Goldmann is certainly wrong when he says that Balzac is the novelist of '*the*' bourgeois order of values *par excellence*: the construction of his works, the distribution and ordering of the characters always evokes the preferences appropriate to '*a*' given period of bourgeois development (and of course to the author's own choices). In the beginning, men of action are the representative heroes: Robinson, the picturesque vagabond, those who act on history.[14] With the change in orientation begun in the nineteenth century, an intellectual struggle is waged for the possibility and the meaning of action with a value content, while during the period of decline, the lived experience (*Erlebnis*) is in principle more important than the 'non-authentic' act. Our relation with the value hierarchy of different epochs can be quite varied: we can as easily condemn the self-confidence of a naive faith in the omnipotence of bourgeois action, as the passive and aristocratic attitude toward lived experience. However, we can hardly deny that the explosion of the fixed hierarchy of values and its replacement by the dynamism of a constantly changing order of values is also an aspect of the increased emancipatory content of the novel as compared with the epic, which we have previously noted. Consequently, the novel is in principle *value-pluralistic*; it does not recognize only a few limited behaviour patterns, only a few fundamental or exclusive virtues. Goethe's remark, 'only the totality of men represents humanity' could be the epigram of every novel. Later, in the period of crisis, this laudable pluralism becomes a sentimental relativism. Lukács often speaks of the false sentimentalism of a great number of contemporary writers toward their heroes, in opposition to the liberating pitilessness of the earlier ones. Behind the Lukácsian contrast of pitilessness and sentimentality, we have the change of a pluralism of values into a relativism of values. In spite of this, it is the pluralism of values that is the formal and structural essence of the genre, expressing and motivating the great conquest of this new epoch: the individual choice of values. Similarly, this pluralism allows in principle a rich and large scale in the portrayal of the human soul, which was inaccessible within the rigid value hierarchy of the epic. Finally Goldmann justly emphasizes (even though his argument is not quite correct) that the novel is an oppositional genre, already by the mere nature of its structure. It takes on this aspect once again, precisely because of its value preferences. Even if the novel responds to the market structure, it never accepts the market's conception of values. Money can play the role of universal means of exchange in the novel, but it can never be placed at the summit of the system of values: it cannot be placed there because that would lead to the destruction of the very possibility of a 'living' representation. As a result of commodity fetishism, the relations among men are reified, but the novel must — at least relatively — decompose this thing-like texture, or simply annihilate itself as a form. This 'decomposition' tends to be less and less successful and this is a decisive element in the crisis of the novel. However, the novel is precisely not homologous to the structure of the market system because behind the dominant market structure, the novel brings 'authentic' human values to the surface — values which, although in a lesser measure, point toward the enrichment of 'human substance'.

Such universal artistic forms as the epic and the novel have to represent systems of general preferences in one way or another. In the case of the epic this was much easier. Aristotle could voice the millenial experience and moral convictions of the Hellenes in declaring that the 'gifts of destiny' are also part of the moral equilibrium of life. In the epic poem, these rewards are the objective outgrowth of purely ethical virtues, each realm reflecting the other. Thus, the rich sphere of manipulation and consumption, described by Hegel to show the objective vivacity of the epic, is in no way marked by reification. The 'living' connection between object and man was greatly enhanced by the particular background of the epic plot, war or travels, where the goods taken from the enemy or hostile nature were in themselves proofs of the human perfection of the hero, according to the scale of values of this genre.

Since it is an oppositional genre and the spirit of capitalism (as characterized by Weber) could never dominate it, the bourgeois epic presented this unity ambiguously from the very beginning. The eighteenth-century English novel (most of all in Defoe) still reflects a radiant optimism which, in the context of human development, sees no problem with the conception of a Mandeville: 'private vices, public benefits'. But protests are already being voiced and not only in the first great dissenters, Swift and Cervantes, but also in Fielding's polemic with the 'café Hobbes' in *Amelia*. With respect to the contrast ('material values' versus ethical values) the novel is characterized by the same conflict that Marx brought to light between the political economy of morality and the morality of political economy. If we consider this philosophical aphorism in terms of the structure of the novel, we can say that, in this respect, the novel is also on the defensive: if it wants to represent characters who have moral value (using any system of ethical values) it must increasingly turn away from the universe of material goods and acquisition. This process is fully completed by the end of the nineteenth century. The already mentioned anonymity of the heroes is increased simply by the fact that the reader almost never gets to know the objective world in which they live, except where the environment is described in order to create a special atmosphere. As a result, spatial representation shrinks not only in an extensive sense (i.e. as a dimension) but also intensively. When the author excludes the activities by which objects are acquired, he is obliged to abandon the essential tools he needs for the intimate portrayal of man. But in this context also the ambivalence of the genre comes out. The objectivity of the world of the epic as a human extension was a 'first immediacy' that had to explode in order for the endless process of production to be launched on the basis of age-long struggles. The relationship of the world of the epic to nature and to hostile human groups — the latter appearing as segments of nature — belonged to the realm of 'restricted accomplishment'. In itself, the satisfaction of the hero at the sight of the material goods he had wrested from the external world stood under the sign of such a narrowness. Moreover, in an organic community, goods of fortune

(fortune, freedom or dependence, etc.) came to the individual by the accident of his birth, and thus as a result of a determination which Marx considered inferior to an accidental relationship of individuals to the powers of existence. The unsettled and disharmonious state of the hero of the novel was superior to that limited harmony of the epic in three respects. First, there the hero of the novel always has a yearning for the infinite — an insatiable desire to possess new objects — which constitutes the human superiority of a society oriented towards the future over the closed world of the epic. Secondly, even when the novel abandons the representation of material values, as contrasted to moral values, it still introduces a fruitful dimension: it considers and forces consideration of the world of objects as a problem. The truly important novel always moves on the level of the consciousness of the species: it not only knows and shows that the increase and extension of objectifications mean the extension of man's power, but a significant novel also makes clear that as long as these objectifications are opposed to man as 'external', alien forces, they are also non-values, and obstacles to the unfolding of human capabilities. It is precisely with respect to the non-authenticity and decline of values in the novel that *The Theory of the Novel* rightfully speaks of alienation as the central theme of the bourgeois epic. Finally, in the novel, the 'gifts of destiny' are acquired through the 'skill' and vitality of the fortuitous individual, and compared with the situational advantages of birth. This represents progress, even when this skill and vitality manifest themselves in repulsive forms.

It is also to Lucien Goldmann's credit to have brought to the forefront of contemporary discussion the 'problematic individual', analysed by Lukács over 50 years ago as the principal character of the novel. Considering its romantic anti-capitalist premises, *The Theory of the Novel* is quite consistent when it describes as totally problematic both the modern individual and the corresponding literary genre, the novel. In the background of the dilemma there is on the one hand the emancipatory fact of the formally free individual, and on the other hand the general specific conflicts of values in a society without community. If we are to remain faithful to our starting point, we cannot unambiguously admit the superiority of the representation of man in the epic or the 'problematical character' of the hero of the novel. The general narrowness of the harmonious universe of the epic appears especially sharply in the quasi-individual quality of its heroes. Hegel and Lukács consider the epic hero as the model of the collectivity, transcending mere individuality. This collective quality of the individual in the epic means that each hero is much more the expression of an *ethnographic virtue* than a unique entity that cannot be duplicated. Marx ironically rejected those conceptions in which the essence of man's individuality was seen in terms of his uniqueness. His irony was perfectly justified: this 'uniqueness' is hardly different from that of a leaf. On the other hand, the symmetry of the Greek vase paintings that is completely free of any individuality, the inter-changeability of hostile combatants (Achilles and Hector, etc.) shows better than any theoretical argument that epic characters do nothing more than fulfil with dignity the function allotted to them in the division of talents. There is no question here of an individuality going beyond natural uniqueness and moulding its own characteristic 'uniqueness' through hard work.

'Collective individuality' offers great advantages to epic representation. First of all there is no *danger of privatization*: Achilles' wrath is just as much a public matter as a private one. Secondly, as a result of the functional and 'non-unique' character of the epic hero, it is never a question *how* certain men become capable of fulfilling such and such tasks. The question raised in the epic is always the following: is there someone to fulfil a certain function? The Greeks are weak as long as Achilles in his wrath does not fulfil his function; Troy's fall is evident when no one fulfils Hector's function. Leaving aside other perspectives, the starting point *in medias res* of the epic has also a more profoundly *individual* meaning: the portrayal of the hero never includes his genesis, at most his genealogy. Finally, the epic never touches on the banal since the individuals are collective, general embodiments of vital powers, and thus the relation between the species and the individual is immediate and direct.

We can understand all the virtues and antimonies of the portrayal of the individual in the novel starting out from Marx's idea that modern man is a *fortuitous individual*. This means primarily that to give the name or genealogy of the hero does not contribute to our knowledge of him and that the situation no longer provides immediate evidence of his character. Only the organic community can give this immediate evidence; it defines the functions that are necessary for its existence — functions which can be understood at a glance — and designates the types of men necessary to fulfil those functions. This is why in the epic *act and character coincide*. In the dominant genre of Antiquity, the classical dictum does not apply: *duo si faciunt idem, non est idem*. The acts of epic heroes are never identical and this is why their character can be judged directly by their actions. As the fortuitous individual gains at least the appearance of freedom by stepping out from the framework of these large collective integrations in order to rely upon his own uniqueness, he becomes, in the exact sense of the term, the problematic individual of the novel. The greatest problem for the novelist becomes the analysis of the hero, and even the possibility or impossibility of this analysis.

Hence we have the numerous dead ends in the characterization of man in the novel, which can only be mentioned briefly here. The general dichotomy of the Self and the outside world in the bourgeois epic often leads to an *a priori* sterile choice in the portrayal of the individual. When the author attempts to 'deduce' the fortuitous individual from the world of 'objects', from his objectifications, the result is the reduction of character to a mass of sociological factors. But when the author chooses to portray the accidental character of the individual — this nebulous entity so difficult to interpret — the result leads him either to ignore or to violate the effective objective nature of the 'world', and to throw his hero into the freedom of his fortuitous individuality. Clearly, this antinomy is excluded from the epic where object and man are one, where Achilles' shield can only be represented from the point of view of the hero's existence. On the other hand, it is obvious from all this that the authentic presentation of man in the novel demands quite complicated techniques and a specific individual inventiveness, especially since the motivations remain uncertain and vague whenever act and character do not coincide. When the novelist stresses the world, the objective and sociological background, in his portrayal of the hero, the modern reader always objects to this on the grounds of a lack of psychological truth, which simply means the following: I believe that this act corresponds to the interplay of social forces but I doubt that corresponds to this individual in particular. If, on the other hand, the fortuitous quality of the character (in portrayal, this is the same as the hidden motivation of his actions) becomes the focal point of the representation, then his deeds are discredited from the human viewpoint and are no longer of interest. Finally, all this has consequences which we discussed earlier from a different angle: the portrayal of the fortuitous individual demands the creation of an *artificial milieu* in order to insure the conditions of transparent characterization. The author of *The Theory of the Novel* says quite profoundly that psychology (in the modern novel sense of the term) is an *Ersatz* for action. But so is inevitably every artificial milieu that the modern writer is forced to create in order to rid his characters, as fortuitous individuals, of all ambivalence and make them seem natural.

On the other hand, these very consequences led to the birth of the *Bildungsroman*, this great humanistic conquest of the bourgeois epic. Here we are not only speaking of a given type of novel, in the narrow sense of the term, to which belong classical masterpieces such as *Tom Jones, Wilhelm Meister, Der grüne Heinrich* or the *Joseph* tetralogy. These differ from other novels only in so far as the educational process itself is purposefully put forward as the goal of the action. (Goethe underlines this by creating a special 'apparatus'.) Every work of this type, even the minor ones, was written in a period when democratic perspectives were alive and promising and called for the creation of a 'new man' to replace the old one. Actually, however, until the beginning of its crisis, the novel always portrayed an educational process — a process of self-education (and this also holds true for later periods whenever the novel does not capitulate to fetishization) — even when the immediate meaning of its subject-matter is a 'reverse education', a losing of illusions. Here too, the dichotomy which was already apparent at the beginning of the history of the novel is once again manifest: Robinson learns confidently how to master nature for the use of bourgeois production and consumption while Gulliver, at the end of his pedagogical tour, understands resignedly that the institutions and mores of his beloved country are unworthy of genuine humanity when compared with the standard of the wise horses. Both, however, must go through a self-education for two reasons. First, because the world is not finished, has no natural character as in an organic community, but is in continuous transformation. Of course, the organic community has education too: every individual who starts out in life must learn the practice of functions related, directly or indirectly, to his self-preservation. But everyone can employ this knowledge with the conviction that it will be valid for the rest of his life: Achilles, whose values resist the attrition of time, cannot be surprised like Don Quixote. The hero of the bourgeois epic must learn capabilities rather than finished knowledge, for the conditions that are given could radically change during his lifetime. Robinson Crusoe, on his island, has to face tasks that are just as unexpected as those of Wilhelm Meister or Lucien de Rubempré. Moreover, the heroes of the novel, as fortuitous individuals, continually transcend spheres of existence: social layers and every new adaptation demands new capabilities. This continuous transformation characterizes not only the period of the rise of the novel: to a large extent, the loss of illusions is a result of the fact that the great heroic dreams of a younger generation as it enters a promising phase of bourgeois society, are irremediably shown to be illusions; thereafter one must re-educate himself in order to continue to live. From Fabrizio del Dongo, Rastignac, to Frédéric Moreau we have the history of the education of whole generations. Increasingly fetishized bourgeois society is harder to understand, and for some it becomes totally incomprehensible. Dickens' best characters are precisely those extravagant ones who grope in the dark and whose timid pathos comes from their total lack of understanding and their ignorance of the world around them. In the epic universe too, there is an unpredictable factor, or at least something rarely known in advance: the will of Olympus or Valhalla. One hero has no inkling of divine decisions, while some other knows them and submits himself to his fate by anticipating events. However, even if the gods have human forms, the heavenly will implies general unpredictability and the supremacy of the universe beyond the limits of the community. This is a fact to which the world of 'restricted accomplishment' must resign itself, since its equilibrium and harmony are based precisely on its inability to go beyond the sphere of life. Whatever is within this sphere, however, is accessible to and recognizable by all. At the same time, the general defetishizing function of art that Lukács discusses in his *Aesthetics* clearly manifests itself in the novel. The action itself is nothing but a struggle against the fetishized character of the world, ending either by breaking through the fetishized limits or stopping desperately before its walls.

Because of the internal structure of the world and of the individual who acts in it, it was inevitable that the bourgeois epic should face the problematic of self-education. In the case of the individual, self-education involves a long, painful and *a priori* equivocal operation, during which the fortuitous individual adapts himself to the 'natural laws' of bourgeois society, to find his way around and to go with the stream or against it. Furthermore, the curve of the theme of self-education is a declining one. While in the first centuries of its history, the novel faithfully imitates bourgeois evolutionism to the extent that it considers each individual as virtually perfectible in both senses of the term, in the decades of the crisis following the French Revolution it develops the contrast of the individual, still capable of developing his personality, with a world which does not give him the opportunity to do so. It is in the second half of the nineteenth century that the still prevalent formula is gradually elaborated: the fortuitous character of the individual and the transformation of the world into a 'second nature' are both regarded as definitive and irreversible.

In spite of the decline of the theme of self-education, during its rise, the novel *as a form* expresses an idea that cannot perish with bourgeois society, nor be discredited by the decadence of the genre. In Marx, 'the fortuitous character of the individual' can mean two entirely different things: it is used to indicate that individuals realize themselves or fail to do so through the accidents of competition and struggle; but it also indicates that an individual's place in a given order or class, his greater or lesser integration, is no longer a personal quality of his, but the result of his own activities. The fortuitous character of the individual in the first sense is the product of one given economic formation; in the second sense it has become the lasting heritage of humanity. Of course, the novel deals extensively with the competitive struggles of the fortuitous individual (the Balzacian cycle deals almost exclusively with these) but its essential tendency is to represent self-realization. Every novel worthy of the name poses the question, 'What can man make of himself?' and does so independently of the ideology that enlightens, motivates or blinds its author. The answers may be hopeful or discouraging, the final result may signify the victory or defeat of humanity; but the process itself, in which a man finds himself or loses himself, creates himself or is annihilated, represents a humanizing value that goes far beyond the function fulfilled by the epic. Moreover, just because the novel takes as its starting point the fortuitous individual and hence the subject of an illusory freedom, the result of the educational process is ambivalent. This is true not only in concrete cases but also in principle. The idea of alternative possibilities as opposed to the predestination of the epic, enters the world-view of the novel through this ambivalence. In stating this opposition we must avoid modern prejudices. Ever since the Marxian theory of history permitted the recognition of history as a process of possible alternatives — and since this viewpoint came to dominate a part of the circle of Marxism — any form that leaves out this notion seems to be retrogressive. This modern viewpoint cannot, however, be applied indiscriminately to the ancient epic. Of course, it is obvious that, when the hero of the epic accepted his destiny or fulfilled it, his fate, his very journey, were predetermined independently of whether or not he knew this. Nevertheless, according to the standards of the anthropomorphic universe of the genre, the hero of the epic raised himself to the level of the gods and he affirmed the dignity of man in that universe. The original public could hierarchically distinguish between mortals and Olympians, but posterity no longer perceives this hierarchy precisely because of the merits of epic representation. Nevertheless, the atmosphere of the genre excludes the very idea that Achilles could become Thersites, or vice versa; as for the comic epic, its effect, which today is greatly diminished, was based on a situation which seemed absurd then and which has now become one of the ordinary techniques of our comic books: the exceptional and imposing was placed in down-to-earth circumstances. In civil society, and in the novel, the possibility of individual development according to alternatives but independent of all community has often enough led to a metamorphosis in which Achilles descended to Thersites' level. But, even at that price, mankind has 'gained' in as far as the characters of the novel are turned towards the future — their own future — instead of projecting from a specific point in the past the unalterable scenario of their existence.

The factors analysed so far can answer many questions about the structure and composition of the novel: questions concerning the essence of an understanding of the form, that are always posed in order to deprecate this new genre or to show its superiority. The most important one is related to the forms of personal contact in the novel.

In the epic, the characters are potential or effective acquaintances. This is due on the one hand to the blood ties that remain quite solid in their sphere of life, and on the other hand, to the limited and well-defined space in which the protagonists move, and finally to the fact that the latter represent 'institutions' or 'functions', the possible variations of which are restricted. It is not just in one single community that the individuals know each other thus; we have but to look at the symmetry of the vase paintings to see that the other collectivities were organized according to identical principles and had the same representative human functions; all those who fulfilled them could not but know each other even without being acquainted.

In the novel, on the other hand, the starting point for human relations is a number of private bourgeois persons who live in houses or apartments, isolated from one another and reciprocally unknown to one another. Initially, this condition is mitigated by the aspiration to constitute a public sphere, from the intimate familial world. However, the contacts within the family never have the all-pervading influence of blood-ties in the epic. Hegel's remark is again relevant: the individual is not the child of the family but, in the first instance, that of civil society. In the epic, the memory of ancestral hospitality is enough to avoid all friction in human contacts or at least to maintain them at the level of polite exchange (cf. the episode of Glaucon and Diomedes), while in the novel, the mere mention of kinship reveals nothing about real personal relations. Moreover, even *romans de famille* cannot concern only a *single* family, and the mutual anonymity of bourgeois individuals completely dominates relations between different families. At the beginning, the novel tries to give the illusion of representing the entire society; even when it was later forced to restrict its domain of representation, it never disowned the principle of this aim. It is obvious that in the spatially-extended units characteristic of modern society, the mutual acquaintance of men is excluded; we can in addition point to the relative isolation of social strata and classes.

All this amounts to only the dry and factual obstacles to harmonious relations in the bourgeois epic. We have already given the essential reason: however, the fortuitous character of the individual reveals only the surface of the personality and not the 'substantial' human traits. As long as belonging to a community was also an essential quality of a person, this quality, the substance of the personality, appeared immediately upon contact with other men. Exceptions arise only when the hero consciously wants to mislead others, as often happens in the *Odyssey*. It was, therefore, impossible to apprehend anyone but in his most personal and most substantial being. Let us look once again at the comic epic. When we do not find Achilles surrounded by the trimmings of heroic life but engaged in his most intimate activities, he no longer has any place in the epic poem and can only be treated in a parody of the genre. Whatever our opinion of Mr Bloom, we could not say the same thing of him. In certain types of community, the recognition of the essence of a person is facilitated by behaviour, habitual gestures or rules of dress. All this means that in the world of the organic community, collective activities and forms of collective behaviour always reveal man in his substantial aspects. In the novel, on the other hand, one has to struggle to get to know this substantial quality; and more than once the action is nothing but this mutual effort of men to know each other, gropingly, among the obstacles of the incognito. Moreover, the novel no longer tends to show its heroes in their objective activities and this is another source of difficulties in the representation of the forms of human relations. We can sum up the obstacles to human relations with Engels's objection to Feuerbach: the existence of man in bourgeois society (and not only that of the proletariat, as Engels said) is not identical with his essence.

In order to overcome these difficulties, the novel develops a specific structure of relations: the fatality that imposes itself on human relations through fortuitous events. The novel starts with fortuitous events, encounters that depend on the will of the author alone, as is suitable for the depiction of a private and isolated personality. Nothing characterizes the relations of isolated private persons more adequately than when two heroes meet each other through a street accident, some 'gratuitous' invitation, a chance remark, etc. But these fortuitous encounters must later on justify a fatality; in other words, they must suggest that the paths taken by the heroes had to follow the given direction. This fatality forcefully asserts itself at the end of almost every novel when, theoretically, the ambiguity of 'this could have happened otherwise' is excluded, when the credibility of the object of the novel is established through the realization of the most probable variant in the realm of possibilities.

In order to clarify the meaning of fatality we must distinguish here three nuances in the word. The first cannot be considered as real 'fatality', in the philosophical sense of the word. It means that 'something must happen' to the characters once they are brought into contact by the author's *Willkür*. Relations have to be established between them, otherwise the story would have no meaning, like those of Thornton Wilder. This is simply a *conditio sine qua non* of the form. (It is, of course, characteristic that, unlike the epic, this form can only arise out of arbitrary and fortuitous encounters.) The second nuance carries the usual fetishistic content: behind every chance event lurks the severe 'law of the universe', in other words, the system of the natural laws of bourgeois society. The established order that is given at the beginning of the novel must justify itself according to a predetermined fatalism. The third nuance resembles what Spinoza called self-determination: men themselves effect what they are and what they become and the result can seem, retrospectively, unavoidable and, if you like, fatal. This interpretation can often be used for love-stories. Think of the relations between David Copperfield and Agnes. For years, the hero and heroine live close to each other, without suspecting their latent love, and finally are united as a result of their own acts and the evolution of their characters. What happens depends on them: it is their own doing. But in its very constitution, the event is so definitive that it can appear not only as a sort of necessity, but as fatality.

Goldmann's theory of the homology of the form of the novel and the structure of the market is most fruitful in this context, for it can rationally interpret the categories of chance and fatality. The encounter between men on the market is entirely due to chance in the sense that it has no other 'rationality' or 'motivation' than the desire to exchange products as commodities. This desire tells us nothing about the 'substance', origin or capacities of the men involved and is therefore purely fortuitous even with respect to them. Their coexistence is also unforeseen: Marx's analysis in the *Economic-Philosophical Manuscripts* gives us an incomparable phenomenology of the encounter and of fortuitous contacts between the Self and the Other. As far as the personality of those who meet is concerned, the occasion and the locality also turn out to be fortuitous: one can deduce from a man's personality neither the moment when he becomes part of the act of exchange, when his product becomes a commodity, the object of successful exchange, nor the circumstances of the unfolding of this operation. Correspondingly, when one considers all this — men, their coexistence, their substance, and the 'eternal, natural laws' of capitalism, laws which seem in every respect to be unchangeable and determining for the various actions of the individual — they prove to be composed of a sum of fortuitous acts. It is clear that, when we speak of the structural resemblance between the action of the market and the form of the novel, we are not thinking of conscious imitation. Marx's analysis shows that commodity fetishism, which is first realized on the market, homogenizes all of social life in its own image and also penetrates those spheres that seem to be the most intimate ones. Thus, if in the work of the artist such 'ordinary' forces of reality as the market or commodities cannot even appear, and if, nevertheless, he orders his characters and actions according to the structure of commodity exchange, or more precisely, according to a similar artistic formula, this is the result of the homogenizing power of generalized fetishism.

The bipolarity of the contingent and the fatal represents to a certain extent a regression compared with the predestined 'linearity' of the epic. On the one hand, the representation of what is fortuitous, of what is exclusively private and hence banal, is inferior to the human universality of the epic poem. On the other hand, the representation of forces of destiny that realize themselves behind men's back increases 'the prosaic nature of the novel'. Yet, as far as the form is concerned, we must draw attention to a *novum*: the tension of the action that arises from the bipolarity of the contingent and the fatal. This tension, based on the elements of unpredictability and expectation, follows from the fact that we cannot know in advance the encounters of the 'fortuitous' heroes, the destinies with whom their own will be entwined, and the nature of their own destiny. In the ancient epic, where human functions are fulfilled, where, moreover, the distribution of roles by destiny is already conveyed to the reader by popular myth, the emotion of suspense arising from unpredictability and expectation is replaced by exaltation when the reader sees the function fulfilled. It is indeed difficult to order hierarchically the two types of impressions. Nevertheless, it seems obvious that exaltation at the fulfilment of the function is an experience that refers to the past just as does the whole emotional universe of the epic hero. The feeling of pleasure is caused by the fact that something already known to the reader is revived in an exemplary form. This transforms simple 'cognition' into shock, into self-knowledge, into self-examination, into catharsis. While following the hero's footsteps, the reader of a novel also does not grope around in a London smog, at least not in works of any importance. It is also true here ultimately that, from its invisible focus, the end of the novel projects back its light and shadow on the faces of its heroes. However, from the point of view of the reader, there is no question of foresight here, but at most a presentiment fostered in a very equivocal way by fortuitous encounters and chance events. It is so much a presentiment that the reader has theoretically the right to question (at the end) the way in which the author terminates his hero's journey. On the other hand, it would obviously be senseless to doubt in the context of an accepted popular myth the 'justification' of Hector's death during the course of the history of Troy. Fortuitous events have thus an *a priori* orientation towards the future, laying out alternatives. In more than one novel this possibility is destroyed by the preconceived and fetishistic logic of 'natural laws'. The question nevertheless remains open in every novel that is a work of art: is the universal context that finally takes shape the result of the free self-determination of the characters or of the bad objectivity of the natural laws of the fetishized world? Correspondingly — and this is also an alternative — tension can arise from the anticipation of elevated human emotions, from the reader's desire to experience such impressions and to enrich his life with them, but tension can also sink down, as Musil noted, to the level of a technique that merely enslaves us and captivates us with the arabesques of chance, without, however, enriching us. The novel, this creation of a structure of consciousness that is conscious of alternatives, also faces alternatives with regard to its own possibilities. The bipolarity of the accidental and the fatal is the structural element of the novel that is most profoundly rooted in its time, that which is most intimately linked to market society: a future epic form will have to transcend it. In every period of historical progress it can happen again that an epic genre of free self-determination will replace the novel's structures based on fetishistic necessity, but the new epic will still remain within the limits of the original model. Nor is there any doubt that since humanity will never again be a single organic community, the purely objective encounter between heroes and their relations will have fortuitous and occasional causes. In two important aspects, however, it seems that the structure of the novel can be transcended. First, man will no longer have slowly to strip off the shell of reification that surrounds other men. As a result the substance of men, their mutually compatible or exclusive essence, will be able to manifest itself at once and without mediation, and this will automatically liquidate the wavering between the poles of the accidental and the fatal. Secondly, of all human possibilities, the one that has been effectively realized (by realization we mean self-realization) will always have additional weight and ontological status as compared with the merely given possibility. Whether it be by the parallel unfolding of the possible destinies of a hero, or by leaving certain potentialities open, or by using contrasting figures who, in their self-realization express one of the possibilities of the other, the new epic genre will be able to grant the idea of the alternative much greater import than the best novels have done so far.

This is where the question of the handling of time in the novel comes in. *The Theory of the Novel* shows in this respect a too radical approach: the novel is considered as the genre of the struggle against the temporal process, a struggle which reaches its climax in Flaubert's *L'Éducation Sentimentale* with the discovery of duration (*durée*) as the only 'authentic' time in a human sense. This conception is just as polemical and exaggerated as the whole of Lukács's summary verdict on the novel, but its element of contrast remains valid: in the epic, there is no flow of time in the strict sense of the term; the novel, on the other hand, is struggling with the dead weight of the temporal process. Even for the epic, though, we must avoid taking these statements literally: every series of actions is in itself a temporal process, such as the one that lasts from the beginning of the conflict between Achilles and Agamemnon until Hector's death. However, the *tempora mutantur et nos mutamur in illis* does not characterize this succession. Lukács notes quite pertinently that Achilles remains young, Nestor old and wise, Helen beautiful, whatever 'effective' time has elapsed from the starting point to the end of the series of events. And this is logical, for the power of lost, evanescent time to change man becomes artistically relevant only if man's change has meaning as far as the work is concerned. It is precisely this transformation that is excluded in the epic: the destinies are predetermined, the education of the characters for the future fulfilment of their human functions is, at most, a background episode; the deformation of the hero to the point of an inadequacy to fulfil his function is either just an episode (the amorous folly of such and such a knight) or a procedure that prepares and leads to the realization of the function (as in Achilles' case). Thus, all processes, the beginning and the end of which show two different states of a character (only there does time play a role that can be used by the author), are theoretically hostile to the structure of the epic. When both Goethe and Schiller point out that all epic forms, as opposed to drama, stress the *how* of the action, they discover in fact the essential characteristics of the ancient epic. The *how*, to use this excessively generalizing expression, basically reveals what we have called 'fulfilling one's function'; from this perspective, the flow of time is just a medium, a neutral terrain where the characters can take the steps that destiny has prescribed them. On the other hand, the fact that the hero of the novel is a fortuitous individual, that the bipolarity of the accidental and the fatal is a basic structural principle of the genre, opens the form onto the future. Thus, the question of the value and character of the temporal process and its power to transform man becomes the vital formal question that must be resolved each time.

The novel has numerous schemata at its disposal to render the problematic of the flow of time: we can only mention a few of them briefly. The 'flashback' that reveals the time-process of a wasted life, and the *Bildungsroman* that unfolds the time dimension of a life of accomplishment are two opposite, yet complementary schemata of the temporal flow. The common characteristic of both is that the heroes are conscious of the temporal process and its importance, whether from the beginning or from a certain moment in their lives, and that they organize their destinies accordingly, or at least have an evaluative attitude towards the temporal process. The schema of the *Bildungsroman* is generally based on the fact that *Tom Jones* or *Der grüne Heinrich* does not know at first what it means to waste time; but awakening from this condition of danger to himself and others, he organizes the rhythm of his life. What we have called an evaluative attitude is mostly current during the period of retreat in the evolution of the novel: Lukács's example, Frédéric Moreau, is the classic illustration of this. But even the passive cult of past experience, which usually registers only the emptiness of its unfolding, and the value given to a particular and arbitrarily chosen moment, forces the flow of time into consciousness and places it in the centre of human self-consciousness. Another schema is the incongruity of the historical temporal process and the rhythm of individual life, in other words, the experience which became increasingly typical in the last few centuries, that there is a profound gap between individual life and the historical process. This ambivalence leads in the novel to an exceptionally rich undulating movement which comes from dreams, from harsh awakenings, from convulsive efforts to make up for lost time, from the isolation caused by premature advances, and through the psychic petrification due to time lags. Of course, there is constant movement in the novel: the hero is like a navigator following the equator of his life, never again able to land in the same world from which he started. Finally, as a logical consequence of the interplay of accidents, the moment becomes of decisive importance in the plot of the novel, the moment of grasped or lost opportunity, the moment which, once the novel has retreated from the field of real action into the domain of inner experience, appears as a substitute for life as a whole, for the flight of time, or at least as the object and the raw material of experience which replaces real action.

The common element of these schemata is that in each of them time becomes a problem, in other words, an unfulfilled task, a project to be solved by man. This is what is pre-eminently human in the novel, in all novels, in the form itself. For it is indeed true that man is never merely a dumb species, a *stumme Gattung*, to use Marx's phrase in his debate with Feuerbach, but there is a certain 'dumbness', something profoundly narrow in the unreflecting, harmonious and passive way in which an Achilles, a Hector, a Siegfried live their strictly limited existence. It is precisely the ethical questions that are lacking, the feeling that man is a moral problem to himself and perhaps an enigma to be solved. On the contrary, the novel, in its very form, unveils the major ethical tension of human life, 'the lack of time', the fact that our existence has an end and that therefore we have to use the temporal process that has been given to us in such a way as to lose neither the fulfilment of the moment nor the totality of higher human development. Different novels can give entirely different, and often unclear or humanly misleading answers to this dilemma, but the form breaks through passive harmony and thus sustains human development.

Our ultimate conclusion, based on the historical-philosophical notion of unequal development, is thus the rejection of the 'problematic' character of the novel. We have discovered the ambivalence of the new epic genre in the fact that it arose from the first 'purely social' society (capitalism) and is dependent on it; therefore it has to contend with all the problems of capitalist fetishization in defending its original structure and bringing it to its full development. Concurrently, the novel has created innovations that cannot be lost in societies that have become social. It does not belong to aesthetics to prophesy or to try to outline the new developments of the epic genre. But it follows from what we have said so far that any dream of a resurrection of the classical epic is but a romantic illusion: the organic community that gave birth to the epic poem and transmitted it is forever gone. Here too, the road forward lies in the conservation of the acquisitions of the bourgeois epic and in their simultaneous transformation. The essence of the structure corresponds to a functional mission: even in its most fetishized specimen, the novel reinforces the reader's consciousness of being a child of the social society; in all its non-fetishistic exemplars, the novel imparts to the reader the knowledge of the maximum possibilities of humanization of which this society is capable. As a form, the novel very clearly shows the limits to which humanization can go in this society and this is for the understanding reader the most salutary sort of catharsis.

NOTES

1   G. Lukács, *Die Theorie des Romans* (Luchterhand, 1965), p. 23; *The Theory of the Novel* (MIT, 1971), p. 30.
2   *Theorie*, p. 26; *Theory*, p. 33.
3   *Theorie*, p. 35; *Theory*, pp. 40—1.
4   *Theorie*, p. 53; *Theory*, p. 56.
5   'But the difficulty is not in grasping the idea that Greek art and *epos* are bound up with certain forms of social development. It lies rather in understanding why they still constitute for us a source of aesthetic enjoyment and in certain respects prevail as the standard and model beyond attainment.' *Marx's Grundrisse*, ed. and trans. David McLellan (New York, 1971), p. 45.
6   Hesiod is the one exception, but peasant novels re-establish the balance on the side of the modern epic genre. Indeed, every time we have a description of a sphere of existence where this material exchange is the exclusive activity or at least the dominating one, the epic structure is necessarily organized around it.
7   Cf. his *Das Strukturwandel der Oeffentlichkeit* (Luchterhand, 1966).
8   Engels says outright that the industrial proletariat nowhere has monogamous marriages and that these generally fall apart as soon as they are no longer bound by the thread of inherited property.
9   *Problèmes d'une sociologie du roman*, 'Introduction', p. 232.
10   Ibid.
11   Ibid., p. 237.

12 Goldmann attributes its invention to Lukács. Presumably, Heidegger merely followed in the latter's footsteps.
13 For an elaboration of this, see Agnes Heller, 'Towards a Marxist theory of value', in *Kinesis*, Fall 1972.
14 It is true that the first objections to this can also be heard quite early: those of Cervantes who sees in action nothing more than the cemetery of values; those of Swift, whose hero returns from action to resignation. But these opposing opinions are also reactions to the dominant schema.

3

What is Beyond Art?
On the Theories of Post-Modernity

FERENC FEHÉR

I

Discussions of the 'end of art' and of 'post-modernity' have recently become the focal point of theoretical discourse both on the right and on the left.[1] It is not my intention here to attempt any redefinition of these ideas which, however topical, are more often than not obscure as far as their conceptual content is concerned. Rather, I would prefer to point out and to some extent analyse certain life syndromes which make these concepts relevant, quite apart from their definitional clarity.

The first complex consists of *sceptical* questions regarding the validity of denomination. Can modern art, many ask, after having become respectable, tamed and perfectly integrated into the establishment, be called avant-garde any longer? If not, can there be any art which is more modern than *this* modern art? (It goes without saying that adding the prefix 'neo' to a noun and calling 'neo-avant-garde' that which is already somewhat obsolete, will not solve the problem.) All these are perfectly relevant questions. Whatever a given observer's attitude to modern art might be, it is clear that the modernist revolution is over. The avant-gardists failed to achieve many of their original objectives, but they did win the battle for respectability. However, a respectable avant-garde is a contradiction in terms. It elicits the doubt that, as far as art and literature are concerned, there may be nowhere to go, that the understanding called 'Art', in general, and spelt with a capital letter, has come to a final halt.

The second complex is constituted by *anxious* questions regarding the institutionalized character of art and literature in modern society. People brought up on the sociological theories of mass society, alienation, fetishism and manipulation (especially manipulation by the mass media) are in any case inclined to regard art as a network of social actions which, as a result of its heavy involvement in crucial public affairs, simply could not have avoided being institutionalized. But institutionalization, as the attentive reader of Max Weber would observe, unfolds in this society under the sign of rationalization. At the same time, to take the obverse of the situation, rationalization is only a refuge in relation to the overall irrationality of our social cosmos. Does art stand any chance of survival if, on the one hand, it is rationalized, like any other institution, and on the other, it is exposed to the all-embracing irrationality of our world?

Thirdly, and this is a statement of *despair*, ours is a world frighteningly close to doomsday, where the social and technological potentials for self-destruction are over-abundant. Is it not simply frivolous to carry on with the business of producing Art in the face of these threats? It is the proverbial 'man in the street' who raises these questions, but he nevertheless echoes Adorno's decisive formulation: can Art be created after Auschwitz?

Finally, there are more limited, but enormously relevant, inquiries into the sociological possibility of distinguishing between 'high' and 'low', shallow and profound, individual and significant versus mass-produced and facile art in a society which, in principle, does not tolerate elites and which is, on both poles of politics, a society of industrially-designed uniformity. It does not take special wisdom to know that without the above distinctions there can hardly be Art, let alone the assessment of art works.

All these theories — some identifiable with one name, some of an anonymous—collective provenance — do not always explicitly predict the 'death of art'. But they are all theories of post-modernity in the sense that none of them radiates any longer the utopian self-confidence of earlier avant-garde movements. On the contrary, directly or indirectly, they all ask questions about the feasibility of continuing the undertaking 'Art'.

II

Peter Bürger's theory of the 'institution of art'[2] is the most lucid and coherent presentation of a theory which predicts, or at least recommends, decisive structural changes regarding the social status of art. The fundamental idea is that during the period of the so-called historical avant-garde movements (the epitome of which was Dadaism), art as such attained to a clear self-awareness, and understood its own long prehistory in retrospect as a history of *institutionalization*. (The decisive movements of the avant-garde are termed by Bürger 'historical', in the sense that they had first represented genuine revolutions and breakthroughs, which have, however, dwindled to the point where their inauthentic heirs follow in their footsteps, pretending to iconoclasm, but in fact longing for the luxury of being purchased by the museum.)

The first category to be understood here is the contrast between the development of art under the aegis of *dominating styles*, which was for Bürger the long and alienated prehistory of art, and a new potential development freed from styles. In this latter development all 'means' of artistic creation (motives, materials, technical solutions and the like) escape the binding context of the particular styles within which they had previously been put to use. In the new era they can be used in any context and in any role as long as it serves the blueprint of the designing intellect. It is obviously futile to point, by way of a counter-argument, to the collages of Picasso, Juan Gris and Braque where even trained eyes, at least at first glance, can easily mistake the work of one artist for the other, for the reason that viewers can identify a *style*, not the individual artist, when utilizing the artistic means as the basis of observation. The historico-philosophical self-confidence of the theory will not be shaken by such a rejoinder, as styles represent for it the first approximation of the much more important concept of the institution of art.

In Bürger's theory one does not find a definition of art as an institution (the theorist obviously regards his key concept as self-evident), but rather very detailed instructions as to how to approach the complex. The institution of art should be understood as the trinity of production, reception and distribution of today's art, all three of which were institutionalized in the prehistory of art, but in a different way in each period. In what follows, I shall give a very sketchy summary of the world history of the institution of art as delineated in Bürger's book.

Bürger identifies three fundamental epochs in the world history of art: art as sacred, in theocratic cultures or in cultures more or less dominated by religion; art as belonging to the system of representative—decorative ceremonies of courtly society; and art as bourgeois, as an object expressive of bourgeois self-consciousness. One aspect of the trinity — distribution

— does not appear historically to undergo any radical changes, according to Bürger. In each world-historical period it is firmly institutionalized by the given particular hegemonic social power elite. However, the situation and interrelationship of production and reception-appropriation is radically different. In the period of sacred art, both reception and production are collective; in the period of art as court ceremony, production is individual, reception is collective, in that it is constituted by the framework, or 'choreography' of court life. In the bourgeois period both production and reception are individual in nature. Here, however, production and reception are only pseudo-individual. For the all-embracing alienation degrades each particular institution in the framework of which art is created or appropriated, and thus voids production and reception of their true individuality. It is this ambivalent situation that provokes the revolt of the avant-garde. As Bürger puts it: 'The European avant-garde movements can be defined as an attack on the status of art in bourgeois society. It is not an earlier arrangement of art [a style] that is being attacked but the institution of art as something detached from the life practice of Man.'³ And there is only one way out: the radical one, the destruction of the institution of art and the total merger of de-institutionalized art and non-artistic life. In this sense, it is an end of Art.

In my view, the main weakness of the theory resides in its unsatisfactory distinction between *objectivation* and *institution.* Beyond doubt, every work of art is an objectivation in the simple sense that it has left the realm of human inwardness (where its *telos* had been conceived) and has appeared, as the end result of inner (cognitive and emotional) processes, as a product which is in harmony with at least some inter-subjective norms and expectations, and in a form in which it may be experienced inter-subjectively. Both the conception of an art work and its impact on the recipients and other objectivations of the world into which it enters, have wider social connotations and presuppositions.

At this point, it is appropriate to recall an important distinction within the very tradition from which Bürger himself departs. I have in mind the distinction between *Absolute Spirit* and *Objective Spirit* in Hegel. Absolute Spirit comprises religion, art and philosophy, the major ideal objectivations of societal life, which are organizing centres of both institutions and everyday activities, but which themselves are not institutionalized. Objective Spirit comprises state, politics and law, to which in a further extension one could now add Church and science. Objective Spirit is the level of institutions *sui generis*, a level to which art does not belong for

Hegel. I think the distinction is important and valid even in the framework of a philosophy which considerably differs from that of Hegel. Perhaps the differentiation between the two levels is too sharply posed in the original version. In a somewhat more flexible formulation one could say that the part of Absolute Spirit which is least able to be institutionalized is philosophy. For, if it becomes institutional, it loses its original sense and significance. The most institutionalizable and institutionalized is religion, even though certain religious sects would strongly deny that the appropriate seat of devotion is the Church, the institution. Art is somewhere in between.

In order to understand this middle-of-the-road position, a tentative definition of institution should first be given, then this definition should be applied to all three aspects of art's existence: production, reception and distribution. Apart from the indispensable element of 'social utility' present within it (one which generally runs counter to *any* concept of the artistic), institution is a type of inter-subjective construct which (a) functions according to rules, ideally at every point, but at least increasingly so; (b) the required human behaviour within which is teachable, ideally in every respect but certainly increasingly so; and which (c) is tendentially impersonal. Institutions will never reach the ideal level of an automaton but they should come as close to the ideal as possible. Now if we turn towards art (which is allegedly completely institutionalized) from the aspect of *production*, we shall immediately see some serious difficulties with Bürger's conception as a whole. The process of producing (if one prefers, creating) works of art is very rarely the direct outcome of any strict application of rules. Even if one applies general rules, as in architecture, in an art which is codetermined by natural sciences, what is being determined is the technology, *not the form*, of the work of art. The only exception here could perhaps be music in which technology and form largely coincide. But if one examines dance or painting, one will see the extent to which the role of rules in creating an art work, while still extant, is ever diminishing. Moreover, this role is reduced almost to nil when we proceed further to literature. The degree of 'teachableness' follows the former pattern: where technology dominates, likewise the rules for successful behaviour dominate. But every intelligent student of any school of music will understand that what can be taught to him is the music of the past, not that of the future, in other words, not his own possible musical production. In all cases where technology plays a diminished role or no role at all, this second constituent of institutionalization diminishes or loses its role in producing works of art. And, finally, as far as impersonality is concerned, the objectivation of art and its institutionalization part ways radically. While the institution in modernity becomes, according to Weber's observation, increasingly impersonal, the objectivation of the work of art bears, in the same period, ever more ostentatiously the hallmark of individuality.

As far as reception is concerned, some of its preconditions have always been institutionalized. The most institutionalized aspects of reception are the *occasion* on which the reception takes place, and the *public reaction* to an art work in the process of reception. But in order to imagine a constellation in which reception—appropriation of art works has become totally submitted to rules, completely teachable, and absolutely impersonal, one must conceive of a society such as that of *1984*, or *Brave New World*. Distribution is admittedly the most institutionalized aspect of the trinity. Arnold Hauser has convincingly pointed out that the allegedly spontaneous propagation of works of art in any social context is a romantic myth. From the smallest and most homogeneous tribal culture to the vast and largely heterogeneous bourgeois civilization of our time, there have always been various social channels, or *institutions*, which have provided for the distribution of works of art, whether created individually or collectively. But granted, then, that the persons living in the given context can exert some influence on the way these institutions function, what is wrong with institutionalized distribution?

Whether we analyse production, reception or distribution of art, then, we shall find institutionalized and non-institutionalized constituents alike, albeit more of the latter than of the former. Therefore the position of art on the Hegelian scale is similar to that of religion. It belongs to Absolute and to Objective Spirit alike, it is institutional and non-institutional in character at the same time, throughout its whole history. (The difference between the two levels is obvious: art does not generate a singular and characteristic form of self-institutionalization whereas religion does.) Therefore Bürger's radical conception of the destruction of the institution of art as an emancipatory act, and a juncture in the world history of art, is a consistent but misleading romantic theory of the *cultural revolution*; indeed, the only significant version of its kind. It is consistent in that Bürger makes a frontal attack on the autonomous art work which he intends to abolish with the gesture of the *happening* or of *provocation*. A provocation of this kind was Duchamp's statue, *Urinoir*, if the denomination 'statue' is not an insult to a product which is no longer an object but rather an act. So also was the Dadaist rally on the occasion of the funeral of Anatole France. And, likewise consistently, the period of post-modernity starts for Bürger when the rebellion embodied in the provocation dies out, and the art work, even if it be avant-garde, is restored to its already obsolete rights.

In referring to Bürger's conception as a misleading theory of the cultural revolution, I not only have in mind the ineradicable difficulties present in his conceptual apparatus, which I have demonstrated so far. There are also two particular *social—moral* aspects inherent in the idea of the merger of life and art which I find problematic. These are the *aestheticization of life* and the *abolition of the paradigmatic work of art*.

In the main, aestheticization of life is a *fin de siècle* legacy of the avant-garde and post-modernity. The new upsurge in the cult of Mallarmé, exemplified in Kristeva's book, is far from accidental. But the *fin de siècle* aesthetes approached the problem from the opposite direction. Even if they had been reluctant to issue a clean bill of health for modern art, their main target none the less was the ugly, prosaic and unaesthetic (daily) life of the bourgeois—technological age. They hoped that this squalid cosmos might be made habitable by the forcible infusion of a sufficiently large dosage of art. The post-modernists, on the other hand, who also of course have fundamental problems with life, are mainly concerned about modern art, this sensitive plant which they cannot hope to rescue except by merging life and art into one compound. In both cases, the criticism should be applied to the aestheticization of life, a criticism which that genuine iconoclast, the non-Marxist young Lukács had addressed originally to Kierkegaard and his so-called 'aesthetic phase'.[4] Lukács was as ardent an enemy of the aestheticization of life as he was of 'scientific ethics', the ethics of the specialized expert. Make no mistake, he warns, if art becomes life, then life becomes art and this would mean an inadmissible influx of aesthetic categories into life. It means that the 'aesthete of life', the genius and the dilettante alike, will treat his or her fellow men as art objects. Modern literature is full of such aesthetes of life, as is our own personal experience. The merger of life and art means that the aesthete of life can pursue artistic experiments on living beings, which is, of course, one of Dostoevsky's main themes. It means that divine egoism, the ethics of the modern artist, which Friedrich Schlegel termed his religion, will vaunt itself unrepentantly and publicly. Life is art, the egoism of the poetic genius suggests, and creating art in modern times allegedly requires exactly this type of morality. It means, to return to Bürger, that in the post-modernist merger of life and art, in which the art work is replaced by the non-objectified happening, the *provocation*, life will become permanent provocation. And it was exactly this type of life, an unbroken series of provocations, that characterized the methodological pattern of the theory, the cultural revolution.

My second objection refers to the abolition of paradigmatic works of art by the theories of post-modernity. This is consistent with Bürger's conception. For the theorist who regards the very existence of objectified and thereby isolated art works as alienation, paradigmatic works will mean something worse, namely the morbid cult of genius. It is not by chance that the German theories of post-modernity manifest such a visceral hatred of the classic Goethe, in whom they correctly locate the greatest instance of the nearly pathological cult of the artist's ego, but whose salutary lessons they nevertheless consistently miss. In reality, the paradigmatic works are not blueprints for imitation, but rather signposts pointing towards new worlds of sensation, emotion and artistic experience. Without these our life would remain just as poor as it would without paradigmatic personalities, who nevertheless should not serve as objects of devotion. And it is this last remark that perhaps elucidates the secret behind the post-modernist hostility towards paradigmatic works. There is a Babuvian—egalitarian zeal, the desire for absolute equality that militates against autonomous works of art, and thereby indirectly against the possibilities for an autonomous human personality in these art works. And given that the paradigmatic work is the utmost concentration of autonomy, the hatred can be accounted for anthropologically rather than aesthetically. But it is precisely this tyrannical (anthropological and moral) streak that makes the radical theories of post-modernity highly questionable.

III

The aesthetic dimension of Adorno's theory of the 'dialectic of enlightenment' embodies the second representative theory of the 'end of art'. What I have in mind is not his posthumously published aesthetic system but rather his theory of music, which I consider to be the heart of his theoretical, and historical, inquiries into the substance of art. Adorno's methodological model is Weber's unjustly neglected masterpiece, *The Sociology of Music*. The Weberian opus has a brilliantly simple fundamental idea. Weber sees western civilization as a structure built up of consecutive and interconnected spheres of *rationalization*. And within this general system he treats music as just one of the rationalized systems. Or, to put it the other way round, music became one of the greatest achievements of western civilization precisely because of its particularly rationalizable construction, precisely because it is the only kind of art which attains perfection by being optimally organized and rationalized. The western rational mind unifies all constituents of musical technology into technologically controlled and teachable configurations of composition. By homogenizing all factors of musical composition, by eliminating accidental and redundant solutions, and by creating a uniform order, music approaches mathematical accuracy and perfection. Bach, for Weber by far the greatest figure in western music, is just as much a contemporary of Leibniz, with his particular brand of *praestabilita harmonia*, and with his mathematical reason, as he was a pious Protestant.

Adorno's theoretical-historical investigations start at the point where this ongoing rationalization of musical forms not only reached its blissful summit but also showed, for the first time in the history of music, the obverse of the process, namely in the late Vienna classicism. The marvellous analysis of *Missa Solemnis* or of the piano sonata *Opus III*, a philosophical morphology which Adorno donated to Thomas Mann for *Doctor Faustus*, locate with unheard-of analytical acuteness the moment in which absolute rationalization turns into anarchy and irrationalism. The felicitous system which had hitherto organized the sounds into an order, a collective existence, suddenly appeared as oppression over their individuality, thus provoking anarchic revolts. The mathematically organized cosmos of musical composition, seemingly the most rational of all possible worlds, unexpectedly reveals the *caput mortuum* of irrationality lurking behind the rational organization. This is precisely the negative dialectic of enlightenment, the transition from high hopes and proud promises of rationality to an *instrumental*, one could say Eichmannian, use of reason, where the word 'reason' no longer has any serious, that is any moral, meaning at all. And Adorno's unforgettable, if often biased, analyses of nineteenth-century and early twentieth-century composers, of Mahler, Wagner, the New Vienna Music, Stravinsky and several others aim to demonstrate this dialectic, namely the necessity of hyper-rationalization and the impossibility of creation of a rational cosmos. Only those composers, who simultaneously transform this deeply contradictory situation into the foundation of their work, succeed in creating genuine compositions. These are the genuinely paradigmatic artists. At the same time, they are, and have to be, very limited in number. In Adorno's hostile presentation Bartók believed himself to have mastered the infernal disorder behind the shining musical façades of his so-called neoclassicism, but for Adorno this is only a pseudo-solution. And Stravinsky, who cultivated unfreedom and unreason in the guise of autonomy and creative order, is likewise a cul-de-sac. It is the lot of only very few to be able to resist the generally anti-artistic tendencies of the modern age, as it draws irresistibly towards post-modernity. The Vienna School of New Music is the last great upsurge of western composing genius. After this, music which is worth being listened to can scarcely emerge as the era of the 'end of music' ineluctably sets in. One can see from the end-result of the analysis that Adorno's remark, quoted above, about the impossibility of creating art after Auschwitz, was more than an *aperçu*. It followed organically from this theory of the degeneration of enlightenment into the Eichmannian use of reason.

Three critical remarks can be addressed to Adorno's theory of post-modernity as an epoch of the end of art. First, the whole theory, together with Lukács's late aesthetics, against which Adorno fought so vehemently but to which he remained so unmistakably close, is an historico-philosophical construct rather than a balanced prediction gained from the observation of the actual life of creators and recipients of art. For me there is nothing wrong in deriving an aesthetic theory from a particular philosophy of history. All representative theories of art, from Hegel to Lukács, rested on premises more or less explicitly gained from a philosophy of history.[5] But all these theories have become the ardent advocates of *canonic cultures*. The canon itself could be positive, as with the classicist Lukács, negative as with the desperate Adorno, who insisted that art describes a negative dialectics, and that after Schoenberg no music could be adequate to the norms of a rigidly conceived Ought. But in both cases, the theorists curtly dismiss all new works which are not in harmony with their strict prescriptions and canons, and simply evict them from their aesthetic paradise.

My second critical commentary is addressed to the hyper-rationalistic character of Adorno's theory of the end of art, a hyper-rationalism inherited from Weber but assimilated much too uncritically. The reason is clear enough: it is Adorno's basic mistrust of the pre- and pro-Nazi cult of the non-rational. But whatever the reason, this exaggerated and exclusive cult of the rational dismissed a large cluster of new needs for art, displayed in gestures rather than in rational argumentation: provocations, psychodramas, exclamations and the like, all inadequately articulate but all expressive of new needs. And as long as such needs exist, no one, not even the supreme arbiter of art, can be justified in declaring new creative efforts as doomed in advance.

The third remark is tied up with the above. While Bürger's theory of post-modernity is the direct and unreflected manifestation of the romantic aspirations of movements, Adorno's theory totally excludes the movements, the recipient along with its collective life dynamic, from the world of creation. This is clear from the hierarchy of listeners in his *Introduction to a Sociology of Music*. In the long list of derogatory labels applied to almost all types of listeners there is a single exception, one type which is accepted as authentic, namely the *professional, the expert*, the high priest of technological rationality. This ineradicable elitism of Adorno's theory not only makes him necessarily pessimistic in a mass society, but also exposes him to surprises regarding creative results, which simply cannoy be predicted from his vantage-point *au-dessus de la mêlée*.

IV

The last type of the theories of post-modernity (or the 'end of art') to be analysed here can hardly be linked up with names, certainly not with so-called celebrated names. It is embodied in the speeches, articles, random manifestos and catalogues of a counter-culture (or several different counter-cultures) which in a way unwittingly assimilate Bürger's argument. They declare modernism dead, some of them explicitly state that the representative figures of modern art have become traitors and have sold out to the art collectors and museums they themselves had earlier so vehemently criticized. But this declaration of war on modernity in the name of post-modernity is not at all sceptical or desperate as is Adorno's theory of a self-defeating rationality, or even Bürger's theory of the unsuccessful revolt against the institution of art. The manifestos of counter-culture could be, and in fact mostly are, facile and shallow, but they are aggressive, optimistic and self-confident. Their main postulate is the abolition of all lines of demarcation between so-called 'high' and 'low' culture as a mystification of earlier, aristocratic periods. In short, their central thesis can be summed up as a conspiracy theory. All distinctions between 'high' and 'low' art are artificial and pre-designed products of a cultural hegemony, invented by the hegemonic forces, distributed by the social channels, mostly the academy and the mass media, dominated by those hegemonic forces. In fact the distinction between 'high' and 'low' does not express any social reality, but rather the exigencies of domination. The contradictory character of the situation as it appears in the documents of counter-culture is correctly summed up in S. Radnóti's seminal essay, 'Mass Culture':

> the public committed to high art has no way to define itself other than negatively and exclusively, by its rejection of mass culture. As a result, it is surrounded by a not unfounded suspicion of snobbery. And high art, on the one hand, by creating dissonance with its own community, as with every other, and the culture industry, on the other hand, by establishing the mechanisms for the effective power of high art, jointly guarantee that the audience for high culture, as a community of taste, itself becomes an integral constituent of low, or rather, mass culture.[6]

It is clear that this definition unwittingly takes recourse to Kant's 'uninterested pleasure'. It is natural that all definitions of the aesthetic in modernity must be pitted against market relations. More importantly, we are witness to a *mutual intolerance of both poles* which was not the case in earlier cultures. All those cultures which maintained an unshaken faith in the hierarchy of 'high' and 'low' considered what they had defined to be 'low' as a necessary constituent of life. And the men of high culture partook of this 'low' culture in just the same way as Victorian gentlemen made use of the brothels which they morally condemned. Now for the first time in cultural history, the relation of both poles to each other is one of unmitigated hostility. Each wishes for the annihilation of the other. In the above, I made use of the term 'conspiracy theory' to describe the attitude of the counter-cultures towards the very definition of a certain type of culture as 'high'. Now it has to be added that men of 'high' culture not only regard the particular culture vegetating in detective stories, tabloid newspapers, discos and the mass media as 'low', but also as *poisonous*, as something to be cut out of the social organism like a cancerous tumour. We clearly face a state of war between the two layers of culture, and such an unusual situation calls for an explanation.

The fundamental question is, where does the differentiation between 'high' and 'low' stem from? In all self-consciously elitist and culturally conservative societies there was a simple answer to this question. In a theocracy it was the social stratum of priests which defined culture; in a court it was the ruler and his entourage. The cultural bourgeoisie, the famous *Bildungsbürgertum* differs from its great predecessors not in that it is less self-conscious, but in that it is more tolerant. Earlier types of culture only recognized the hegemonic types of cultural values and attitudes (the 'high') as properly cultural. The 'low' was defined as non-culture but, paradoxically, it was tolerated as an appurtenance of a life in which the duality of mind and body was tolerated as well. The very gesture of admitting both 'high' and 'low' into the sacred realm of culture was a concession in the same spirit as the emancipation of the Jews by bourgeois liberalism. But the concession proved destructive for the cultural self-consciousness of the society dominated by the *Bildungsbürgertum*. Very soon, the newly emancipated group demanded total equality and exercised, through its very existence, a terroristic cult of homogenization and reduction of all expression of needs to the same level.

In particular, there are two factors which promote this unruly relationship between the self-definition and practice of 'high' versus 'low' cultures. The first is the problematic democratism of the *technological* age, in which the art work leaves the protected shelter of museums and of its singular-unique existence, for an arena in which it becomes accessible to hundreds of millions and in which it exists legitimately even when copied. This epoch had a well-known and passionate advocate in Walter Benjamin, who in his famous essay, 'The Work of Art in the Age of Mechanical Reproduction', saw only advantages, and hardly any disadvantages, in the newly created technological constellation.[7] I, for my part, would regard this new epoch as problematic, or at least as both problematic and advantageous, for this complete undermining of the distinction between high and low, shallow and substantial, profound and empty, is the false transcendence of the cultural barriers created by cultural conservatism. This transcendence is legitimate and radical in that it recognizes everyone's equal need for, and equal right to, self-creativity; but more importantly it is a false transcendence in that it accepts all acts of self-creativity as acts of equal value — a position which is potentially tyrannically collectivist.

The second factor promoting the discord between 'high' and 'low' culture is to be found in the *universal standards* of present cultural production and consumption. Cultivated people who are familiar with the semi-religious aura that surrounded Gauguin's escape to Noa-Noa learn now with bitter contempt that thanks to satellites, those people in Noa-Noa and other Pacific islands watch the same Incredible Hulk whilst chewing on the same Kentucky Fried Chicken as do people in Phoenix, Arizona. But those smiling disdainfully tend to forget that these equalizing tendencies make it possible for those products, which they deem worthy of belonging to high culture the world over, to be selected and judged according to unified principles. It is not necessary to analyse here the advantages of a human culture which is unified, even if at a very abstract level. My problem is rather, the contrary. It is a truism of aesthetic theory that we are no longer living in a world of *sensus communis*, in a homogeneous community of taste, indeed that there are no such communities any more. The question to be asked is rather whether such communities are at all possible. In this respect the otherwise salutary universal standards and their life-basis, namely humankind as a common ground for artistic evaluation, work against, rather than for, the unification of taste. Not only would it be impossible for humankind as a whole to become one single community of taste — this would indeed be a totalitarian nightmare — but also, and more importantly, the effective abolition of *local communities of taste* would abolish cultural *mediations* as well, those beneficial gradations through which the hierarchic ladder of value judgement of every cultural community has come about up until now, a hierarchy which has been passed on to us, and which we must accept even if we reconsider its particular judgements again and again. But whether or not we accept or reconsider the traditional value-hierarchy between good and bad, low and high, there is a *hierarchic* legacy and we, living in a cultural vacuum, lacking in local communities of taste, are not going to pass on any such legacy — or so it seems — to those coming after us.

But I definitely do not intend to create a new romantic myth of an artistically God-forsaken period, nor to suggest that we are now facing more than a crisis of certain forms of life. In particular, there are two colliding tendencies in the life of cultural production, reception and distribution which have not yet found the social channels, the institutions, through which they can reconcile their contradictory positions. On the one hand there is an influential tendency towards establishing a cultural pseudo-democratism, a world of false equality which I analysed above. Its partisans regard all hierarchically ordered value-judgements concerning art objects as attempts at creating power hegemony. This is a false trend, but one which preserves the ancient dream of the universal rise of Everyman to the world of culture. The zealots of unqualified self-creativity demand that all self-creative needs should be equally recognized. This is, without any doubt, a radical need. On the other hand, there is an equally strong and ineradicable tendency in everyone's life, in all types of human activity, including artistic activity, to distinguish between true and false, shallow and profound, valuable and worthless. These fundamental types of need are now on collision course. But for me this does not mean that the 'end of art' is imminent. For we *are* in the period of post-modernity, with all the discords that such a transition period implies, but we are definitely *not* in a post-artistic epoch.

Epilogue

A quite unexpected, strong and convincing piece of evidence of the ineradicable need for art reached me after I had presented this paper at a seminar. A woman of extraordinary sensitivity sent me a letter from which I publish, with her consent, the following long paragraph. A personal document is, of course, nothing more than a gesture. But gestures are always indicative of needs, and this need is very deep-seated. In fact is it compelling:

> The proposition you investigated, namely the 'end of art', has in my ears the resonance of 'the end of language', 'the end of thought', 'the end of imagination', 'the end of search for truth'. Nothing short of a nuclear holocaust could bring it about. . . . To me art has always been an absolutely essential part of my daily life and my communication with people. It has so many functions I couldn't describe them all. My mother tells me that when I was tiny I scorched my fingers on her iron and suppressed sobs by saying '*ralle, ralle, ringer,* I have burnt my finger', which made crying unnecessary, brought me praise and admiration and from then on served as a family watchword to warn all of the dangers of heat. I still tend to cope with distress in this way. When my sister died the distress was too great; for weeks I had a vision of her eluding me in a dark fairy-tale forest. I tried to make a story of this, but there was none, nothing I could write down and formulate. At this time my father found century-old poems and fables that had the range and flexibility to hold my grief and that I recited to myself, living in them as I had in the forest, but meaningfully, not compulsively. As a teenager I was subject to strong, sometimes suicidal moods that a doctor, had he been consulted, might have cured with pills. My cure was to find in my by now, vast reserves of sentence rhythms and strophe patterns the one that was the rhythmical embodiment of the mood. I would walk it, skip it, hum it to myself, much as one has a tune on one's mind, and eventually it would

often fill with words. In a period that seemed a chaotic crumbling of everything that was 'me' the stern and challenging form of the sonnet presented itself and my unconscious, not my conscious mind, compressed into this unbelievably flexible form of fourteen lines twice fourteen times everything that needed to be taken into consideration. I 'worked on myself' with these poems, experiencing them not as my creation but as something that had been given to me to help me to cope, which they did very successfully. The alternative would almost certainly have been a nervous breakdown. When my eldest daughter reached her teens there was a period when she wanted to ask me hundreds of things and yet she didn't seem to be able to talk. Again my unconscious came to the rescue and presented me with a cycle of sixteen stories in quick succession, which she read avidly each day when she came home from school. The stories were not about me nor her but they were the needed link. When the children were little they always wanted to hear stories about me 'when I was little'. I didn't like the idea of turning my life into stories, particularly as children tend to insist that the story must never change, but I did write a cycle of stories for them that played with facts of my childhood in a fictional setting and they had a wonderful time trying to work out what was 'true' and what was 'made up'. In the context of this game I could talk to them about a great deal of things, including myself as a child. Children seem to have a desperate urge to know who their parents are. Last week I had two letters to write, one to a person dear to me who was dying and whom I could not visit in a hurry. What I said had to have the full depth of a final farewell and yet sound casual, even lighthearted and not frighten her. The other was to someone to whom I had ceased to write for certain reasons, and who wanted me and didn't want me to explain. In the latter instance a dream came to my aid. It could be lightly recounted — a small indulgence in madness — and, placed in a context, mean a whole range of things, explain — I checked on this — virtually anything that might need explanation without directly giving away anything or betraying anyone else. In both cases I would have been helpless without art. At one stage the children and I were in fear of permanently losing a landscape to which we were deeply attached. In this case I took a collection of material, cloth, yarn, etc. and we walked from site to site, discussed what made it so unique and then I set down and 'made' it for all of us, i.e. wove it, knitted it, embroidered it etc. etc. I could go on this way indefinitely, for there is really not a day where I do not have to resort to literature or art. The size and nature of the audience I aim at varies; on the whole though I feel happiest when I am writing for one person and the circumstances surrounding his need create the form of my expression. In nearly every such case, however, I am aware that this person stands, potentially, for hundreds or thousands, who are as welcome to this 'work' as he is. To generalize: literature is for me the expression and bestowal of human freedom, which in my philosophy of life is the very kernel of human nature. I myself live a life restricted physically and mentally by dozens of different things. I need literature quite as urgently as food and drink and there could never be too much of it to explore.

NOTES

1 See for example, Juergen Habermas, 'Modernity versus post-modernity'; Anthony Giddens, 'Modernism and post-modernism'; Peter Bürger, 'Avant-garde and contemporary aesthetics'; and Andreas Huyssen, 'The search for tradition: avant-garde and post-modernism in the 1970s', all in *New German Critique*, 22, Winter 1981.
2 Peter Bürger, *Die Theorie der Avantgarde* (Frankfurt, Suhrkamp, 1974).
3 Ibid., p. 66.
4 See Georg Lukács 'Esztétikai kultura' [Aesthetic culture], in *Ifjúkori művek* [*Early Works*] (Budapest, Magvető 1980).
5 I have analysed the necessity and the antimonic character of aesthetics derived from philosophies of history in (with Agnes Heller) 'The necessity and the irreformability of aesthetics', chapter 1 of this volume.
6 Sándor Radnóti, 'Mass culture', chapter 4 of this volume, pp. 88−9.
7 In *Illuminations*, tr. Harry Zohn (Fontana, 1973).

4

Mass Culture

SÁNDOR RADNÓTI
Translated by Ferenc Fehér and John Fekete

The legitimation crisis of art, and its struggle for emancipation, are two sides of the same coin. This complex process has given rise to a dichotomy in modern art between high and low, popular and elite, kitsch or mass culture and art *sui generis*. The emancipation of art means a dynamic pluralization of ways of seeing and aesthetic styles: a freedom of options, an increase in the scope of artistic activity, a growing possibility for self-determination in standards and values, and a critical elaboration of traditions. But the existence of a multiplicity of art works that transgress the rules at will is only possible against a homogeneous background. The development of this multiplicity involves the elaboration of unified concepts of art. Two things have thus become combined during the struggle for the emancipation of art. One is the particularization of art works: artistic originality becomes a function of the artist's internal rules rather than external ones. The second is the integration of art works within a general concept of art.

In this fashion, disconnected areas have become subordinated within a unified concept of art and, in this process, traditions have come to be reinterpreted. During the second half of the eighteenth century, universal conceptions gradually displaced the canons of individual arts, genres and conventions, and the so-called natural systems of beauty universalized from them. Although these new conceptions could identify with selected traditions and claim to provide the sole definition of real art, they also contained an inherent contrary tendency to become independent of particular art works and occasionally even superior to them in order to attain greater generality. Now, the metaphysical mission of art works emancipated from their subordination to metaphysics requires self-determination. This is achieved by each art work, but it is also accomplished by the philosophical contemplation of art works that inevitably confronts them with postulates derived from this contemplation.

German Romanticism was the first artistic movement where the universal concept of art integrated several heterogeneous trends and became an independent entity: this was Friedrich Schlegel's famous *progressive Universalpoesie*.[1] The emancipation of both art and art works can equally be seen in the first philosophies of art. Schelling postulates the freedom of the product of genius, that is, he starts with the freedom of individual art works. To that end, he has to create a general concept of art that excludes unfree works. He separates aesthetic products from common artistic products as follows:

> all aesthetic creation is absolutely free in regard to its principle, in that the artist can be driven to create by a contradiction, indeed, but only by one which lies in the highest regions of his own nature; whereas every other sort of creation is occasioned by a contradiction which lies outside the actual producer, and thus has in every case a goal outside itself. This independence of external goals is the source of that holiness and purity of art, which goes so far that it not only rules out relationships with all mere sensory pleasure, to demand which of art is the true nature of the barbarian; or with the useful, to require which of art is possible only in an age which supposes the highest efforts of the human spirit to consist in economic discoveries, it actually excludes relation with everything pertaining to morality.[2]

This leads necessarily to an independent concept of art based on freedom. A new mythology cannot be invented by any single poet, but only by a new human species for which there can be more than *one single poet*.

If a new integral mythology, the great Romantic aspiration, were to come into existence, autonomous art works and ontological concepts of autonomous art would cease to exist. All universal concepts of art undoubtedly contain such an aspect of self-dissolution and the 'tyranny of freedom', the wish to subordinate or annihilate other concepts of art, in spite of the fact that the fundamental experience to be absorbed by them is precisely the freedom and multiplicity of art works. Freedom and multiplicity also mean that our relation to artistic activity is no longer self-evident. The reverse side of emancipation is therefore a legitimation crisis. The general concept of art is called on to solve the crisis, to justify artistic activity. The reality of this concept is one with a practical realization which stands or falls with each art work and each act of reception. But, at the same time, the practical realization in every art work stands or falls with the reality of the concept. This is why the various general concepts of art do have independent substance; this is why what is considered art within a given artistic movement, tradition or culture has a certain type of priority over the individual work.

This 'pre-concept', which I call 'will to art', is, of course, far broader than its conceptualized and ideological component, the autonomous and universal concept of art. But it is precisely that component, the conceptual integration of various wills to art, which is most characteristic of modern art. The universal concept, the great ambition of modern art, can never come to a standstill and its priority can never become permanently fixed in any one form. It can never become singular. In terms of cultural history, the universal concept of art can only exist in the plural. Over the last 200 years, fixed legitimacy has been replaced by the incessant re-emergence of legitimation in a dynamic process that is more accurately characterized as a mode of existence than a crisis. Individual art works claim their freedom not only against the old non-autonomous status of the arts, but also against all universal concepts of art deduced from philosophy of history or metaphysics as well as against all concepts of art constituted through traditions, movements or any other art work. This declaration of independence, however, is bound to generate a new concept of art or else lapse into arbitrariness and relativism. The dispute between a concept of art and an art work is not a contradiction between theory and practice, as is often misunderstood, nor a methodological debate between deductive and inductive interpretations, nor a struggle between consciousness and spontaneity, but rather a tension between two fundamental constituents of an aesthetics in the process of emancipation, and hence inherent in each work of art and in each interpretation.

The universalization of this dynamic is related to the radical transformation of the structure of artistic reception. Oliver Goldsmith remarked: 'The patronage of the public had replaced the "protection of the great",'[3] the cultural history of the past testifies to an infinitely rich variety in types of reception, each definable in sociologically exact terms; by contrast the concept of 'public' is abstract, its consistency heterogeneous and fluid. It is precisely this abstractness of the public audience that emancipates the artist — although not in the heroic (if exaggerated) way recounted in Renaissance anecdotes about artists — as a simple result of the unpredictability of the orientation of the public. The world of practical risk is dominated by the ideal of predictability, and this ideal, as mediator between artist and public, in itself demonstrates the disappearance of the immediacy of this relation and its increasingly abstract character.

It is convenient to employ here the analogy of the free wage-labourer selling his labour power on the market. Leo Lowenthal analysed eighteenth-century English culture from this aspect, depicting the emergence of the cultural market with the artist as producer and the public as consumer and the development of mediating institutions: publishers, booksellers, lending libraries and magazines orienting taste. This sociological constellation to a certain extent accounts for the usage and elaboration of varying styles by artists who produced works in the transitional period both under the patronage of the public and the protection of the great.[4]

Both the art and the culturally receptive behaviour of the *public* are market mechanisms, their principle of organization is identical with that of the market, and abstract in that the creative and receptive subjects confront each other freely, detached from their traditional contexts, and in concentrated masses. Before capitalism, a public always emerged where market mechanisms developed. The free wage-labour of the cultural market opened a different type of freedom for art as well, the freedom of *non*-participation in this production. Apparently, this refusal contributed considerably to the emergence of the universal concept of art by distinguishing the resulting art works, and contrasting them to the products of mass culture: 'productive art'.[5]

The most widespread image of modern art is the artist standing at the crossroads of market temptations and his own inspirations. An artist is one who says 'no' to the world for he does not recognize his home in it; an artist is one who *can* say 'no' to the world for he creates a new one. The idea that the work of art is a 'world' is a modern idea. As to whose world this is — whether it represents the millenarian promise of the realm to be appropriated by everyone with patient cultivation, the earthly paradise of the select and anointed few, or the exclusive territory of the law-giving genius — answers may differ in direction and content. So much, however, is certain: that this world as a rejection of the existing one, in actual fact belongs to only a few. The art work, as a distinct world, is a prefiguration of a new world-view, a forecast of an aesthetic state or a report about the existence of an aesthetic caste — in short, the utopian home of man, the human species, definable democratically or aristocratically, and even compressible into the artist's personality.

The universalization of the concept of art and the increasing individualization of art works have constructed this utopian edifice. Similarly, the grand unity of the arts and art works, embracing epochs and peoples, plus the isolated totality of individual works, have to some extent severed the hermeneutical interconnections and drained the inner substance of works of art. It is a modern idea and a modern experience that the art work is form, that its intellectual construction can be derived above all from its aesthetic nature, not from its substantive orientation and commitment, and that it is precisely this kind of freedom that can make the enjoyment of aesthetic reception independent of ideological adaptation and, in this sense, disinterested. Form turns against everyday life, and artistic appearance, as Schiller had hoped would happen, must vanquish reality and itself become reality.

All autonomous, universal concepts of art entail the claim of an aesthetic universe. An abyss, created by the radical 'no' uttered by art, separates art and reality, however the latter is interpreted. Art extracts itself from reality, the most obvious testimony to this being the distinction between art work and 'artifact' (as a 'piece of art in reality'). Schelling's theoretical separation of aesthetic product from common artistic product — and, five years earlier, Friedrich Schlegel's distinction between the free rational arts and the mechanical arts serving the needs (in the form of 'the useful' and 'the pleasant') — draw attention to a sharp contrast between high and low art. Both regard the emergence of this contrast as the characteristic feature of modern art. Schlegel writes:

Entirely indifferent to all form, and thirsty for nothing but artistic *material*, even the more refined audience demands nothing from the artist but *interesting individuality*. If something only has an effect, if the effect is only *strong* and *new*, the audience is just as unconcerned with its manner and context as with the unity of a single effect with a completed whole. Art does its part to satisfy such needs. As in an aesthetic flea market, *Volkspoesie* and *Bontonpoesie* are offered side by side, and even a metaphysician will not seek in vain for something to suit his mood. There are Nordic or Christian legends for lovers of northern mystical horrors, cannibalistic odes for poetry lovers thus inclined, Greek costume for lovers of antiquity, tales of knights for heroic tongues, and yes, even *Nationalpoesie* for the dilettantes of Germany. But it is in vain that you gather together these great floods of interesting individuality from all quarters. The legendary keg remains eternally empty. With every pleasure the desire becomes only greater, with every enjoyment the demands are only increased, and hope for final satisfaction recedes further and further. The new becomes old, the unique commonplace, and the spur of charm is dulled.[6]

How does this characterization differ from the following one?

But since the spectators are of two kinds — the one free and educated and the other a vulgar crowd composed of mechanics, laborers and the like — there ought to be contests and exhibitions instituted for the relaxation of the second class also. And the music will correspond to their minds; for as their minds are perverted from the natural state, so there are perverted modes and unnaturally colored melodies. A man receives pleasure from what is natural to him, and therefore professional musicians may be allowed to practice this lower sort of music before an audience of a lower type.[7]

The first difference obviously lies in the calm and composed acknowledgement of the existence of low art. But this is probably the least interesting aspect, for the reader of this passage is still groping in the dark as far as Aristotle's real position is concerned: shortly before the lines cited Aristotle sharply rejects any tolerance of this kind. But is the structure of the two distinctions similar? The public, a market abstraction in the modern age, is in Aristotle divided from the outset into two distinct social strata, two independent groups of recipients with correspondingly differentiated types of art. In the given case, a perverted variant of vocal-instrumental musical performance corresponds to 'the vulgar crowd', although one in which the perversion of the original artistic character and even the natural laws of music can be recognized. In other episodes of cultural history, from which no documents remain, it is even conceivable that there was nothing in common between the 'arts' of the two groups, and that the educated had no idea that the vulgar pastimes of the uneducated or the alien barbarians could also be art.

At any rate, Aristotle does not have a universal concept of art. He relates various arts — not all of them — to one another, by way of distant analogies. But precisely for that reason he is far from inclined to detach art by reflection — *Herausreflektieren*, as Gadamer would put it — from the context of content and impact. Thus, in the above quotation, music appears in the context of relaxed entertainment, cultivated pastime, 'killing time' in a pleasant way, and the education of citizens.[8]

It is only in the modern age that high culture and an industrialized low culture aiming at mass production confront each other as split, obverse fragments of a conceptual unity, two independent, self-contained, yet interrelated complexes. As Lowenthal sums up the situation: 'The counter-concept to popular culture is art.'[9] Both are offspring of the bourgeois epoch: a 'yes' and a 'no' to the same mechanism with regard to the emergence of mass culture and the culture industry. It is obvious that the ideological midwifery of a universal concept of art assisted in the birth of all modern art works. Whether in tragic, messianic, classicist or naturalist-educational form, it always embraced the realm of social utopia. Indeed, it would not be desirable to sacrifice the radical critique and the utopian standard inherent in this construction either to an historical-materialist or a hermeneutical reconstruction.

Yet I would like to reverse the direction of interpretation and return to a previously mentioned idea. According to this view, the interpretation of mass production and of the culture industry in the economic terms of the market fails to account for the homogenization of the concept of mass culture. This massive, closed unity that re-emerges in every redefinition cannot be explained by *production* for the market, because this constitutes a total system and therefore the market mechanism transformed into an absolute, rational, social explanatory principle. The assumption of the unity of mass culture is just as much an ideological construction as the absolute generalization of the market, and it is needed precisely for the purposes of another ideological construction: the self-definition of the concept of art. It presents a dystopia, the negative counter-image of a positive utopia. Lowenthal's dictum can be reversed: the counter-concept to art is mass culture.

In other words, it is not only art that explains mass culture by denying it, but vice versa. According to the previously cited passage from Schlegel, the vast substantial richness of needs and the unlimited possibilities of interest, entertainment and enjoyment follow the same pattern. If we recall that the culture industry did not yet function at the end of the eighteenth century in Germany when the contrast between low and high culture was elaborated for the first time, then it can be legitimately maintained that the concept of high art is not merely a theoretical reflex of a culture in the process of capitalization, not simply a response to the commodification of art and its rationalization in terms of profits — even though it is this, too — but rather the conceptual integration of those mechanisms as a precondition for the unification of the 'free rational arts'.

It is worth considering the full logic of the dichotomy between high and low art, starting with the hypothesis that it was high art itself that fetishized mass culture. How and why could this happen? My interpretation will conclude in the genesis of dynamic society and even the market mechanism will play a role in it, but in a different way. I would like to return to the argument that modern art and modern art works started to wage a war of emancipation because the self-evident character of artistic activity had disappeared. The atmosphere of freedom in this situation was somewhat rarefied. The function of the art work in life became much more indeterminate, or else variously determinable and hence the artist's role in life became more abstract. For me, it is a series of shots from Tarkovsky's film, *Rublyov*, that most remarkably expresses the paradox of the disappearance of the self-evident character of art: the paradox of its simultaneous freedom and abstractness. At the nadir of his deep crisis of separation from sacred traditions, Rublyov, the icon painter, throws his rag, still moist with dye, against the white wall, a place destined for holy paintings in the prescribed order of canonic forms. In front of our eyes, the formless trace of the rag turns, in unity of emptiness and freedom, into an artistic form.

But abstractness is not displaced in the openness of the art work, the autonomy of its contents, or the pluralistic modalities for perceiving and experiencing it; abstractness is also incorporated within the universal concept of art. Indeed, this concept is always abstract to a certain degree. Culture abstracts itself from material culture and, stepping outside its original local context, represents the universe of those intellectual values that can be selected relatively freely and consciously: it represents the possibility of detachment from direct life relations and their reality. Culture, art and the art work become values for their own sake; culture itself, in opposition to all previous establishments and all religious cultures, becomes the leading cultural power.

In this situation, art's frame of reference becomes questionable. It cannot take its new reference points from a closed context of life and traditional interrelationships, but has to adopt to the new dynamics breaking through these interrelationships. Art becomes its own frame of reference by defining its own concept and distinguishing itself conceptually. New and old, high and low, comprise the two conceptual pairings within which this conceptual distinction and definition come into existence. The old will be identical with the ancient, the archaic (folklore), the grand style that unifies everything, the naive and the natural. The new will be identical with the non-actual, with exploration, dedicated quest, thirst.

The new will discover, or fail to discover, the unity of the old with the eternal home of art and, on that basis, either set up the old as the measure for itself (in a form ranging from simple imitation right up to establishing the most general metaphysical measures) or else satisfy low needs.

This simple schema of the emergence of the universal concept of art, the elaboration of reference points, standards and counter-concept out of art's own materials, the definition of modern art in the mirror of the ancient, and of art in the mirror of pseudo-art, becomes, of course, incomparably more complex as soon as it becomes dynamic, and consecutive universal concepts of art come to be based on the negation and rediscovery of one another. But there is an incipient contradiction in the interrelation of the two pairs of concepts, and this tension contributes to the evolution of the dynamic. In the distinction between genuine and false, high and low, the leading values must be originality, individuality, novelty. Yet, on the other hand, in the antithesis between new and old, the old must, in some fashion, be paradigmatic. This latter constellation is also new, since the paradigm is not provided directly but by a selected tradition. The *edle Einfalt, stille Grösse*, or noble simplicity, of Greek art, popular art, the homogeneous culture of pre-Raphaelite art in Christian Europe, national archaic art, the primitives are all rediscovered.

Such rediscoveries are at the same time constructions. Passing on a selected tradition is always a more problematic and violent process than the direct and self-evident inheritance of traditions. The old may become obsolete and antiquated in this process, noble simplicity an empty and dictatorial canon of classicist academicism, popular forms and homogeneous culture may turn into an irrationalist myth, Schillerian naivety, perhaps into narrow-mindedness, and the cult of naturalness into blind faith in a scientifically manufacturable naturalism. A relay race of universal artistic doctrines develops in which the very gesture of radically confronting the old becomes an artistic value for its own sake and the very criterion of art.

The strategy of the avant-garde (or modernism) thus takes shape well before the word itself is coined and the related self-consciousness of the movement emerges. Part and parcel of this strategy is to identify any doctrine regarded as antiquated with low, kitsch, mass products. Most of the new concepts of art push their direct ancestors into the counter-concept, mass culture, the more radically the more they promote their own novelty.[10] Meanwhile, the culture industry is established for the mass-production of the latest artistic innovations. Similarly, fashion, a more embracing and more fundamental category than the industrial production of culture, also becomes the *colporteur* of the latest, original, artistic innovations. In this sense, the ever-new universal concepts of art find ready-made materials through which they can manifest themselves as long as they universalize them into low or mass culture.

This alternation of obsolescence and innovation, and the parallel submergence of formerly high art in the sphere of low art (even as formerly low art may become the foundation, as Tinyanov showed in *The Literary Fact*, of a new high art) has constituted the general, and accelerating, development of the last 150 years. We can recognize in this trend an orientation to the market and its need for the systematic introduction of new products. Novelty has become so much the predominant value in art that it has subordinated and to an extent even excluded other values such as beauty, harmony, proportion, completeness and objective form. The orientation to the market, however, cannot be reduced to the fact that culture has become a sector of the economy. It is not adequate to suggest that the industrial organization which caters to mass consumption provide stimuli that partly coerce artists to escape from mass culture into the ever-new, and partly induce them to experiment at their own risk with novelties that will later be absorbed by mass culture. I do not question the existence or possibility of such manipulation, but I consider that any reduction to this particular tendency as the determining factor is one-sided.

One may say that the two great forms of articulation of modern art are the artistic movement and the isolated art work. One can note as a matter of record that all criticism of the avant-garde takes as its standard the great isolated art works. The critic constructs his own antithesis between the new and the old, and confronts the new with a catalogue of old masterpieces perceived as isolated, as separated from their own contexts of tradition. Only those really isolated art works of the present age are then found to meet this standard in as much as they 'swim against the current'. On this logic, modernist avant-garde, too, is included in the category of the mainstream 'current', the pseudo-aesthetic sphere of low culture consisting of works that, unconsciously or against their intentions, serve the world rather than run counter to it.

Without dealing with this critique of ideology, I want to direct attention to the common structure it shares with its adversary. The market, not in its reductively economic, but in its overall cultural sense, has an impact on even the most isolated art works, in so far as the work relies on an unknown and heterogeneous public reception and distinguishes itself by a global opposition to any other actual or potential procedure for achieving artistic effect. This reliance on an unknown public becomes the existential basis of the universal concept of art. Universality, and artistic expansion beyond the borderlines of a closed community and a homogeneous scope of ideas, are inseparable from the assumption of a common authority for the validation of values and a common standard of value applicable to the whole universe that is complementary to the material market, and where the difference between cheap and valuable art becomes interpretable. Individual works and movements enter this market mechanism as 'property'. Originality, an independent conception of form, a characteristic selection of materials, a new concept of art — these are all either the private property of individual artists or the collective group property of trends and movements. (The great anonymity of authors, as Simone Weil correctly understood, is only conceivable in a world order in which art has no value for its own sake, that is, no universal concept in the sense under discussion.) Exchange-value in this context is identical with the new value of general recognition, although this act of exchange, in contrast to material exchange, has no temporal limitation; it can be even merely imaginary, and there is no quantitative criterion for universality.

It is from this constellation that the fundamental value of novelty and the universalization of low culture into a counter-concept can be understood. All art works count on having recipients; this expectation is a structural element of the very work itself. To repeat: the art of the bourgeois world epoch calculates on an abstract (open) and free reception that is capable in principle of integrating recipients from totally alien cultural-intellectual backgrounds. Since it wants to sustain itself, this abstract calculation can be defined only negatively: by its *non*-everyday character, *non*-this-worldly character, grotesque features, peculiarity and dissonance with reception.

Each modern art work generates a tension between taste and the idea of form which can be properly measured by the historical separation between artistic taste and the perception of quality. Because it is *not* only *one* community of taste that a new art work confronts but in principle all prior communities of taste, every novelty becomes valued for its own sake in an abstract sense, and each particular community of taste becomes the adversary of the autonomous art work and of the universal concept of art. Every particular community of taste is hostile to an art work with a claim to universality — the community of taste from which the work arises, because it resists expansion; alien communities of taste, because their traditions resist intrusion. Thus, a universalizing claim becomes evident not so much in the creation of a dissonance with *one* particular community of taste (except to the extent that that one represents all others symbolically) as in unifying all particular communities of taste within the general category of low culture. Of course, this process is advanced by the weakening of particular communities of taste and the emergence of a world community of tastelessness. But the adversary of the universalizing tendency is not only 'bad' taste. Its very mode of existence is tension with all existing conventions of taste. The other side of this same process is that the art work becomes insular, a universe, a monad.

If we were to draw the radical, but justified, conclusion that the universalization of the concept of art comes into conflict with taste itself, this would coincide with the experience that the high art of our age is not a culture-creating art. The slow process of cultural evolution is ill served by the furore over the ever-new, the insular individuality of the art work, and the corresponding devaluation of purely value-preserving or sustaining art and art enjoyment (as expressed in the current atmosphere surrounding such categories as epigone or dilettante). More precisely, if it is true that generating dissonance with common taste is the very mode of existence of modern art; if Walter Benjamin's discovery is valid that Baudelaire expected to be received by an inattentive, distracted public longing for entertainment, and for that reason employed calculated shock effects; if it is true that it was in 'cette longue querelle de la tradition et de l'invention' (Apollinaire) that the greatest modern art works were born; and if it is true that Mayakovsky's famous dictum, 'we are going to slap the face of common taste', is only a reckless and extremely provocative formulation of the typical behaviour of the modern artist, then the high art of our age is paradoxically indeed culture-creating art in that it creates its opposite, mass culture. It generates a culture of life in order to articulate itself in tension with it.

The situation of the modern audience for high art is symptomatic in this respect: the public committed to high art has no way to define itself other than negatively and exclusively, by its rejection of mass culture. As a result, it is surrounded by a not unfounded suspicion of snobbery. And high art, on the one hand, by creating dissonance with its own community of taste, as with every other, and the culture industry, on the other hand, by establishing the mechanisms for the effective power of high art, jointly guarantee that the audience for high culture, as a community of taste, itself becomes an integral constituent of low, or rather, mass culture.

Up to this point, I have been talking about emancipated high art and its self-interpretation as rooted in its form and mode of existence. This self-interpretation, the universal concept of art, has a double structure. On the one hand, it is a *tendency* that acquires formative existence with the modern will to art, that is, in the life of art and in the art work. On the other hand, it is also a *consequence*, as an ideological utopia that remains a concept whose material actualization would lead to self-contradiction. So far, I have been speaking of reception as an integral part of form and artistic intention. Reception, however, as it occurs in actual recipients, raises new problems. The discussion began with the self-interpretation of art, that it belongs to the sphere of high culture. At this point, however, the question arises whether there exist universal criteria which, apart from such self-interpretation, would divide the realm of art in two.

In his essay 'The Structure of Bad Taste', Eco takes notice of a great change in art and postulates a dialectical relation between avant-garde and kitsch. 'The arousal of effects produces kitsch in a cultural context where art is not regarded as an inherent technology in a series of diverse operations, but as a form of consciousness that is generated by the creation of form for its own sake and that makes disinterested contemplation possible.'[11] Bad taste and kitsch are characterized by forced prefabricated effects and the endeavour to reproduce the typical effects of art: 'when common and popular culture no longer sell art works but their effects, artists react by moving toward the opposite pole and concerning themselves neither with arousing effects nor with the work itself but with process leading up to the work.'[12] Kitsch, then, has a concept of art and provides the appearance of art. 'The anthropological situation of mass culture is circumscribed by a continuous dialectic between innovating suggestions and justificatory adaptations; the former are constantly betrayed by the latter because the majority of a public which enjoys the latter in fact believes that it is engaged in the enjoyment of the former.'[13]

Clearly, the conception that I have set out is identical to Eco's. However, his attention is focused on the birth of avant-garde strategy as a reaction to kitsch gaining ground, that is, under the forcible impact of the 'abuse of art' by the market economy. That it is not only the relation between avant-garde and kitsch that is dialectical, but also their relative priority is not Eco's concern. The result is a somewhat pragmatic delimitation of the problem. Eco strictly separates off within mass culture the communication of messages and everything that does not possess a concept of art or claim to be called art; he only criticizes what remains.

We may call this latter kitsch, and identify it with bad taste, as Eco does, but then the extremely important question of the relation between bad taste and tastelessness still remains open.

On one hand, the very conceptual framework of Eco's sceptical-realistic position excludes all those programmes and ideas that would aim to transform the tastelessness of a mass culture overwhelmingly indifferent to taste and to elaborate cultures in which the objects, 'messages' and pastimes in everyday life would be characterized by good taste and purposefully created forms. On the other hand, Eco uncritically maintains a separation between life and art. This is natural in as much as he is one of the scholars who in the past decade have most influentially summed up the experiences of two centuries of art's struggle for emancipation. His famous phrase, the 'open work of art' (to be compared with Goethe's *oft gerundet, nie geschlossen*) refers precisely to the capability of the modern art work to cut the anchors of unambiguity that bind it to any particular frame of reference or community of recipients. In modern reception the same thing happens to ancient art works as well, since in their case the very fact of reception already points to openness, or more precisely, in a formulation somewhat different from Eco's, to 'being opened'. On the question of whether there exists a universal criterion for assessing low and high art, it is precisely the modern reception of ancient art works that may provide relevant experiences.

It is commonly known that certain classic works become part of mass culture and sink to the level of kitsch. For instance, Adorno mentions this in his study 'On the Fetish Character in Music and the Regression of Listening', in connection with certain Beethoven symphonies. Eco's explanation is that in such cases it is openness that ceases to exist: the varieties of reception fail to enrich each other and one particular mode of reception becomes schematic and prevalent to the point where the work attains a redundant unambiguity. Through this process, the 'stylistic potentialities' of the work are exhausted and kitsch is what appears thus exhausted.

This is a convincing explanation. The question, however, is whether we could not also imagine a reverse process in which 'closed' kitsch is opened and received as a work of art (for instance, Ernst Bloch 'opened' Karl May's work, probed beyond its crust and explored it; nevertheless, he defended 'happy endings', *colportage* literature). But Eco himself is compelled to answer this question in the negative since he considers openness *not* to be a subject-object relation but an objective structure, a potentiality provided in solid objectivity. He writes, kitsch, which by definition refers to 'being exhausted',

> is based on a relation between surprise and the unexpected which ought to arouse in the recipient an interest in the particular structure of the poetic message. In fact, this communicative relation now faces a crisis. But this crisis does not predicate anything about the structure of the message which, from an objective point of view, if all references to a historically situated receptor are eliminated, has to remain unaltered. The message must still contain the communicative potentialities brought into it by the author when he had in mind an ideal addressee.[14]

This, however, is a double impossibility. Historically-situated reception cannot be eliminated either from our own reception or from the artist's 'ideal addressee'. Should we wish to 'reopen' Leonardo's work, as against the kitsch-Gioconda, we cannot blot out from the history of reception, which is the life of the art works, the episode of its transformation into kitsch. (Indeed, the term 'episode' is already evaluative, polemic-laden and expressive of a chosen perspective.) There is, undoubtedly, in a sense different from Eco's conception, an atemporal reception, a resurrection of the art work, side by side with its temporal reception, its continuous life; indeed, the latter must ultimately lead to the former. But this atemporality does not mean an objectively or metaphysically 'fixable' *a priori*, since it is not the abstract fixation of the actual moment of genesis of the art work that is at issue but the elimination of the elapsed time between the creation of the work and the life of the recipient. This supra-historical approach cannot eliminate the concrete, unrepeatable historical time in which this act of elimination itself takes place. The very word resurrection alludes to this, and what has been resurrected flows back historically into the life of the art work. The two types of reception can briefly be characterized in the following way: the first is the permanent presence of a given work in a culture; the second is the individual (in other words, always reinterpreted and differently interpreted) repetition of its genesis.

Open and closed: these concepts cannot be universally evaluative. The work remains open as long as it is not 'being opened' by someone. The emancipation of art leads with logical necessity to the recognition that there is no artistic value in itself. As we have already seen, the value of an art work in its specific capacity as a work of art is a value for its own sake that is *posited*, and it presupposes positing art's universal value for its own sake. (For the universal concept of art posits value: it contrasts a non-value, in the form of mass culture, to itself.) As acts of individual freedom, both fall short with respect to their universality, on account of the equally free acts of individual receptions and of positing other universal values. If the history of its reception is the life of an art work, then reception cannot be determined to be true or false by revealing some objective value structure abstracted from reception. Indeed, there can never be such a determination at all, only a value debate about what is low and what is high art. The whole process of the emancipation of art is nothing but this value debate.

What stage has this debate reached? The most remarkable factor is the increasing openness of works of art. This is not the place to discuss what may be the limits of the openness, the disintegration of reference, or the reduction of redundancy in music, theatre, film, poetry or the fine arts. What seems to be beyond doubt, however, is that the process itself is none other than the strategic integration of the universal freedom of reception into the art work itself or, put differently, the acknowledgement of the impossibility of such calculated integration. The artist accepts the hypothesis that even his own relation to his work can only be one reception among many; he declines a large part of his distinguished role of guiding interpretation in the creative process. It is doubtful that these new trends, sometimes called the neo-avant-garde (or post-modernism), will bring about a grand style. At any rate, they proclaim a new attitude that criticizes the universality intrinsic to all search for a grand style and challenge as inexact or false the very designation of post-modernism or neo-avant-garde. The argument is that the new development means precisely that the tendentially terroristic energy of the modernist avant-garde is renounced, playfully or ascetically.

Such renunciation of energy mutilates the universality of the concept of art at two decisive points. First, this view implies a reduction of interest in whether a given work is a work of art. The game, the experiment, the document and the action come to rival, as values for their sakes, the concept of the art work. Second, in connection with the first, there is a reduction of interest in the universality of the valuation of these products for their own sake, that is, in the principle of their universal receptivity. This does not contradict what has been said about the calculated integration of the universal freedom of reception; it simply means acknowledging something that also belongs to freedom of reception, namely, that many do not wish to receive a given thing at all. The end-result of such a recognition may be that artistic activity and life activity become nearly identical. This would mean that only one who lived it could become its recipient, the references of a way of life would come to replace the references of artistic form, and the calculated strategic integration of the unknown recipient would be abandoned. Such sectarian introversion is already evident in a number of modern artistic currents. Under these conditions, the autonomy of art and life, art and the universal concept of art, disappear. As a consequence, the myth of the universaliztion of low culture disintegrates as well.

Would this then be the resolution of the dichotomy of low *culture* and high *art*? Would autonomous and universal concepts of art be annihilated, and art fragmented into the infinitely variegated and once again self-evident artistic activities of small groups and sub-cultures that either ignored or tolerated one another? And, provided there were no hierarchy in the eventual relations among small groups, could a creative and productive aesthetic universe of freedom arise in the place of universal art, where everybody could be an artist and the aesthetic sphere would not be isolated or in transcendental opposition to life but an immanent ethos? This utopia, based on existing tendencies, along with its inherent values and standards, is important, but not as an alternative to universal art. To renounce the latter would represent a serious loss in value. We do not need the annihilation of art, but a reform (or reform movement) that would eliminate the antithetical complementarity of art and mass culture and regard the aesthetic ethos of small groups as a culturally innovative dilettantism that must remain equally subject to criticism as to the integration of its universalizable artistic values.[15]

In summary, and in anticipation of what follows, my own view is that the pacification of the universal concept of art, the conclusion of the *war* for the emancipation of art, is now necessary. The last chapter of Georg Lukács's late *Aesthetics* bears the title, 'The War for the Emancipation of Art'. I no longer share my teacher's philosophy of art, but I must reach back to his categories. First of all, as is by now obvious, I regard the existence of this war of emancipation as an indubitable fact, and since art cannot have a value for its own sake in a religious universe, I also accept that art's war of emancipation, its self-interpretive, universalizing dynamic, is primarily directed against religious universalism, at least at the point of art's genesis. But I cannot share Lukács's view that aesthetic this-worldliness and religious transcendence are so contradictory in substance that, if we attend to this conflict, some of the great artistic periods will appear to be mere 'counter-movements' or 'preliminary stages' within the mainstream of aesthetics, and some essential kernel of 'this-worldliness' can be extracted from the transcendent religious shell of Dante or Giotto's work. On the other hand, I consider it one of the most profound characteristics and most magnificent achievements of emancipatory art that we can become the recipients of Dante or Giotto's work as disbelievers, without a community of ideas or religious consciousness.

Further, Lukács's diagnosis of modern art is that, in the modernist avant-garde, an aesthetic attitude is subordinated to religious consciousness (religious in its structure, its doctrine) and religious need. If we shift the emphasis of this line of thought away from the avant-garde, and say 'substituted' instead of 'subordinated', then the assessment in a sense characterizes the whole emancipation struggle of art. Goethe and the age of Romanticism, Lukács says at one point, 'was the prelude to the transformation of an object-oriented religious universality into a religious need confined to the subject'.[16] Universal and exclusivistic concepts of art do satisfy religious needs and provide substitutes for religion, but this is not only characteristic of certain problematical trends within art, as Lukács contends, but serves as the necessary energy-source in the struggle for emancipated autonomy.[17]

It is to the distinctness, the utopianism of autonomous art that the religious need attaches itself, or rather, this utopianism partly accounts for the quasi-religious structure of universal concepts of art. Kant's term for the ability to appropriate sensuous and aesthetic phenomena directly was intuitive reason in contrast to discursive reason, 'moves from the synthetic universal, or intuition of a whole as a whole, to the particular — that is to say, from the whole to the parts. To render possible a definite form of the whole a contingency in the synthesis of the parts is not implied by such an understanding or its representation of the whole.'[18] This can refer equally to the intuition of the whole of the divine teleological consciousness that has arranged nature and the teleological consciousness of the artistic genius that has created a masterpiece. Obviously the direct, aesthetic 'appropriability' of the art work, and hence also its dysfunction (i.e. the suspension, pluralization, and opening up of its everyday functions and claims) is a precondition for the autonomy and universality of the concept of art.

In the course of its conceptual emancipation, art assumed quasi-religious features and reproduced categories of grace, mystery, divine promise, salvation, prophetic expectations, revelation and the absolute. Arnold Schoenberg writes in one of his letters to Oskar Kokoschka in 1946 about one of the latter's admirers: 'unfortunately, like my own followers who admire Hindemith, Stravinski and Bartók as much or even more, he too has too many gods, Klee, Kandinsky, etc. Yet "thou shalt have one God" . . .'[19] It was with a purpose that I selected this bizarre document. It clearly shows the limits of the religious need attached to art — limits that emerge simultaneously with the need itself. These are the other artists' freedom to universalize their own concept of art, the recipients' freedom to be familiar with and to prefer 'other gods' and finally the situational specificity of universalization today, as over the last 200 years, that, to maintain the claim of universality, the artist has to take the work to a spiritual market and reckon with the varying contextualization of recipient strangers. Artistic pluralism, having provoked conceptual unification, also prevents it from being completed; in other words it stands in the way of a final triumph of any one of the rival concepts of art.

The first condition for concluding the war of emancipation of art and attaining this emancipation has been actively at work in the concept of art since the beginnings of this war. I am referring to the universality that evolves from individuality and which has to be sustained as universal on the basis of its individuality. If this evolution is an act of emancipation, then against the militancy, even tyranny, of freedom must stand the self-communication of freedom, Marcuse's free fantasy without its self-revocation: *solidarity* in freedom. This individual universality, in solidarity, by its nature (not its content), with other individual 'samples' of universality and with acts of individual reception, does not represent an annihilation of aesthetic universality but surely its diminution. Against the idea of the infinity of universality and the eternal validity and immortality of the art work, it emphasizes finiteness — in the sense that in each epoch, each human act of reception, it is not some eternal life of the work that carries on but a new life that begins. It is a finiteness and recommencing anew that ensure the co-constitutive role of the recipient.

This, however, presupposes a further scaling-down, in the form of renouncing the idea of perfection as a component of universality. I do not mean here canonic perfection, which was renounced long ago, but the conviction (expressed in many ways) that the value of the art work excludes the contingent character of its parts. But can contingency be excluded from the notion of the whole that is constituted by intuitive reason? Reception may well represent a process in the self-creation of the work where contingency can come as an actual end; in a hierarchical aesthetics, this could be called an artistic peak experience. But, because of its rarity, this cannot exhaust the entire sphere of aesthetics, nor, because of its finiteness, can it be solidified independently of actually given recipients, into a domain of eternal, objective value. There is, none the less, some extent of solidification, but it does not take place in actual artistic reception where the art work is given life, again and again, but rather where the work lives its life virtually as a reservoir of the former: in culture.

This brings us to the second condition for a successful conclusion to art's war of emancipation. The autonomous and universal concept of art essentially takes into consideration only the arts at the top of the hierarchy. Its expectation is that an art work adequate to the concept of art should evoke a peak experience, have a cathartic impact, and alter the recipient's life. Forming hierarchies is legitimate, as is the utopian hope expressed by Rilke's famous line. But the segregation of the peak of the hierarchy from the rest sets up a confrontation between high culture, the corpus of great works, and low culture, the homogenized corpus of other artistic activities and products of the most diverse character. The reform of the universal concept of art should have as a goal not to ostracize from the concept of art the non-universal arts (e.g. art that is not valued for its own sake, art that is regional or even narrower in scope, non-objectified artistic activity, which is decorative, entertaining, didactic or utilitarian in nature, the art of conservative epigones aimed at maintaining and preserving values, or dilettantism).

These varied modes of practising the will to art should not be excluded from the concept of art, either on grounds that they are devoid of individuality (e.g. clichés, series, non-individuated traditional forms, variations on a theme or imitations), or on grounds that they are devoid of universality (e.g. in having reference to only *one* tradition, community, group or particular entity). The concept of art should not exclude the constructs of any autonomous idea or form for lacking in taste, nor that wide area of culture that guides us upwards to the individual-universal art work. Again, this calls for solidarity — solidarity with the human need for art that lurks behind all these products and human activities.

Such a reconstruction of culture, a broadening of the concept of art, and a scaling-down of universality cannot, however, mean either the

be 'opened' in every individual receptive context and which can be detached
from its given context.

NOTES

1   For Novalis poetry was absolute reality, and every individuality partook of truth
to the extent it was poetic. Boccaccio was Tieck's model when he integrated his
works into his *Phantasus*. But here, art works were extracted as individual
fragments from a conversation constructed by its participants out of mutually
entertaining art works; meanwhile the framework itself, no longer a story but
rather the concept of art turned into a way of life, was called on by virtue of its
generality to display a higher order of reality.

2   F. W. J. Schelling, *System of Transcendental Idealism*, tr. Peter Heath
(Charlottesville, Va., 1978), p. 227.

3   Quoted in Leo Lowenthal, *Literature, Popular Culture and Society* (Englewood
Cliffs, N.J., 1961), p. 6.

4   The most obvious example is Hogarth, who, according to Frederick Antal, in
keeping with his changing subject-matters and types of public, made conscious
selections from the artistic arsenals of mannerism, baroque, rococco, and
classicism.

5   On the one hand, the criticism derived from Marx that takes notice of the
subjugation of art and culture to the yoke of the market, and on the other, the
Romantic idea that defines art as resistance to market temptations and to common
life, vulgarity and prosaic bourgeois life in general, are in spite of the elitist
inclinations of the latter not so radically opposed as certain scholars contend —
for instance, J. Davidov, in analysing the philosophical problem of the relation of
art and the elite. The economics and the Romantic viewpoints are rather
complementary. This is demonstrated not only by the late syntheses of the two
traditions in Adorno, Benjamin and Marcuse, but also in Marx's *Theories of
Surplus Value*: 'Milton, who wrote *Paradise Lost* for five pounds, was a *non-
productive* worker. By contrast, the writer who delivers factory hack-work to his
publisher is a productive worker. Milton produced *Paradise Lost* for the same
reason as the silkworm produces silk. It was an activity wholly natural to him.'
Even if the conception of artistic activity as natural is ancient, contrasting it to
'societal nature' is a thoroughly Romantic idea. Art is that which is not produced:
this is the thesis of the Marx citation.

6   Friedrich Schlegel (1795), *Ueber das Studium der Griechischen Poesie (Seine
prosäische Jugendschriften,* vol. 1) (Vienna, 1906), p. 91.

7   Aristotle, *Politics*, tr. Benjamin Jowett (New York, 1943), VIII. 7. 1342a,
pp. 335—6.

8   Obviously, it is not possible to sketch in an outline the prehistory of distinctions
between 'low' and 'high' art: cultural history provides an infinity of variations. It
is even questionable whether we are entitled at all to speak of a 'prehistory', since
the work itself presupposes a teleology and a linear evolution of cultural history of

which we can find no trace. What can be called 'low' and 'high' in various periods of medieval culture may refer to a comparative definition of the cultural status of unequal yet independent estates or an undifferentiated will-to-art according to different recipient strata; or to a contrast between some regional culture, eventually left without history and memory, and the then prevalent international Latin culture. But all these concepts are unrelated to the modern concept of low and high art. It is not necessary to take a stand as to whether medieval culture (or one of its periods) is an integral whole in spite of its many particular facets, or whether it is legitimate to speak of two or perhaps more cultures basically independent of each other. It is not necessary to decide whether medieval culture unifies complementary (feudal and urban, clerical and secular) cultures, or whether it is unified in its intention to integrate or marginalize the various types of *ars barbarica*. Whatever the case, in this culture (or cultures) the particular arts, and within them various traditions, genres and artistic techniques, are separate entities and there is *no* common generic concept of art comprising all the arts and only the arts. That *ars* does not mean such a universal concept is well known. In this world there is no art, only arts; nor, therefore, is there any counter-concept to art as art.

9   Lowenthal, *Literature*, p. 4.
10 Whether those have a narrow or a wide audience does not matter: Bayreuth's elite did not turn in Nietzsche's vocabulary into the Bayreuth mob because the quality and quantity of that public had changed in proportion with the changing judgement, but simply because Nietzsche's concept of art had changed.
11 Umberto Eco, 'La Struttura del Cattivo Gusto', in *Apocalittici e Integrati* (Milan, 1965), p. 72.
12 Ibid., pp. 74–5.
13 Ibid., p. 78.
14 Ibid., p. 102.
15 Such criticism, in the interests of reforming the universal concept of art, must paradoxically always consider whether the art-creating small groups have truly renounced the universal concept of art or in fact are really neo-avant-gardes with a false consciousness, with the result that their inner openness and outward closedness (a closedness not in the aristocratic but in the defensive—tolerant meaning of the word) are mere ideological appearances. I am thinking of two critical possibilities. In the first case, these groups have *not* resigned their claim to elaborating a universal concept of art, and what had seemed to be such a resignation was in fact nothing but the continuation of the old dynamic, a new recycling of discontinuity, provocatively elevating something from low culture to the rank of high culture. If criticism demonstrates that such is the case, it is then clear that the high—low dichotomy has once again been reproduced, although this in itself has no direct implications for the value of art in question.

In the second case, the concept of art is renounced but, in spite of an ascetic and resigned sectarian spirit, the militant universalizing endeavours are *not*. This attitude also has deep roots. Let me mention Bertolt Brecht, whose name alone remained on the blackboard when, in Jean-Luc Godard's *La Chinoise*, the small anarchist group wiped the names of the giants of high culture off it. Brecht found the contradiction between life and illusionist art intolerable, and therefore gave up the concept of autonomous art in favour of the utility and applicability of the art work in life. In this way he was able to draw closer to mass culture; or, more precisely, for Brecht it was not the primitive fable, the *colportage* novel, the 'whodunnit', the exoticisms of harbours, colonies and vagabonds, the cabaret, jazz music, obscene erotica, or jocular and didactic effects of the 'sub-art' of carnivals and market-places that meant low culture, but rather an oblivious absorption in high culture without any life consequences. A search for direct life-effects instead of artistic ones (which of course resulted with Brecht in immortal artistic effects) was inextricably bound up with a militant doctrine that possessed 'firm knowledge' of the determinate direction of the development of human society, and wanted partly to share information and partly to shepherd people in this direction.

Also in this second case, some such doctrinal background inevitably exists, and it is the doctrine that the small artistic groups desire to distribute and universalize even as they renounce the concept of art. They may totally reject high art, together with the values of the past, as the spoils of the conqueror. (Nietzsche's cool remark that slavery is essential to culture was later converted into *Kulturkritik* by Walter Benjamin.) Herbert Marcuse, in *An Essay on Liberation* (Boston, 1969), pp. 25–6, writes: 'The aesthetic as the possible form of a free society appears at that stage of development . . . where the higher culture in which the aesthetic values (and the aesthetic truth) had been monopolized and segregated from the reality collapses and dissolves in desublimated, "lower" and destructive forms, where the hatred of the young bursts into laughter and song, mixing the barricade and the dance floor, love play and heroism.' This liberation, conclusion: human emancipation has to be realized against the will and the interests of the great majority of human beings. In the cultural revolution of small groups, that is, in militancy that transgresses to boundaries of their own circles, free fantasy turns into its opposite — a fantasy practising coercion — and no trace remains of the openness and freedom of reception. The reform that could put an end to the dichotomy of low culture and high art will not be born of 'mixing the barricade and the dance floor'.

16   Georg Lukács, *Die Eigenart des Aesthetischen* (Neuwied and Berlin, 1963), vol. II, p. 872.

17   The canonization of various arts was followed and replaced by an autonomous aesthetic creation of artistic norms, and the normative—teleological structure of the aesthetic entity thus emancipated reconstructs to a certain degree the primary teleological structure that in past religious cultures has comprised the world itself. This is why aesthetics plays such a key role in classic and Romantic German philosophy, as a mediator (Kant, Fichte), the hierarchical summit and general *organon* of the system (Schelling), the guarantee of human individuality and universality (Schlegel) on the hidden structuring principle of the system, as in Hegel's philosophy of history where universal history is constructed teleologically by self-conscious speculative dialectical reason, and where the art

work itself, as a created totality, a teleologically constructed *world* that is simultaneously organic, 'natural', and a goal for its own sake, becomes either the model or the residue of the creation of the world, but in any case an 'other-world' distinct from the given world.

18　Immanuel Kant, *The Critique of Judgment*, tr. James C. Meredith (Oxford, 1952), part II, para. 77, p. 63.

19　Arnold Schoenberg, *Briefe* (Mainz, 1958), p. 254.

20　Hans-Georg Gadamer, *Philosophical Hermeneutics*, tr. David E. Linge (University of California Press, Berkeley, 1976), p. 405.

5

On the Drama of Euripides

G. M. TAMÁS
Translated by Ferenc Fehér

The bloody and bloodsucking gods, Hercules the hero, the phosphorescent *corps*, the daimon, the seducing Olympian — the reader trembles like aspen leaves, like the laurel shaken by Apollo. Finally, finally, he is allowed to be drawn, in a trance, to the intemperate classic, the barbaric Hellene. Finally, finally, he is violated by this supernatural power of steely frame. Finally, finally, he lies prostrate under the force which centuries have testified to be nothing but a school of humanity. Enough, says the reader, enough of equity, of forgiving our weaknesses and guilt. We are fed up with 'pro- and anti', with the rule, the exception and the consolation, we are sick and tired of the half-hearted weighing-up of intention and consequence, of understanding, of embracing the cause of the frail and the weak, of castrating the heroes, of dissolving genuine power into powerless wittiness. We no longer need caution and moderation. Let the valley catch fire, let the whole forest blaze as a single torch, let us feel the spirit of intoxication coursing through the blood in our veins, let us rove the tracks designated by fate, let us dance, let us not meditate any more! This is how the reader talks, and when he does, he talks Nietzsche.

Euripides is the most tragic of poets, says Aristotle. Euripides is a shabby modern literatus, says Nietzsche — and in the wake of him come all those ashamed of being just that. And, again in the wake of Nietzsche, this is the judgement of culture where thought is suspect, albeit thinking is practised.

What, then, is the issue on the agenda?

Nietzsche wrote his book *The Birth of Tragedy From the Spirit of*

Music in 1870—1, during the Franco-Prussian war. The book fed on the hope that non-Christian art, religion and philosophy were still possible. Wagner's pagan-German musical voices, Schopenhauer's bitter and elegant disillusionment, were for him proofs of such a possibility. And should something non-Christian be possible in Europe, the humanist dream might be realised: something which is Greek could be revived. But for this to happen, everything should be obliterated that had indeed been Greek but had, none the less, led to Christianity. The great heretical theologian of our century, Simone Weil, was clearly aware that a path, just as wide as the one broken by Ezekiel, leads from Cleanthes' *Zeus Hymn* to the Gospel. However, considerably earlier, Nietzsche, the antagonist of Christianity, had known this as well. The demonic philosophy of Socrates, he remarked, had contaminated art and religion with thought. A religion without a gospel is unacquainted with revelation. Inspiration is just as crucial to it as it is to art. Of course, not even Nietzsche would go so far as to state that Socrates had changed the dogma of Greek religion. In fact, the dogma of the Old Testament exuding the odour of the blood of the sacrificial lamb would be entirely alien to Socrates.

According to Nietzsche, Socrates' guilt was to seek a universal truth. And a *moral* truth, valid for everyone, creates the lowest possible level of equality. It serves the interests of those who are not outstanding or powerful, or even exceptional. For the Greek, a supporter of competition, *agon*, assumes self-consciously the sin of envy; it labels hubris all that which is excessive and immoderate; rejects and punishes it. The greatest possible hubris was that of Socrates: he had duly expiated it. None the less, Nietzsche contended that a low spirit had become vocal in this hubris: the envy of triumphant life, which is at the same time prepared for death, alias the spirit of the mob. Nietzsche did not mind that it was democracy — usually identified with the spirit of the mob — that had put Socrates to death. Much as he hated democracy, at this point he was in agreement with it. The philosophers charged with irreligiosity (*asebeia*) had well deserved exile and the potion of hemlock, for it is inadmissible, in terms of faith, to apply human norms of morality to the bloody, intemperate and lecherous gods standing above human beings. Socrates, the Sophists, and their fellow, the playwright Euripides, went as far as to believe that an evil god is not a god, but the mere fabrication of fanciful rhymesters. For them, theodicy — in other words, the answer to the question of how and why god tolerates this-worldly evil — was more important than the slaughtering and ecstatic faith itself. In terms of this theodicy, evil reigning supreme in this world was all the more evil as deity itself was good. Good is not a mere wish but the crowning of the universe.

For Nietzsche, this lukewarm faith of good created the rule of the feeble-minded weak, by having curbed the violence of the powerful. It paralysed thereby the god-creating arc of the sword cutting into the heavens and the high seas. The envy of the fool, the untalented, the uninspired, the crippled, the mongrel, pulled down the demi-god, the aristocrat, the law-giving and law-breaking man into the dust. Contemplation frustrates action. The natural hue of life is sickled over with the pale cast of the contemplative study of the true and the good. 'Crito, we ought to offer a cock to Asclepius,' Socrates-*moriturus* remarked. I am going to die, therefore I am in debt to the god of *healing. Ergo* life is illness, death is recovery, Nietzsche explained.

Philosophy is then the demon of death.

And the goal of Nietzsche (which he believed to be Greek) is: sanity, recovery from decadence, from drabness, from perversion, from the servile morality and the maid-servant melancholy of the Gospel. In *The Twilight of the Gods*, before his breakdown, he no longer believed in the Wagnerian phantasy of music inarticulable in words and essentially inarticulate, but his hatred of Socrates was unabated. Nietzsche thought he observed the mark of the vilest, *suppressed*, inclinations on the face of Socrates. Socratic conversations are distorted, sublimated eroticism. But elsewhere he remarked, Socrates is the great eroticist. Nietzsche was desperately concealing something here, hence the blatant contradiction. Greek culture had been considerably fashioned by homosexuality, while in Nietzsche's age, already and as yet, homosexuality influenced only the *sub*-cultures of aristocratic cliques of Oxford and Cambridge, of the elite of Prussian army officers. It is completely understandable that, living in Wagner's milieu, Nietzsche regarded homosexuality, under the impact of the shallow and tragic story of Ludwig II, King of Bavaria, as a distinct form of decadent perversion. It is beyond doubt that the love of persons of the same gender plays practically no role in Greek tragedy, whereas its share in lyric poetry, in the comedies of Aristophanes and, in particular, in the Platonic dialogues is tremendous. Should the tragedy indeed originate from Dyonysian fertility rites, it would be comprehensible that no barren love is put on stage; but this origin is far from a certainty.[1] As we have learned, the performance of the Attic tragedy was a communal—state act. It was the logic of causality and necessity that provided general guidance in it, in a peculiar way indeed, but strictly and consistently. In contrast to moral philosophy, however, in tragedy not only does action have consequences, but so do comportment and affections, and moreover, position. However, there is only one position in which the natural situation of human beings has an ontological consequence: when a child is born. In the Old Testament and the Greek tragedy the offspring is punished for the culpability of the parents. It is indeed guilt for which punishment is meted out, but the cause of expiation is simply that *there were* parents.

One would misconceive the essence of religion, should one believe that the devotee regards this constellation as right, or contends that god regards it as right. Moral logic has always been possible. Only faith suspends judgement and states that *this is how* things are; and the religious man goes on believing in god. The truth of faith is invariably empirical. This is how the devotee has to contemplate: I see the fabric of fate — it is woven by the gods — fate is terrible — gods are terrible — but they are gods — and I go to do my duty.

Man does not conceive a child with man, woman with woman. In homophily there is only the act. The act generates affection. Affection, in turn, generates the act. A *third life*, becoming independent of both, cannot be born of it. Nietzsche was right to believe that tragedy is erotic and religious, but he was wrong to contend that the philosophy of Socrates is not religious and not erotic. There is Socratic religion and Platonic eroticism — they are only different. Thinking (moral analysis) contemplates action; religion, being. The assertion of 'being as such' is in itself a religious hypothesis. For Nietzsche, the religious suspension of judgement (*epokhe*) was tantamount to pessimism. In his book on tragic Greek philosophy (1873) he asserted that it was Socrates who had initiated optimism, i.e. that which is non-artistic, teleology (in other words, belief in purposiveness), 'holding on to the good god', man who is good through knowledge and the suppression of natural instincts. From the aspect of the tragic world-vision, the learnability of virtue is indeed nonsensical. Tragic virtue (*arete*) casts off universal standards, it represents the uniqueness and exclusivity of creation (*poiein*). 'Knowing what' is not the measure of man, but of the cosmos, it is not practice (*prattein*) on which man is weighed, where we learn something of someone; it is where someone learns something of something.

In the dramatic poems of Euripides, in contrast to the tragedies of Aeschylus, religious and heroic myth is undoubtedly replaced by philosophical religion. Therefore, the myth enclosed in the poetic text became ambivalent and polivalent.

Even if Nietzsche misjudged the Athenian philosophy of the fifth century BC, he was, needless to say, well aware that in it, thought (*noema* and *logos*) had been built on art. The only question is whether thought, even as reflected, as contemplative, can be tragic.

Nietzsche's ideas on all matters Greek were often criticized, but invariably from a classicist position, from the vehement pamphlet of Wilamowitz to the cool and respectful Platonist critique of the George circle.[2] Classicists — from Lessing and Winckelmann to the last *Aesthetics* of Georg Lukács — are only prepared to conceive works of art in a sensuous medium; at this point they are perforce in agreement with Nietzsche. Classicism intends to keep apart thought and sensuousness (*aisthesis*), in order to achieve harmony between the two. So did Nietzsche, or so he believed: otherwise culture will be bled white. In fact, Nietzsche reversed the achievement of Euripides: he implanted the spirit of tragic art in philosophy.

Can thought be tragic? Those answering in the affirmative and in the negative alike depart from the plays of Euripides. Gilbert Murray, in his fascinating, modest and miraculously profound book[3] remarked that the modern reader is confused by what Euripides had learned from rhetoric of sophistic provenance, as the Greek rhetorical ideal was lucidity (*sapheneia*), in contrast to what is now called rhetoric. Euripides interrupts the plot, his protagonists utter wise *gnomas*, pursue sophisticated debates, infer the conclusions from the two premises of syllogisms — in other words, they do all the things that could also be done by the well-trained modern reader. However, the latter does not expect wisdom, but romantic ambiguity, puzzles, mystique. For him, art should not be too clever.

But why do the majority of modern readers and audiences reject Euripides? Why was he rejected in ancient times as well? for Euripides was never in his life a 'box-office hit'. Let us analyse the many reasons in turn.

This rejection has had, in the past and in the present, one root in common. It is a general consideration that speculation is *external* to action, and drama is about action. So far so good. But in what way is drama about action? In the way that the protagonists speak of their actions, they prepare them by dialogues, comment on them in monologues. But this speech has to create the appearance of having an act, not a speech character. This can be achieved by the dramatic speech in that it alludes to myth or, later, to consensus which replaces myth; in other words, by not creating the impression that the speech is spelling out something that is being invented now.

The data appearing as sensuous evidence accepted via faith, whose usual form we consider as generally known, is nothing but fate. From another aspect, fate is nothing but our conception of human nature in the sensuous form of myth which has been made congruous with this conception. In other words, it is something general, yet beyond dispute, for no theses can be asserted of it, only stories recounted. Of course, all this is only possible so long as everyone still believes in myth, or at least pretends that he or she does. When the value of myth decreases, the non-tragic period sets in. Even non-tragic periods may have their tragedies where, as one of the masters of modern hermeneutic states, the spectator sitting in the auditorium catches the message of moral transcendence that has been relayed to him from the stage in the *camera obscura* of his solitude. In modern, non-mythical tragedy the happening on the stage itself is external (transcendent) in that it is altogether moral, not religious, in nature. It is 'not a problem', while moral argumentation is, to its very heart. The same author wrote of ancient theatre that play is *accidens* in it, the by-product of the sense of religious festivity.[4]

Once the lights of the festivity are switched off, myth no longer lurks behind everything. However, Euripides demonstrates, unlike modern, non-mythical tragedy where the stage itself is the sublime or blood-soiled moral transcendence, unlike Shakespeare whose clownish features presuppose the solid, decorative and sensuous pessimism of a disillusionment with Christianity, that not only act-like but also speech-like speech acts can be tragic (at least within the drama where speech happens); streams of blood might flow by in the meantime with the phlegmatic indifference of *quod erat demonstrandum*. First, as we shall come to see, philosophy itself intruding into the plays of Euripides is tragic itself. Secondly, fate, at least in the sense that it appeared up until now, can naturally only be represented in the cultic space. But, in Ancient Greece, the fluctuations in the social status of myth did not necessarily undermine the cult itself. For in Athens religious cult is obviously not a mere symbolic replay of divine stories, in other words, not a mere rite, but cult *sensu stricto*; cultivation, the metaphor of the city-state as well. Not for nothing did Hegel mention in his *Aesthetics* that in classic art artists and poets were also *prophets and pedagogues*. They announced and revealed what was absolute and divine for man. The tragic poet was directly required by the seriousness of cult to teach. Even when the evocative, cathartic, reviving power of religious myth, as well as the feeling of the *necessary* affiliation with the myth binding upon the religious man (a feeling of necessity, of evidence, of 'so it is, and so it must be') were weakened, the city cult still remained religious. Its cultic, that is to say cultivating and culturing functions, became ever more important. Not every thought, not every artistic idea stems from the lessons provided by history and politics.

But whatever the source of moral judgement may be, no one in Athens could avoid these lessons. It was judgement that took place on the stage of tragedy, and on the stage of Euripides it often happened in a way that shed light on the impossibility of making judgements. And it is precisely this that appears as tragic in the act-like dialogues of moral beings (and, after all, a drama of Euripides consists, apart from music and the powerful *carmen lugubre* of the Chorus, of precisely such dialogues). For these moral beings are thus abandoned to an amoral fate which is no longer self-evident, not given with certitude and *a priori*. Evil gods are not gods, only the good ones, Euripides says. Yet, Cypris, with her malicious intentions, may punish Hippolytus, and not because he has committed a crime of any kind but, as it were, out of jealousy. Just as loose women can hardly bear to have reserved men around them, so Aphrodite is annoyed by the chaste hunter, Hippolytus, the devotee of Artemis. In a peculiar way, Cypris does not punish him by arousing his love for his stepmother, rather she wounds the unhappy Phaedra. Both Phaedra and Hippolytus are innocent: demonic forces drive them into wrong-doing. In vain are they moral beings. Amoral fate reigns supreme over them, a fate only worthy of terror, not respect.

Chamfort remarked correctly that the other name of providence is contingency. Fate which is unpredictable, haphazard and uncertain, is an explicit refutation of the image of divine order. Thus morality itself becomes absurd and impossible. Goodwill is to no avail, it remains a derisory effort opposed to the demonic. Tragic guilt becomes relative. Responsibility is destroyed. It is not by chance that, in a characteristic context, Aristotle links the pertinent problems with the name of the tragic poet: 'Is there a degree of truth in the paradoxical lines of Euripides:

> *"I slew my mother" — four words tell the tale.*
> *Willingly both or both unwillingly?* [Alcmaeon]

When a wrong is done it is never without the consent of the wrong-doer. Is it then really possible for a man to have injustice done to him without the consent of the wrong-doer, or does that never happen? Secondly, is suffering wrong always voluntary, always involuntary, or sometimes the one and sometimes the other?'[5]

In a sense, the tragedies of Euripides are nothing but the pondering of these problems. However, the considerations do not come from the writer, from outside as it were. The protagonists themselves spell out the motives of their decision, their inability or their obligation to decide. Understanding the motive and comparing it with that of others, respectively the incomprehension and solitude arising from the incapability of comparing, the incongruity of all these with the divine will, and the incongruity of the latter with fate — this is what the drama itself is all about.

How then shall one discern ''twixt these and judge?,' Orestes asks in *Electra*.[6] And Phaedra states bitterly: 'That which is good, we learn and recognise,/Yet practise not the lesson . . .'[7] The plays of Euripides are not parables, their protagonists do not present an unambiguous morality. Moral conflict, moreover, the dilemmas arising from contemplating morality, represent subject-matter here to the same extent as in the Aeschylus myth or the religious-uplifting experience of the historical present formed *a priori* does.

It is sophistic philosophy, the traces of which we can constantly unearth in Euripides, a tragic thought.[8] It was Gorgias of Leontini, the greatest personality of fifth-century BC sophistics, who had discovered that speech was one of the demonic forces capriciously manipulating the strings of human existence. Greeks had, of course, always been aware that persuasion (*peitho*) is a genuine power, but Gorgias added in his plea for Helena that *logos*, because of its natural amphibiousness, deceives man easily, that wrong can be inferred from right, that therefore word is just as irresistible as *Eros* or fate. Equivalent and contradictory statements can be asserted of the most general subjects, each and every ultimate truth is a puzzle. 'What is measure then?' asks Euripides. And Protagoras, the Sophist answers, 'The measure of all things is Man.' And what is Man? Man being the measure of all things, thus himself as well, the measure of his act and the weight of this act is the word that can be uttered of him. Equality before *logos*, the measure, remains valid even if *logos* is tragic, for we are aware of what good is even if we do not act it. *Peitho* combined with *logos* can lead us to truth, but it can be the means of deception as well. Not even the most discerning man can be safe from this. Man is the measure: a universal and irrational one, therefore also the barbarian, the woman and the slave is Man. *Andromache, Hecuba, The Trojan Women* show us that the Hellene can be worse than the barbarian woman. So does *Medea*: a barbarian is one who acts barbarously. The dividing-line between 'internal' and 'external', 'we' and 'you' is transposed: it will become *invisible*, and if it is, it will be a regulative principle, a rule which transgresses the limits of order set by the logic of seed and blood. Jocasta, of all people, says:

> *Nature gave men the law of equal rights,*
> *And the less, ever marshalled foe against*
> *The greater, ushers in the dawn of hate.*
> *Measures for men Equality ordained,*
> *Meting of weights and number she assigned.*
> *The sightless face of night, and the sun's beam*
> *Equally pace along their yearly round,*
> *Nor either envieth that it must give place.*[9]

Let us have no misunderstanding: an invisible order is not a rational order. Men are equally unhappy in the visible and the invisible. But an invisible order opens up the human heart for the poet to a much greater degree: even those who have been invisible will now be seen. It was Athens that made people perceptive of the invisible order. And yet Athens followed its own bloody, tribal gods. Within, democracy; without, tyranny. True, Victorian England was no better. Neutral Melos is confronted with the demands of the emissaries of Athens to join the commonwealth or the island will be occupied, the men slain, the women and children sold as slaves. The people of Melos answer that humanity will not tolerate such tyranny. The Athenian rejoinder is simple: For you, this is a matter of life or death. The poor people of Melos answer that the gods will then. . . . The next Athenian rejoinder is equally laconic: we shall take the risk; we are as religious as you are. And Melos is trampled underfoot.

The reform of Cleisthenes replaced blood-ties by territorial principles. The representatives of the ten 'tribes' constituted by this principle presided over the General Assembly of the *demos* in rotation. The year likewise was divided into ten months. The *agora* was placed in the spiritual and actual centre of the city, the distinction of communal and individual, public and private, was substituted for that of sacred and profane, which up until then had been crucial. The organizational and urban reform was, at the same time, spiritual and political. It is not by chance that Plato in *The Republic* placed the *acropolis* in the centre, in lieu of the *agora*. Space and time changed as well: the duodecimal system protected by the twelve great gods of the Pantheon disappeared, the cultic space surrounded by the profane became spiritual and shaken. Among others, the function of tragedy was *to fill* this space with the community of the city-state spiritualized in itself. Tragedy spiritualized the ancient cult, transformed it into an artistic and state duty, in other words, into a profane obligation, which of course meant denying it a portion of its freedom. Literary and musical merits are to no avail, there is no appeal against consensus. Euripides harangued patriotically against Sparta in vain, the audience did not buy his brand new humanity, and publicly professed religious scepticism. The reform of Cleisthenes reshaped the *polis*, the city-state, according to spiritual principles but did not spiritualize it.

J. -P. Vernant states in his study of the changes in Greek spatial conceptions[10] that the relations of the Athenian citizens to the *agora* as centre became symmetrical and interchangeable — only, of course, after Cleisthenes. (The system of rotation and selection by lot rested on this.) This spiritualization of human relations intensified the feeling and cohesion of citizen solidarity to the extent that the spiritual relation to any life exterior to the city-state could no longer be established unless Athens was the dominating spirit, and the outside world the obedient body. In the General Assembly the rule of an obsessed *peitho* was unleashed: minority positions were declared hubris and persecuted. Spirit had to function within the body politic, in silence: having become explicit and vocal, it was no longer recognized. Socrates, Euripides, the Sophists embodied the spirit of Athens: but they made it explicit, therefore they had to atone. Aristophanes ridiculed the spirit of Athens; in that sense he disguised it, so he had success. His ridicule constantly aimed at the juncture where the spirit of Athens would become universal and collide with the egotism of the city-state, with male and Hellenic selfishness. This is how in Aristophanes the feminist Euripides will become a mysoginist, his high-bred mother a common market-woman. Aeschylus was still able to spell out the truth, for it was the selfish and sublime truth of the mob: it could not be extended to others, it was no one else's business. The truth of Athens of Cleisthenes and Pericles could not be spelled out for, because of its spiritual-abstract character, it could be applied to and claimed by everyone. The secret of freedom became a state secret. Kleon, the most bloodthirsty of all the *enragés* of the demagogues in the Athenian General Assembly, was perfectly right when he said that not even a democracy can govern territories suppressed by it in a democratic, only in a despotic manner. From this also the conclusion could be drawn — in principle —

that democracy must not subject other states to itself if it wants to remain a democracy. However, Pericles was already fully aware that we had undoubtedly embarked on the wrong course, but should we stop following it, we would perish. The Athenians were calmly and soberly aware of their crimes, but if this was the will of fate, they kept committing them, dreading vengeance, holding on to their spears.

Euripides was one of them. He shared his fellow citizens feelings, but he disapproved feeling so. Not indignation, but compassion, bitterness and general uncertainty dominated his passions. There is, of course, a difference between good and evil: the evil will expiate, but the good will suffer a downfall as well. Guilty and innocent will be punished alike. The difference exists and it is important; there is no reward; the gods are unjust; fate is blind. In the case of the most intellectual and the most philosophically-minded of tragic poets, word was no longer magic: it was one of the inscrutable demonic powers. Word no longer depicted ill-fate: it *was* ill-fate in itself.

In Sophocles' *Oedipus Tyrannus* reasoning, logic, the rational word, all served to make lucid and scrutable what happened. In the dramas of Euripides they all served to promote what was fated. The protagonists were driven in the fateful direction by their own speech. The lives of Euripides' protagonists were so much conversation, quarrel, argument and rows. Speech can be the cause of anything just as any other act. It happened for the first time that tragedy, *as drama*, used its material, the word, for something other than the portrayal of what was beyond it. Tragedy became total: passion, contingency and nature were joined by *logos*. There was no longer remedy. And the much berated psychological expertise of Euripides, ironically deemed to be so un-Greek, serves to awaken us: compassionate, consoling and soothing words burst out of a disgraced, cruel and ferocious soul in an authentic way. If we need consolation we have to accept the terrifying maenad, the half-frenzied driven by his Furies, the lecherous and ill-fated murderer who offer it. Tragedy became philosophical, therefore all that which can be conceived by intellect will be included in the tragic. Blood does not only drip from the trembling hand; the voice, the view, the soul, too, are guilty. The oppressed knows what compassion is as he is longing for it — as long as he is oppressed. Does Clytaemnestra commit murder? So does Electra. The Trojan women groan in bed beneath their husbands' murderers; *phallos* and sword imprint the order of the victor on them. And what are they panting for? Revenge.

Brecht, who somewhat like Euripides made drama philosophical, epic, in our century, wrote in his *Theatrical Organon*:

> The theatre, as we find it today, does not show the structure of society (depicted on the stage) as influencable by society (in the auditorium). Oedipus who has sinned against some principles, which maintained the society of the time, is executed, the gods take care of that, they are not criticisable. The great individuals of Shakespeare, who carry the stars of destiny in their breast, run amuck vainly and fatally without restraint, they destroy themselves. Life, not death becomes obscene in their collapse, the catastrophe is not criticisable. Human sacrifice everywhere: Barbaric entertainments! We know that the barbarians have their art. Let us create another![11]

Euripides was not a barbarian. However, had he been a Hellene in the manner of Aeschylus, while being aware of what he was indeed aware of, he would have been a barbarian. In Aeschylus, cultic and theatrical space coincided, for the latter was the metaphor of the city: the victims were sacrificed to the voracious gods. As long as the performance lasted, all that which was divine and human was present, everything was sanctified by being *there*. Whether good or bad, the cultic space was limited by the metaphorical boundaries of the city, Greek was inside, all others outside — and only this was relevant. Order prevailed: judgement was made inside, at home. Fate was terrible, but it was not alien. In Euripides, cultic space only *intersected* theatrical space; gods kept absconding from the play. Clearly, they were elsewhere, perhaps even in foreign lands; we were not in the same place with our gods. Neither was the theatrical space the metaphor of the city any longer. For the real line of demarcation between barbarian and non-barbarian was drawn in the heart just as Christianity appeals to us to be circumscribed in spirit, not in body. Visible order, in terms of which the man, the king, and the fortunate gain the upper hand, is merely disorder, because it is the good, the noble-hearted, the humane who ought to be on top of the world, even if a woman, a slave are cursed by the gods. This is how things ought to be, but Euripides had hardly any hope that this would ever happen. The invisible order cannot prevail, precisely because it is real. And once *real*, it has no time to become generalized, for it fits into the elements of the world, even adds a new dimension to them, it submerges in the visible and becomes demonic. Adorno wrote in his essay on Beckett[12] that the *epiphany* (divine apparition) of the meaning of the drama as metaphysical content was a rule in ancient theatre. In Euripides, the *total* meaning of the drama, indeed, appeared in retrospect and as a summary, but shattered, as an arbitrary element of the play, as a will'o-the-wisp. The whole meaning may appear as partial too, being an apparition instead of an epiphany. The thought hovering above, beyond and beneath the drama is compelled to become a play which makes both play and thought nightmarish.

It is not contemplative and analytic reason that desiccates tragedy, rather it is reason interfering with ominous events that becomes tragic precisely for not having been able to abstain from interference. Once it fails to remain *totally* outside, reason cannot impute unambiguous moral meaning to the drama. It is the eventual emergence of total meaning that makes this meaning so ironical. We might ask, if it could not help, on the scene, during the unfolding of the plot, what good is it as a conclusive judgement?

The tradition of scepticism has preserved a sophistic consideration for us: 'Good is either the decision or that on behalf of which we decide.'[13] In Euripides the *good choice* and choosing *the good* are equally tragic, for evil always exists, for time passes, and the end-result of collision and combination cannot but be suffering. Evil can follow from good, good cannot follow from evil. Taking into consideration time as well, we stand little chance.

The heroine of *Alcestis* decides not to let Death drag her master and husband, King Admetus, into the underworld. Pheres, the father of Admetus, could sacrifice himself instead, he had had his time and the young powerful man is much more valuable, but the selfish old man refuses to die. This is what Alcestis says:

> *O Sun, and the day's dear light,*
> *And ye clouds through the wheeling heaven in the race*
> *everlasting flying!*

And this is the response of Admetus:

> *He seeth thee and me, two stricken ones,*
> *Which wrought the gods no wrong, that thou shouldst die.*[14]

Man must live, and woman must die for man; this is not a dilemma but a mishap. Alcestis' farewell is a simple one:

> *Darlings, farewell: on the light*
> *Long may ye look: — I have blessed ye*
> *Ere your mother to nothingness fleet.*

Whereas the rejoinder of Admetus is visibly exaggerating, because his attitude is insincere:

> *Ah me! for thy word rusheth bitterness o'er me,*
> *Bitterness passing the anguish of death!*
> *Forsake me not now, by the Gods I implore thee.*
> *By the babes thou wilt orphan . . .*

Alcestis indeed thinks that:

> *Howbeit this*
> *Some God hath brought to pass: it was to be.*[15]

It is her understanding that man is more important, that he should survive; therefore she is prepared to die. Admetus has almost the same understanding, with the slight difference that it is more important *for him* to live. He rebukes his father for not having embraced death instead of his beloved wife, for the queen is much more needed by him. But the old man snaps back:

> My *cowardice!*
> *This from thee, dastard, by a woman outdone*
> *Who died for thee, the glorious-gallant youth!*[16]

The value hierarchy of the three protagonists is similar; but the moral roster of Alcestis is more general and it is unselfish. The fable-character of the story relieves Euripides of the duty to pronounce judgement. It is not the fact that according to Alcestis and Admetus the value of the male stands so much higher than that of the female that is so significant but how differently the same thing is conceived by each of them. For if the male is more valuable than the female, he ought to be more courageous, more prepared to be sacrificed than his woman. But, apart from this, the same belief means life for the one, death for the other. Thought is ambivalent: if we choose a hierarchy of value, the selection between particular people already follows from it, and we no longer have a choice. At best, Admetus could decide to his own detriment, and thus restore equilibrium. However, this would mean the rejection of the value hierarchy shared by both of them.

It was Claudio Paduano who observed[17] to what extent the word *philia* (affection) takes over from *eros* (love) in *Alcestis*. And yet, the less passionate and instinctive the more personal emotion is a demonic power: it lures Alcestis to the underworld. The moral conviction of Alcestis, the selfish weakness of Admetus, these are not the passions we usually regard as frenetically tragic. And yet the consequence is extreme: Alcestis dies. Hercules enters the god-forsaken stage. Admetus, the polite host, conceals the mournful event from him. In the unknown house Hercules gets drunk. The facts are revealed. Hercules becomes very much ashamed of himself, and saves Alcestis from the clutches of Death. Admetus proves his faithfulness in front of the veiled Alcestis. The resurrected must not be approached for three more days, but the story will finally have a happy conclusion.

What happened here?

What enormous power had to be invoked in order to destroy the evil demon of a morality which measures with unjust standards? The drunken Hercules garlanded as Dyonysis descends to the underworld to fight Death and regain Alcestis, who has yet to be purified, and offer sacrifice to the gods of the underworld, and then she returns to life. When Hercules confronts The Girl and The Master, Persephone and Hades, the Chorus, not in vain, mentions Orpheus. The hero has an intimate relation to Death, the tomb, oblivion. One has to descend to the inferno, shake the pillars of the underworld, evoke all the obscure daimons and clouded remembrances in order for heroic commiseration to reach the heart of the non-symmetric, non-Cleisthenesian morality. The barbarian soul will only be redeemed from guilt and death by the *son* of Zeus.

The son of Zeus and the mortal Alcmene — whose essence was, however, so well understood in *Amphytrion* by Kleist — descended to hell, triumphed over Death, assumed the guilt of Admetus and redeemed him from his guilt. The Son saved the simple-minded, frail and deceived Alcestis from the shadow of death; sunshine is pouring over her.

We can see not only the contours of Dionysius and Orpheus, but those of a more oriental man-god emerge from the person of Hercules. Euripides introduced the philosophical thought into tragedy, and mystery was revived. The new thought, exactly where it seemed to be the most

detached from the tragic, moved the archaic element to utter its thundering words.
If the depth is silent, it is only *logos* that can make it speak.

NOTES

1   See Ulrich von Wilamowitz-Moellendorff, *Euripides Herakles* (1895), Introduction, II.
2   K. Hildebrandt, *Nietzsches Wettkampf mit Sokrates und Plato* [Nietzsche's Competition with Socrates and Plato] (1922).
3   Gilbert Murray, *Euripides and His Age* (1918).
4   Hans-Georg Gadamer, 'Über die Festlichkeit des Theaters' [On the festive character of theatre'], in *Kleine Schriften* [*Essays*], II (1967).
5   Aristotle, *Ethics* [The Nicomachean Ethics] tr. J. A. K. Thomson (Penguin, Baltimore, Maryland, 1965), Chapter 9, Book V, 1136a, p. 162.
6   *Electra* tr. Arthur S. Way (London, Heinemann), p. 373.
7   *Hippolytus*, tr. Arthur S. Way, London, W. Heinemann and Cambridge, Mass. Harvard University Press, 1921), lines 380—1.
8   See Mario Untersteiner, *I sofisti* (1948) esp. V, 2—3.
9   *The Phoenician Maidens,* tr. Arthur S. Way, lines 538—45.
10 Jean-Pierre Vernant, *Mythe et pensée chez les Grecs* (Paris, Maspero, 1974), I.
11 B. Brecht, *Kleines Organon für das Theater* [Little Theatrical Organon], in *Gesammelte Werke* [*Collected Works*], vol. 16 (Frankfurt-am-Main, Suhrkamp, 1967), pp. 676, 33.
12 Th. W. Adorno, 'Versuch, das Endspiel zu verstehen' [An attempt to understand *End Game*], in Th. W. Adorno, *Gesammelte Schriften* [*Collected Works*], vol. 11 (Frankfurt, Suhrkamp, 1974).
13 Sextus Empiricus, *Hupotuposeis*, III.183, in Sextus Empiricus, *Opera*, rec. Hermannus Mutschmann (et J. Mau) Lipsiae, in aedibus (B. G. Teubneri, 1958—62), 3 vols, v. 1.
14 *Alcestis*, tr. A. S. Way, lines 244—7.
15 Ibid., 270—5, 297—9.
16 Ibid., 696—8.
17 *La formazione del mondo ideologico e poetico di Euripide* (1968), IV.2.

6

Aesthetic Judgement and the World-View in Painting

MIHÁLY VAJDA
Translated by John Fekete, Trent University

Painting and Representation

All ages and societies have painted differently. Looking back from our own day, it seems that there has only been one epoch in the history of painting that endeavoured to reproduce the visible world (of 'nature').

It is possible to ask whether painting is at all capable of reproducing the visible world, of creating the illusion that what is visible in the picture is 'real'. The question is valid, but *does not, in itself, belong to the sphere of aesthetics.* Only if we have already made the prior decision that painting *must* reproduce 'reality', can this question properly be raised within the framework of aesthetics. Should we not regard the reproduction of the visible world as the task of painting, and should we conceive of the visual field of painting not as a reproduction of the visible world but rather as a modality of the visible which, if not independent of the visible world, is not identical to it, then the possibility of reproducing the visible world becomes a matter of indifference from the aesthetic point of view. The question can be referred to the psychology of perception, subsection 'sensory deception'.

What this would mean, however, is that the question would lose relevance for all but the most extreme naturalistic aesthetics. Of course, this statement too would be acceptable only to proponents of yet another extremist aesthetics, pure actionism: those who adopt the standpoint that the art work is a production precisely because, as far as possible, it *re-produces* nothing of the independent visible world. In this context one may again enquire whether this is at all possible; whether it is possible to create a visual field of such character that it is impossible to 'read into' it something other, something independent of it, something that we have seen prior to it. This question, too, belongs to the psychology of perception and not to aesthetics.

From the point of view of aesthetics, the question must somehow be reformulated to enquire how the *relationship* between the visual field of painting and the visible world (exterior to but not necessarily independent of art) developed in the history of painting. The distinction between 'realist' and 'anti-realist' aesthetics will not reside in the former's demand of the most faithful possible reproduction of the visible world against the latter's demand of the repudiation of resemblance between the painting and the visible world. The realist aesthetics recognizes that the picture does not have to reproduce the visible world, just as anti-realist aesthetics recognizes that the painting does, in certain respects, reproduce it.

But the aesthetic testimony of Gombrich's fine *Art and Illusion*, for all that it does not work with aesthetic problems proper, is that the fundamental principles of realist and anti-realist aesthetics in the fine arts remain purely rhetorical and in practice uninterpretable until the given aesthetics demonstrates where — in which works of art, what types of painting — they see their ideals realized. Gombrich's work shows that even the picture that we experience as most materialistic does not — *cannot* — reproduce the visible world (not even the photograph is identical with its object!), while at the same time we can read very definite reality elements into an altogether abstract scheme, even an ink blot or splotch of paint. Gombrich's work deals exhaustively with problems in the psychology of vision and reaches very convincing conclusions, so that I need not refer to these problems below. That a significant, genuine work of art 'must reflect reality', or, alternatively, that it always creates a new reality that has never existed before — these two, apparently diametrically opposed, propositions are equally applicable to Tintoretto and Picasso (or even Mondrian!).

It would seem completely absurd, nevertheless, to say that Tintoretto's paintings have no more to do with an independent visible world than Picasso's. There exists an epoch in the history of painting that we can call the epoch of *illusionist painting* — in spite of the impossibility of totally accomplished illusion and in spite of the partly ridiculous, partly disgusting character of efforts directed to that end. We can formulate the framework of such efforts in the following way: art in this epoch sought to realize its goals (which, except in the case of naturalism, did not resolve into the reproduction of the visible world itself) in such a manner that the resulting painting *should be intelligible* as *the visible world* that could be seen through a certain 'window' (the picture frame) from a fixed viewing point situated at eye-level above the ground.

This formulation, I should stress, comprises the *boundaries*, not the common principles, of the efforts of modern European (and associated) art. These boundaries separate modern European art from the art of every other society and historical epoch. The first appearance in fifth-century BC Greece of illusionism in the fine arts represents in a certain sense a prefiguration of the modern 'Renaissance'. We need to be clear about this, but it provides no obstacle to delimiting our enquiry into the epoch of illusionist art to European modernity. If, according to our formulation, we consider the creation of illusion not primarily as a particular project but rather as an untranscendable framework, then our investigation of strictly aesthetic questions will not be disturbed by the psychological problematic of the relation between the visible world and the 'reproduction' of it that can be effected on a flat surface.

It is not much open to dispute that illusionism, even as a general framework, has not always been a feature of art, and that the effort to achieve it is characteristic only of the epoch mentioned above. It is wrong, however, to identify illusionism — the endeavour to bring into existence a type of painting that is interpretable as the visible world — with the demand for the representation of reality, or for representation at all. The proposition that representation is to be identified with the reproduction of the visible world is, after all, not that self-evident. In a certain sense, any painting represents, even a purely decorative painting, but by no means does it always represent the visible world. The question must be posed: Is there any way, in abstraction from historical demands and conditions, to distinguish between the decorative and the representational kinds of painting?

In individual cases it is difficult, sometimes impossible, to separate decorative and representational art from one another because, as Lukács says, 'many kinds of transitional forms come into existence, not only out of historical, but also out of aesthetic necessity.' But, he immediately adds:

As difficult as this frequently makes situating individual cases aesthetically with precision, as assured remains the possibility of drawing the theoretical boundaries. These are brought into being precisely by the preponderant role of abstract reflection. Wherever the objects of the concrete external world are built into aesthetic systems, everything depends, first, on whether these objects are first and foremost reproduced according to their independent inner structure or whether they are shaped to decorations within the meaning of the abstract forms — in other words, whether their existing depths are employed to burst open the two dimensions of ornamentation or whether their original objectivity is reduced to what in a given instance is the necessarily abstract signification of the essential; second, whether the actual objects — which in reality and hence in their concrete reflection, exist inseparably from their real surroundings — are represented in the aesthetic formation as elements of such interconnections or whether they are torn from these connections in order to be transformed into abstract—decorative moments of abstract relations.

From the outset, since this too is an individual case, Lukács wards off the undoubtedly polemical edge of the question of whether the row of figures above the pillars of the San Apollinare Nuovo should be regarded as ornament or representation. But this is an individual case that is ultimately characteristic of its period. The whole of Byzantine style — not only with respect to mosaics, which are, after all, not paintings, but with respect to paintings as well — evokes a sense of uncertainty about how to situate it. We may say, of course that, whether it decorates or represents, it does so only incidentally, and only *for us*, the art world of later periods, since its own original function, which served the liturgy of eastern Christianity, was not aesthetic in character. And we may generalize: among all that the contemporary art world regards as art, the number of works that originated explicitly as 'works of art', that is, as objectivations meant to fulfil a primarily aesthetic function, is infinitesimal.

I do not wish to deny that beauty has *always* played a role in the history of mankind. Not only have human beings always wished to give beautiful form to their most diverse objectivations, but there has always existed the aspiration to decorate, *beyond* whatever beauty was intrinsic to their pure functionality, those objects whose function was to serve the manifold purposes of the most varied types of human activity. The earthenware pitcher, if made to appropriate measure, is as beautiful in form, as is, or can be, a modern suspension bridge. If the earthenware pitcher is supplied with 'geometrical' decorative elements, or if the stone railings of the bridge are ornamented with carvings, then, it is fair to say, the makers of these objectivations are striving for *beauty* itself. Nevertheless, decoration — whether of objects of use, cult instruments, or anything else, and whether it is 'representational' or consists of strictly abstract forms — always remains decoration: it serves to increase the beauty of objects and objectivations that serve other purposes. The object that *exists in order to be beautiful*, that serves and actualizes only aesthetic purposes, is the exception in the history of the arts.

Is there any justification, then, for the distinction between decoration or *embellishment* and the *work of art?* It is not easy to decide. There is no doubt, however, that such a distinction is not intelligible in every historical epoch — since mankind has always made beautiful objectivations, but has created the objectivations of beauty only in determinate periods — and that, in any case, it is not to be confounded with the distinction between *decorative art* and *representational art.*

According to Lukács, decoration is 'abstract form' and the decorative element is 'the abstract—decorative moment of abstract relations', in contrast to the work of art whose represented objects 'exist inseparably from their real surroundings'. But decoration can as readily be abstract—geometrical as 'representational' — thus the art on classical Greek urns remains decorative even though it may be more beautiful, more individuated, and more artistic than the purely geometric decorations on earthenware pitchers — in the same way that the work of art, or the painting specifically, can be worldly or abstract.

We need not take sides here on the question of whether the so-called 'abstract' and 'non-figurative' in modern art is a product of the crisis of art, to be regarded as a problematical historical phenomenon that contradicts the essence of painting. We have to acknowledge that it *exists.* Kandinsky and Mondrian are painters, not 'decorators'. If we were to regard their canvases as pure decorations — and why not? — then our debating partner would be right to retort: Ultimately, even Rembrandt's paintings are nothing more than decorations for the homes of the wealthy Amsterdam bourgeoisie, or at least Rembrandt was not, or would not have been, opposed to his work satisfying that function, or that function as well.

Then if, along the lines of such a response, we too advance a step further, the distinction between art and decoration begins to disappear altogether. Were we to consider every painting decorative — whether abstract or representational in form — if it serves to beautify some material objectivation which is just as capable of fulfilling more or less its entire function independently of the painting placed on it, and were we to consider every objectivation a 'work of art' if its function is beauty as such, then we would be constructing yet another distinction whose 'practical' application leads to hair-raising results.

It is true, on one hand, that it seems artificial to regard easel paintings as decorations for the bourgeois home — without doubt, this would be the 'natural' place for Rembrandt's paintings, though I am convinced that his enthusiastic admirers would not regard his paintings as decorations for the bourgeois home, but rather the bourgeois home as the natural place for the works; why these canvases *had to* end up in museums, and to what extent this is problematical, belong to a different enquiry — but by contrast it would be rather difficult to deny that the altar picture or the fresco decorating a Christian church are decorations of objects that fulfil a cult function. For us, however, the decorations of the most divergent cults and cult objects unquestionably fulfil an artistic function as well. To give two worldly examples: Simone Martini and Ambrogio Lorenzetti's frescoes on the walls of the chambers in the Palazzo Pubblico of Siena are decorations of the building itself, and inseparable from it.

We shall not get out of the thicket of increasingly fine yet, 'practically' speaking, increasingly useless distinctions until we recognize that both the decoration versus art distinction and the decorative art versus representational art distinction — indeed, all endeavours to make such distinctions — rest on a *specific aesthetic conception*, on a specific formulation of the task of painting. The presupposition that underpins this conception is that *the task of painting is to represent the world*. If we take this as our starting point, as Lukács did in his *Aesthetics*, then, in setting up the decoration/art opposition, we need not take into account the placement of the painting — whether it is an independent object or else placed on some object that serves other purposes — and simultaneously the decorative art versus representational art distinction tends to collapse into the decoration versus art distinction.

This distinction lacks *any functional element* of the kind mentioned above; it is built on seemingly pure 'content'. Behind this distinction in content, however, the functional element is none the less present in a different form. The *work of art* itself is *posited* as a function. The aesthetic sphere is posited as a relatively differentiated domain among the various kinds of objectifying human activity — hence beauty cannot be a central category of aesthetics of this type — and beyond this, it is posited that the sphere of objectivation characterized by an exclusively aesthetic intentionality, namely the separate sphere of art differentiated from all other types of objectifying activity, is a sub-domain of the sphere of cognition where purely ideal objectivations are created. First and foremost, art is cognition, the reproduction of the world rather than its production — or, more precisely, the productive side is subordinated to the reproductive.

These aesthetics take as their ideal the great world epoch of painting that we have called the epoch of illusionist painting. Of course, they do not contend that the representation of reality is to be identified in painting with rendering the visible world. When they distinguish between decoration and representation on principles similar to Lukács's, however, then ultimately they do identify the representation of reality with the pursuit of illusion in the sense given above. After all, even Gothic painting does not represent its objects so that they appear to our eyes 'reproduced according to their independent inner structures' or as they 'exist inseparably from their real surroundings'. They do not 'burst open the two dimensions of ornamentation'.

There may, of course, be many reasons for this. If we offer a direct explanation without further ado — that the visible world in its own structure, as it existed for the people, at least painters, in the Gothic period, was totally identical with our own, but it was not what they wished to represent and hence their art differs from ours — our account seems quite arbitrary at first. There may indeed be innumerable causes for the unalterable fact that every society, virtually without exception, has masters who work with paint and brush and yet bring into existence paintings that differ so greatly that even the slightly practised eye immediately notices their decisive stylistic differences and is able, moreover, to identify the origins of a given painting in time and place.

We may look for the causes of this phenomenon, in their many concrete variations, in the following moments:

1 All painters in all societies have endeavoured to create illusion, but the members of different societies see differently, even in the concrete physiological sense. Since their vision is not uniform, what passes for the perfect reproduction of the visible world in one particular age does not appear that way in others.

2 All painters in all societies have endeavoured to create illusion, but the means that given societies accept as the means of illusion differ fundamentally from each other.

3   The periods in which painting endeavoured to create illusion have been exceptions. The majority of societies did not consider it at all the task of painting to 'reproduce the visible world'.
4   All societies have endeavoured to reproduce the visible world but only exceptional societies have been capable of it.
5   Painting endeavours to reproduce the visible world; the question is simply, what dimensions and aspects of visibility does it wish to reproduce?

I believe that with the exception of cause (1), it is possible to adduce intelligent arguments for each of the others; what is more, causes (2)—(5), although they contradict each other in certain respects, have equally played a role in the development and transformations of the modes of artistic formation. The reason that the hypothesis of alteration in the physiology of vision is absurd is that the human organs of vision have not undergone any significant transformation since the conclusion of anthropogenesis, much less in the past 200 years. But if someone should nevertheless suggest that it may be possible with identical organs of sight to see differently in the concrete physiological sense of the word, then we are in a position to propose the following.

Let him ask a modern painter his opinion of which resembles more closely the visible world accessible to an observer placed at a fixed point at a fixed time: a photograph or a painting, both made from the same given point at the same given time. The painter will reply that the photograph, naturally, resembles the world more closely, but he will immediately add the question: why should he, as a painter, have as his task simply to copy nature (or more precisely, a given section of nature)? If someone needs such a copy for some special purpose, of course he does much better to order it from a photographer.

Before we begin to analyse the causal accounts listed above, we need to confront a seemingly decisive objection to our train of thought so far. We began by calling into question the possibility of separating decoration and representational art or, more exactly, we contended that the separation itself cannot be based on an objective distinction, that the very attempt to draw such a distinction conceals from the outset a specific underlying aesthetic standpoint concerning the visual arts. We argued that representation and decoration were not separable from one another, and that the endeavour to represent comprised the demand of only a delimited period of painting. As a result, our reflections readily *permit* us to conceive of artistic endeavours that diverge from those of modern European art as being equally representational, but not to be regarded as either successful or unsuccessful representations of the visible world. By contrast *if decoration and representational art are paired as opposites* (according to form, not function) *then representation will always be taken to mean representation of the visible world.*

Lukács is not vulnerable to the charge of favouring 'photographic naturalism' and, indeed, has repeatedly experienced the problematical character of impressionism, precisely because the latter had finally been successful in carrying the principle of naturalism to the limits of possibility; nevertheless anyone who reads Lukács's distinction quoted above carefully will discover that ultimately Lukács, too, *understands representation as the most faithful possible approximation of the visible world.* After all, if representation were not understood this way, then what would be the basis for denying a representational character to embellishment? Even the most abstract decorative element can be conceived as the representation of something!

Anyone looking for well-founded, precise and many-sided evidence to substantiate this proposition is advised to read *Art and Illusion*, a text that is all the more convincing in that it restrains itself from raising aesthetic problems. Gombrich's argumentation clarifies unequivocally that a psychological, not an aesthetic, question is involved in whether a given figure is accepted as a representation of some real object. I wish neither to reproduce Gombrich's argument, nor to clarify what is to be understood by 'psychological question' (which is undoubtedly interconnected with historical problems). We need to clarify only what is meant by the phrase 'not an aesthetic question': that it is not confined to figures and representations with 'artistic claims'. When a child's matchstick figure 'represents' a fat man, nobody regards the given figure as either artistic or decorative, yet if asked whether the given figure *really* represents a fat man, everyone will agree that even this hurried, unquestionably abstract figure drawn in an unskilled child's hand really does do so.

What is involved here is the relationship between signification and representation. Genuine reflection on this relationship necessarily leads to the proposition that we not only do not know how, but that it is in principle not possible to draw a rigid distinction between the signification of something with the aid of lines (drawing) or colours and the 'representation' of the same thing. In consequence, ultimately, every embellishment can be conceptualized as a simplified representation (thus, indeed, the majority of ornaments were probably not, in fact, originally 'abstract') and every representation, even of photographic fidelity (indeed, photographs themselves!), can be described as 'abstract', not a rendering of the visible world but merely a signification of the object. Indeed, the original visible world itself cannot be rendered in its reality by anything other than its original, 'perfectly faithful', spatial model.

We have not yet responded, however, to the second moment of Lukács's distinction, that the ornament renders the object in isolation from its surroundings, while the representational work renders the object, without separating it from its real surroundings. But the question is: What is the extent of the object? Let us take the following example: an ornament patterned on a leaf versus a landscape representing a forest. The leaf (whose degree of abstraction need no longer, on the basis of the above, occupy our attention) is undoubtedly torn from its surroundings, plucked from the tree, and the object is isolated, on its own, no longer in its original surroundings.

And the forest? It too is an object, and it too is torn from its surroundings! The picture frame lifts the represented 'object' as definitely out of its surroundings as is possible, whereupon the imagination is free to construct the landscape, to imagine more forest around the given section of forest, or else meadows, villages, towns. As far as the picture is concerned, the imagination simple acknowledges — and only as long as this is acknowledged is the picture conceptualized as a picture — that the picture has torn the represented object from its real surroundings, simply because it has not represented the entire universe. Gombrich agrees with Nietzsche that representing nature would mean representing the infinite.

Beyond the two Lukácsian criteria we might raise a third, if we still wanted to experiment with a separation (unrelated to function) between the ornament and the representational picture. This would rest on the duplication versus the singularity of the represented object. When I mentioned earlier the mosaics of the San Apollinare Nuovo, I had this aspect in mind. There is no doubt that the row of very realistically formed figures acquires its ornamental character, and gives rise to our feeling that decoration rather than representation is their essential aspect, by virtue of the fact that all these figures, at least on first sight, appear to be uniformly similar. Here, only 'first sight' matters, since even the most abstract repeated figures only appear identical on 'first sight'; even two 'abstract' leaves cannot be perfectly identical. With the aid of our chosen 'technique', however, it is once again not difficult to dissolve the boundaries: for example, nobody would regard Simone Martini's *Maesta* as ornamental in character, even though its figures too are strikingly uniform.

Very likely, I have been working with exaggerated examples, perhaps also over-sharpening the moments I highlighted. It has been my intention to do so. At the same time, I have not wished, either up to this point or hereafter, to deny the possibility that these two types of art can be distinguished. All that I wanted to 'prove' was that such a distinction is not compatible with a general concept of representation as 'the representation of reality'; the basis of the distinction (bracketing functionality) is the identification of representational art with art that endeavours to create illusion.

Now, in possession of this 'proof', we can calmly begin to examine causal accounts of stylistic changes in painting. According to what has been said, we need not commit ourselves in advance either to the position that painting somehow always represents reality or to the position that, in effect, it never does. Both propositions are acceptable and both are 'true' in a certain sense — particularly because, in the end, there is no daub of paint on canvas into which one could not dream the entire world, and no photograph so faithful that the observer could not need to dream something into it in order to constitute it as a world. If, therefore, the concepts of reality and representation have, one by one, eroded to this extent — this is the basis of the complementary truth of the two opposing terms — then there is really no reason to exclude from the start any of the causal accounts (2)–(5) as a way of explaining changes in style.

Before briefly considering these causes in turn, however, we need to answer another question. Is it at all possible to conceptualize the history of the 'stylistic changes' in painting as the history of changing relations to *the visible world*? More precisely, is it legitimate to hypothesize only such causes as can be brought into connection with the visible world, that is, with the relationship to the creation of illusion? What motivates a hasty (and perhaps rash) affirmative is that painting is connected unequivocally and, strictly speaking, exclusively with the sense of sight; it is precisely its exclusive connection with visual sensation that distinguishes painting from all the other arts (except mosaic art which, at the present high level of abstraction required by the author's inexperience with artistic techniques, can safely be regarded as a sub-category of painting).

Next to music, which is connected equally exclusively with the sense of hearing, painting is the other 'pure' artistic genre. Sculpture, even if its works are likewise enjoyed through the eye, is not connected to vision exclusively. In the case of sculpture we can choose to have recourse to our tactile sense to enjoy the work. Apart from our respect for 'Visitors are forbidden to touch the exhibits' signs, what makes it *possible* for us to do without recourse to tactility is that vision is capable of assuming in almost every respect the function of touch. In principle, the blind may enjoy sculpture and acquire, without verbal information, an exact awareness of what the sculpture represents, but the blind cannot enjoy painting, and only indirectly can they form any idea of it.

Does the fact, however, that painting is so exclusively bound to the sense of sight mean that it is necessarily coupled to the visible world outside the painting? This, as was noted, is denied by the adherents of extreme artistic actionism on the argument that while the painter inevitably *produces* some kind of visual field on the canvas, this has — or need have — no reference to the visible world that is prior to and independent of the painting. The reason that I am referring to action painting and not abstract or non-figurative is that the abstract incorporates in its very name the ingredients of a *relation* to the visible world from which it 'abstracts', and even the non-figurative is not *necessarily* a denial of the visible world since, for example, it can choose to highlight colour as a moment of it.

I should remark that I consider total autonomy from the visible world simply an absurdity. It would require that both the creator and the beholder of the work of action painting should cast out of the mind every other visual memory and should forget that they had ever seen anything other than the canvas before them. In Gábor Karátson's attractive phrase: 'There is no art without nature.' But even if we decline to take a stand in this matter, it remains the case that, apart from action painting in the modern period, every style that has ever existed in history has had something to do with nature, the visible world, so that we are in a position to conceptualize even the hypothetical transition to pure actionism in terms of a relationship with the visible world — as complete abandonment of it.

Let us look briefly at our points (2)—(5), beginning with (5), which is true because it presupposes what is to be proved. It regards everything that is a painting as the reproduction of the visible world; that is, it seeks out the visible world that corresponds to the painting, not the means of painting that are adequate to render the visible world. If every bizarre vision comprises the visible world, if the drop of water under the microscope, with its own bacterial flora, comprises the visible world, then in effect every painting is a rendering of the visible world, even if the painter is perhaps unaware of it. In the latter case, it would be the critic's task to bring to consciousness what is purely 'subconscious' for the painter, to demonstrate where and in what manner existed the 'original' of the vision made objective in the painting.

Certain modern theorists of art indeed have recourse to this kind of argumentation. There are those who thereby wish to 'defend' the modern 'abandonment' of the world visible in everyday life. In as much as modern European painting, by the middle or the second half of the nineteenth century, acquired the capacity to render the everyday visible world as perfectly as possible, painting has been forced to experiment with other sorts of visible worlds, with getting on canvas the 'sights' that unfold in the deep layers of the psyche or in the scientific instruments that effect a manifold increase in the efficacy of our visual organs. I do not want to deny the right of this kind of artistic experiment to exist, nor that such factors may have played a role for certain modern painters or in the development of schools of painting. But I cannot find such explanations satisfactory when they aim to account for the development of modern painting *in general*. They are not satisfactory because they are *defensive* in character: they hope to escape the grip of realism with its system of requirements by effectively accepting it, albeit with a certain internal insincerity.

Points (2) and (4) are closely interrelated. They represent two polar formulations of the same thing. As noted, it is not disputable that painting in every society, with the exception of the modern current that we have called artistic actionism, has had something to do with the reproduction of the visible world. No doubt, the reproduction of the visible world on a two-dimensional plane can never be perfect, if only because it is in principle impossible to paint in such a way that the observer, looking at the picture from two *different* points, would not *have to* take notice that he is dealing with a picture and not with 'reality itself', and because the painting *must* be delimited. Therefore, since the reproduction is not perfect, it becomes in a certain sense merely a matter of convention what is acceptable as an *adequate* approximation of the visible world. It really depends on social consensus, therefore, what is or is not regarded as painting that creates illusion.

Still, it is not disputable either that the painting does not consist of purely arbitrary marks that some accept and some do not accept as the signification of the visible world — the painting, after all, is not a verbal expression. There is no doubt that, in the end, having perfected its means, only modern European painting was successful in approximating, as far as is possible, the world visible from a fixed point through a defined 'window frame'. All these questions are tremendously exciting, but I do not want to pursue them here. Gombrich's book offers a thorough, many-sided examination of the pertinent problems to which I have nothing to add as far as the objective side of the matter is concerned.

I suspect, however — here turning praise to reproach — that Gombrich did not only restrain himself from answering aesthetic questions, but rather is unable to provide such answers. Not because they lie outside his competence as a psychologist of art, but because he is unable to decide a strategic question: should he or should he not conceptualize the history of painting as a *connected* history, one which displays the presence of a process towards grasping the visible world with increasing perfection? Sometimes he responds in the spirit of our point (2): the visible world is not reproducible with perfection; it has been approximated sometimes one way, sometimes another; ultimately it is not worth striving for such reproduction. At other times he inclines more toward the solution proposed in point (4): humanity has kept perfecting the means of reproducing the visible world.

It seems to me that he is unable to decide because he does not acknowledge that the reproduction of the visible world in general and the reproduction of the visible world in painting are connected but should be distinguished. Strictly speaking he has created not a psychology of art but a psychology of the reproduction of the visible world, a psychology of illusionist representation. Man has, indeed, increasingly perfected his means. I find it probable that an Egyptian 'painter-artist' would not have been capable of doing something that today anyone can do, even if not endowed with any artistic talent, so long as he can draw well: to represent the visible world according to linear perspective. But the Egyptian probably never aspired to this, either. What has today become virtually an ordinary, everyday skill has been developed in art by the persistence of a demand for the reproduction of the visible world. (It is another matter that this demand has a bearing not only on art but on numerous other social factors as well.) In this sense what has a history is not art but rather a definite human capacity.

Combining points (2) and (4), of course, we can develop a sufficiently solid conceptual account of changes in artistic style not to frighten anyone away. With the aid of certain concrete historical explanations, such an account is valid for every turn. We can take as our point of departure the fact that when man 'began' to paint, he painted what he saw, as best as he knew how. In determinate societies, finally, a consensus arose as to what would be accepted as 'correct' representation. In as much as each person learned to represent from another, everyone from those more skilful, each generation from the other, the (artistic, not artistic) representations of a society fundamentally resemble one another. When all is said and done, static societies draw and paint in a virtually uniform manner over thousands of years, and their art, if it changes at all, changes very slowly and organically.

In two instances, however — only twice during the whole of human history to date — something happens: in classical Greece and in the European Renaissance, style is transformed suddenly, non-organically. Something (bracketing explanations for the moment, since the fact still stands even if we cannot explain it) moves people suddenly to strive for the increasingly perfect approximation of illusion. First in sculpture, where the Greeks immediately carry the task to perfection, and then also in painting (where the creation of illusion is incomparably more complicated), slowly the means are perfected in the belief that increasingly realistic formation will result in works of art which increasingly comply with the *a priori* rules of harmony (proportion, compositional structure, colour relations).

We cannot plan to trace here the development that characterizes the European bourgeois epoch. But there is no doubt that — with certain sudden stops, across the sometimes tragic inner struggles of innovative artists, leaping ahead now here in Europe and now there, and giving up all its earlier 'prejudices' — painting increasingly comes to approximate the visible world, 'the world visible in everyday life'. This is true in every respect, as much in the increasing secularization of themes as in the increasingly successful elaboration of linear perspective and, correlatively, its harmonization with the perspectival effects of colour.

And this is true not only as far as form is concerned, for example that even in painting the treasures of Christian myth, the occasional scene here or there can be conceptualized as an wholly everyday scene drawn from the painter's own age. (There is no longer anything other-worldly in a birth of Christ or in a *pietà*. It is a common observation that even the early Renaissance was no longer able to paint the Ascension because already its means had become unsuited for representing something that could not have happened to a *human being* anywhere and at any time.

Such events could only be convincingly represented as long as the represented world also differed in its other respects from our this-worldly, everyday world.) It is also true in the sense of the increasingly conscious undertaking of painting that anything can be the object of artistic creation. 'Anything' is, naturally, an exaggeration. And here, it is from the thematic side that we have arrived at the impossibility, in principle, of reproducing 'the' visible world: painting has never really tolerated every subject-matter.

Even at the end-point of this development, the period of naturalism — impressionism in painting, the conceptualization of the nature of representation as the most faithful possible approximation of the visible world still incorporates the element of social consensus. (Finally, even the most naturalistic formation is none other than the virtually perfected revision of a definite, historically generated scheme; Gombrich rightly conceptualizes the evolution of the representational capacity as the constant refinement of this scheme.) The protest against impressionism was not only motivated by the fact that it violated the centuries-old rules of harmony that had been judged sacred and invulnerable by the academies, but also by the fact that the beholders of the period had internalized the academic rules as the rules for the faithful representation of the visible world, with the result that impressionist paintings failed to appear realistic to them.

Today, everyone *accepts* that impressionist painting is a real approximation of the visible world. There is a sound basis for such acceptance. Impressionism really is the perfect solution, as well as the commencement of dissolution, within the determinate system of requirements which the Renaissance established for the vanishing-point of representation and the space of painting.

Would this construction, designed on the basis of points (2) and (4), be contradicted by the account offered in point (3), to the effect that only certain exceptional periods endeavoured to reproduce the visible world? In all probability not. It is certain that the existence of such an endeavour is a decisive aid to the development of suitable means, and it is certain that the effort directed at improving the means in turn strengthens the demand for illusionist painting. In the ultimately 'naturalistic' sense in which we have come to interpret-conceptualise the reproduction of the visible world, it is indeed the case that only exceptional periods endeavoured to create illusion, and this does not contradict either that other periods in a certain sense already regarded as reproduction of the visible world what we would not remotely regard that way, or that other periods simply did not have the same capacity as modern European painting for creating the same kind of illusion.

In our search for the causes of stylistic changes in painting we began by definitely rejecting one thing: the hypothesis of a physiological transformation in the mode of seeing to provide a causal account of changes in the requirements governing painting. We should stand decidedly by our position on this score. But is it unambiguously established, following our discussion of points (2) and (4), that merely the requirements for representation have changed — from society to society, and period to period — and that the mode of seeing, in a broader sense of the word, has not changed? Is it not true at a minimum that, in parallel with changes in the modes of artistic formation, people have looked at the world differently? As the system of requirements for representation changed, representation itself changed in compliance. And as representation changed, as the system of requirements for it changed, people began *to see* differently.

Only in the twentieth century can we see a natural landscape *à la* Cézanne or Van Gogh. Does this follow from Cézanne, Van Gogh, or our vision? In order to avoid any type of mystification, one would be readily inclined to say that, naturally, only from Cézanne and Van Gogh; that following in the steps of two geniuses, looking at them and loving them, people learned to see differently. But is this answer really less mysterious than its inverse: people began to see differently, and the constitutive epochal genius of Cézanne and Van Gogh consisted precisely in that they knew how to paint in accordance with the new way of seeing and that they put an end to the contradiction between the new way of seeing and the old painting, something which significant painters since Barbizon had tried, in vain, to accomplish?

The mystery in the first answer concerns the nature of Cézanne and Van Gogh's genius. What is so great and significant about them, that after them Europeans can no longer see 'without them', are unable to avoid reading their canvases into the landscape and the world? Why do they happen to be the ones to compel a new way of seeing, and what is it in their painting that compels? Yet everyone, from either a 'realist' or an 'anti-realist' perspective, agrees that these are the first two great figures in the development of modern painting. The mystery in the second answer concerns the meaning to be assigned to that change in vision which the two geniuses were capable of formulating—expressing: What accounts for the change in people's ways of seeing? Whether we prefer the first, more activist and anti-realist, conception or the second, more realist, 'reflection'-based conception, we are bound to run into difficult, and so far unanswered questions.

An empirically-oriented theorist, with no desire to believe in the 'world spirit', will prefer the first answer. He would wish to stay with the model that we sketched above on the basis of points (2) and (4): man began to draw and paint. Occasionally, he succeeded in making something which he accepted as the reproduction of the visible world; he came to be fond of his schema, and soon no longer saw it as a schema but read the world into it. Still, he could always improve something in it. And since there exists no perfect schema on one hand, and no schematic outline which would not be acceptable as a representation, on the other, there are infinite possibilities for painting. As Gábor Karátson well and justly says: 'Only the whole of painting together is capable of expressing "the world of our sight", all that the human eye is capable of. . . . Painting realizes the possibilities of sight *seriatim*.'

We might almost be inclined to be satisfied with this kind of answer and henceforth reject the overstrained character of every Hegelian kind of rationalism and every belief in the 'world spirit'. Let us face the problem squarely: the Marxian proposition about an inherent standard, the Lukácsian concept of realism which is its legitimate, if somewhat narrower, heir, Lajos Fülep's faith in the unity of 'art and world view', Max Raphael's conviction which defines his entire theoretical activity in aesthetics, to the effect that seeing is not abstract 'but indeed very concrete and determined, among other things, by both the individual and (particularly) the cultural attitudes of the given historical period' — all these lack that self-evident naturalness which resides in the crystal-clear logic of Gombrich's thought-processes and in the model we developed on the basis primarily of his ideas.

Let us consider the Marxian aphorism: 'man knows how to employ the inherent standard . . . and therefore he also creates according to the laws of beauty.' What is this inherent standard? Does it reside in the functioning of man's material objectivations? Is the earthenware pitcher that is best suited to storing and pouring water also the most beautiful pitcher? Is it the most beautiful because it is the most suitable? Do we become accustomed to considering the most suitable as the most beautiful? Or does beauty itself possess some Platonic idea which finds, or fails to find, expression in the proportions of the object? Does the standard implied in the function provide the beauty, or do the laws of beauty announce the inherent standard?

We have already noted that this question, posed in its generality, is unanswerable. After all, if we look at an aspect of the matter that so far we have hardly touched on, as Raphael says: 'we are dealing with a type of object which, in its totality, is inaccessible to our cognitive approximation.' If art or, more narrowly, a given artistic period, the *oeuvre* of an artist, or a work of art, points beyond itself at all — of which we are convinced — even then it merely *points beyond*; 'what it has to say' can be formulated only in its own language. If it could be formulated otherwise, then there would be no 'need' of art. But if its statement can be made *only* in its own language, then it is impossible in practice to offer an explanation of the interconnections between a period and a work of art, this latter comprising a way of seeing the world which (it does not matter) either finds expression in it or is constituted by it. The two — period and art — cannot be transcribed in the same language.

The changing relationship with the visible world is what genuinely characterizes the 'history' of painting — indeed, this is its meaning. Different causal reasons can be offered, either singly or all together, to account for stylistic change — that people in different ages accept different things as the reproduction of the visible world; that there are epochs when neither painters nor those who commission, enjoy or behold paintings consider it their task to reproduce the visible world, and epochs when they do; that only exceptional societies have been capable of reproducing the visible world, at least as circumscribed by certain definite stipulations; that different periods have expected painting to reproduce different visible worlds. But in so far as we are enquiring into the task of painting, strictly speaking we are asking about the cause of these 'causes', and we would like to know precisely why it is that man relates in a number of different ways to the visible world and its reproduction.

It is not worth disputing — and there is no intelligent way, really, to dispute — that 'European' civilization, and only it, succeeded in reaching the 'peaks' of illusionist painting, and that only this painting was capable, within the frame of the possibilities, of most fully rendering 'the visible world'. There is no debating this, even if we know that what we are to consider as *the* visible world is quite ambiguous and that what we are to consider as the perfect reproduction of this visible world is completely ambiguous. What can and *must* be said on this score has been said by the psychology of art (more exactly, by the psychology of the reproduction of visual sensation and visual perception). The real question, or at least the one germane to aesthetics and philosophy of history, is why it happened to be precisely modern European culture which *strove* for the reproduction of the visible world.

Right up to the end of the nineteenth century it was possible to give an unequivocal answer to this question: because only modern European culture was *capable* of it. Capability gave birth to demand, the first successes of the Renaissance intoxicated painters and admirers of painting alike, and fired them with a passionate fever: to create total verisimilitude, to render three-dimensional space in the two dimensions of a canvas. 'Se non è vero, ben trovato' is an anecdote about Giotto and Cimabue. It is said that Giotto was still working in Cimabue's workshop when he painted a fly one day on the nose of one of Cimabue's figures. The master, on returning to the workshop, saw the fly and several time tried to chase it away. He did not notice the joke until his eye nearly touched the painting. Yet who *today* would see Giotto's fly as alive? Today, by contrast, we know that the possibility and capability of perfectly reproducing the visible world by no means *always* gives birth to the demand for its actualization as well. Painting in the twentieth century aspires to just about everything except rendering the visible world in its everyday sense.

Illusionism in Painting and the Aesthetic Judgement of the Bourgeois World

Illusionism is the characteristic feature of a definite epoch in the history of painting — of an epoch where the 'average', even the 'normal' judgement of taste embraced only paintings that neither fell short of nor surpassed the boundaries of illusionism and where the ideal of beauty, in spite of variations according to time and place, always remained within the framework of illusionism. The acceptance or the rejection of illusionism can and should be handled by reference to the distinction between judgement of taste and aesthetic judgement,[1] in the same way as the aesthetic relationship to any other concrete style of painting, painter's *oeuvre*, or single work of art.

Naturally, the relationship to 'illusionism' — since the latter is not a school of painting but rather a boundary or limit which not a single painting, painter or school of painting transcended over a long historical epoch — does not demarcate any concrete taste or any concrete ideal of beauty. Just as illusionism serves as the untranscendable framework for the endeavours of painters and schools of painting during a well-defined epoch in the history of art, so it can also be conceptualized from the side of reception as the framework for that epoch's most diverse artistic tastes and ideals of beauty. If a beholder — an aesthetician or critic with a significant role in the formation of the ideal of beauty, or else an 'ordinary', 'average' appreciator of art — does not want, or is not able, to accept as a real painting anything that transcends the framework of illusionism, this is (or is not) a matter of purely subjective taste to the same extent that the relationship to painting(s) in general is (or is not) a matter of purely subjective taste.

What is not open to question is that there exists an epoch of painting when the possibility cannot even arise that anyone would accept as a significant work of art any painting that transcends the framework of illusionism. We may also contend, perhaps, that, as far as this framework is concerned, this epoch is almost as rigidly dismissive with respect to the non-illusionist art of preceding societies and ages as are these latters' constitutive tastes and ideals of beauty with respect to the art of others. It may not be accidental that it is simultaneously with the breakdown of illusionism and its constitutive taste and ideal of beauty in the second half of the nineteenth century that the European type of artistic taste begins to accept the art of every other society and period virtually universally — in other words, that taste now begins to become unambiguously universal.

There is no doubt that illusionist art, taste and ideal of beauty already comprise a step toward accepting as one's own something that is not directly one's own creation. Illusionism is a mere framework within which we encounter a far greater variety of possible forms than in earlier art. The breakdown of illusionism is a further step in this direction towards the existence of a greater variety of creativity and, at the same time, as far as artistic taste and ideals of beauty are concerned, towards the acceptance (as objects of artistic reception, if not as examples to be followed) of a broad (or perhaps complete) spectrum of art from preceding societies and epochs. (It seems beyond question that the sphere of what is artistically receivable has, since the development of bourgeois society, always been broader than the sphere of what is acceptable as the art of any given moment; but it also appears beyond question that these two spheres expand or contract collaterally. This matter requires detailed historical study and I cannot deal with it here, but I do not consider it insignificant for illuminating the problem complex of this essay.)

It is beyond dispute that painting in our period has passed beyond the boundaries of illusionism. Whether figurative or non-figurative, and regardless of which aspirations of which 'ism' are being actualized, it is not debatable that paintings born of our period, with very few exceptions, show no desire to be interpretable as the visible world. Any 'ism', whether intellectual or perfectly reliant on the senses (even to the extent of refusing to tolerate as interpretation the verbalism to which it gives rise), can be brought into relationship with the visible world, in the sense examined above, but never does it wish to represent it.

It is fair to wonder whether this tendency of painting, which has been in train for nearly 100 years since the decay of impressionism, is the product of crisis, as many claim, or marks the art of a new era, an art which can be accepted or dismissed (on grounds of taste: it pleases—it does not please; or on grounds of aesthetic judgement: it is beautiful—it is not beautiful), a possibility of choice that can never be excised from modern society, but which has to be acknowledged as the art of our age.

The present author favours the second alternative, as the reader will already have gathered from the train of thought to this point. The aesthetic judgement is based on the judgements of taste, and the artistic taste of our time (it would be ridiculous to call this into question after nearly 100 years) has gone beyond the bounds of illusionism. We cannot claim that painting in the last century has failed to 'fulfil its own taste'. However, in as much as there are still those for whom illusionist painting remains an (inaccessible) model and example, and who treat contemporary painting as a crisis phenomenon (purely because it was not able to fulfil its own task within the framework of illusionist painting, whether this is said explicitly or not), we have to ask: What gave birth to the demand for illusionist painting, and what put an end to it?

Before experimenting with an answer to this question, I feel an obligation to explain its intelligibility. With respect to pre-bourgeois art, I adopted the position that the question of why certain specific stylistic traits characterize the art of a particular society is not meaningful. I held that although all the stylistic traits could be derived from the diverse heritage of the period, this derivation would be irrelevant in the face of the irrevocable fact that the given art is connected to the given society, as far as the members of that society and the art world of later ages are concerned. What would be the sense, then, with respect to the connection between illusionism and bourgeois society, of saying more than that they are irrevocably interconnected and that, therefore, it is perfectly irrelevant what originally gave birth to the demand for illusionism?

Several factors underpin the intelligibility of the question:

1 Illusionism is purely a frame within which innumerable variations of style and schools have existed. Indeed, within this framework, bourgeois painting had endeavoured to create something new each day, as it were. Why did the will for novelty not decompose the framework itself, or rather, why did it explode the framework all at once?

2 Illusionism is not the art, or the framework for the art, of closed societies. Societies that reproduced themselves in identical forms over centuries or millenia also reproduced their own art organically; their society, their art, and they themselves formed an indissoluble unity within their consciousness. The bourgeois, by contrast, is severed from the umbilical cord of community. For him, it has never been in the nature of things that what once exists cannot be otherwise, except, perhaps, where the frameworks are concerned (to anticipate our conclusions), precisely those frameworks which guarantee for him the possibility of severance from community, but in such a manner as also to assure his survival!

3 The reflective consciousness of this epoch has a distanced relation to itself. With respect to art, as in all other respects, it constantly attempts to legitimate what it does as the right thing to do; it attempts to call its own activity into question in order to confirm its legitimacy all the more through triumph over doubt. Why is it that the aesthetics of this period (and the very existence of aesthetics in the modern sense is the consequence of this reflexivity) never raises the question of whether painting might pass beyond the framework of illusionism? Put differently, why are decoration and representation in the visual arts unequivocally separated from one another?

What then gave birth to the demand for illusionist painting and what put an end to it?

I am convinced that the art of the bourgeois epoch is just as symbiotically bound up with a world-view, a fundamental attitude, as the art of earlier periods and other societies. But the bourgeois epoch may be the only one whose art is inseparable from the contents of its entire vision of the world.

The attitude or world-view that gave birth to artistic illusionism is none other than bourgeois rationalism, the same view or vision of the world which also gave birth to science. On its account, our world is solid and circumscribable, a world of objects strictly determined in their motion by objective regularities. If we wish to live our lives as freely as possible, it is this world, the visible world of nature, that we must come to know, and the regularities that exist within it or behind it but not independently of it; our freedom is identical with the recognition of the (invisible) laws of the visible world. The task of art (including painting), just like the task of science, is the cognition of the visible world, the disclosure of the essentials present in its contingencies.[2] Their means naturally diverge from one another, but their tasks are the same.

Cognition, of course, cannot make the *entirety* of the world into safe and secure territory; the visible world will always contain things we know to be threatening to us. Nevertheless — and here, in the capacity for cognition, lies the possibility for autonomous man — he can secure his own limited milieu for himself totally; he can come to know it perfectly; and therefore he will be able to move around in it with complete safety.

It was not by accident or incidentally that I used the word freedom in the above attempt at synthesis. I am convinced that it was only possible to bring into existence significant works of art within the framework of this ideology as long as the faith that cognition is freedom remained genuinely alive within it. Once this faith is lost, once the achieved and closed world of objects becomes alien to man (even his own product becomes alien to him), once bourgeois ideology feels that its own ideal of freedom is unrealizable, that it is a lie that determination is freedom, then it is no longer capable of producing great art. To cite Lukács:

> the bourgeoisie either had to give up this ideology, or use it as a cover for quite the opposite activities. In the first case, the result was an absence of ideals, an ethical morass, because, by virtue of the place it occupies in production, the bourgeoisie was incapable of generating any other ideology than that of individual freedom. In the second case, the bourgeoisie was facing the ethical bankruptcy of its internal lie: it was constantly forced to act in opposition to its own ideology.

Illusionist painting is given life by bourgeois ideology.[3] This is how it appears to painters, as well as to ideologues and aestheticians. To cite Gábor Karátson's admirable formulation: 'The glassbox of central perspective . . . in effect expresses the world view of the bourgeoisie and came into existence at the same time as the bourgeoisie. It was like a closed, safe room.' 'For the bourgeois, this was the familiar room of central perspective in contrast to the uncertainty of the external world of nature.' Karátson gives articulate expression to what must have been the thought of van Eyck in painting the Arnolfini couple. The small world in which the two people stand is perfectly known (mirror!), even if it does not point beyond itself. Man moves freely in its interior.

All this, however, comprises the ideology, the view of the world, which gives birth to illusionism itself. Bourgeois ideology — whose classical epoch is characterized by the concurrence of opinion among its most antithetical variations that the world is given, whatever its form, and freedom means learning to move around in the world as given — provides the framework which the painting of the period has to acknowledge. We should remember that, according to our characterization, illusionism itself is a framework. The artistic exploitation of the possibilities extracted by this framework opens up the opportunity for numerous, fundamentally divergent styles of painting that can be described as illusionist. All those who have wanted to paint pictures that would be interpretable as the visible world have shared a common conviction, one of whose elements has been the confinement of the task of painting within the framework. This common conviction, however, has been capable of encompassing the most diverse vision of the world and of permitting the development of the most diverse styles of painting.

In sum, what assumes shape and form in illusionism as a framework is the bourgeois world view, that of men severed from the umbilical cord of community; and in various illusionist styles, the various visions of the world which now acknowledge the framework of this world-view and flesh it out (by this time in ways that are not, in every respect, verbally paraphrasable), now clash with it in some aspects. The beauty and harmony present in the different styles that emerged within the illusionist framework at the start manifestly demonstrates that the concrete visions of the world that painters of that epoch had do fit harmoniously into the framework of the bourgeois world-view, in complete conformity with it; indeed, that determination and freedom, in a certain sense, are genuinely not yet antithetical. (In as much as there is no freedom, only freedoms, to use Agnes Heller's phrase, it is also evident that freedom, in all its forms and kinds, is a process, not a state, and under no conditions the absurd reconciliation of determination and freedom. It is not possible to undertake the analysis of this philosophical problem here.)

As soon as the illusions of the bourgeois world-view start to be exposed, harmoniously beautiful representations of the visible world become unrealizable. (The last such realization, though one that by today seems increasingly problematical, is Leonardo da Vinci's painting.) To be more exact: the striving after harmonious representation proves to be falsehood — academicism on one hand, kitsch on the other. The creation of beautiful form — or the reception of a form as beautiful — more and more decidedly becomes possible only through techniques for disturbing harmony. (We need only think of any of the great artists from Michelangelo, Tintoretto and Rembrandt onwards, or rather of those whom a progressive vision of the world is able to accept today as genuinely great artists.) What emerges more and more is a new vision or sense of life that is no longer capable of registering or taking in the forms of the visible world without mediation.

It is interesting, however, to see what an indirect route was followed to the effective breakdown of illusionist art. Nineteenth-century painters found forced harmony according to the rules of academic art unacceptable. Yet the first experiment at refusal of the visible world was an experiment to render an *'unorganized'* visible world, to take illusionism to its extremes, that is, an endeavour to assure that painting should not only be interpretable as the visible world but that it should truly render the visible world itself. This was the experiment of naturalism—impressionism. A reader who has found our argument at all persuasive will not then find inadmissible the proposition that the kind of vision of the world which achieves form in naturalism and impressionism is one that has not yet come into direct conflict with the world-view that equates cognition and freedom, but is no longer capable of acknowledging the narrow material world of bourgeois life as the world in which freedom is realized. It represents, with increasing 'freedom' from formal obligations, but it no longer wants, or knows how, to take up a position. In consequence, precisely because it does not want to assume a position, painting finally *becomes* unequivocally *ideological.*

In its passionate effort not to falsify the world — not to disseminate some untrue creed present in either academicism or in the already emerging kitsch — naturalism finally destroys itself as art. To cite Konrad Fiedler: 'Its powerful refusal of everything that it stamps with the mark of falsehood, concealment, or the embellishment of the truth in the world view of the past does not protect it from similarly regarding as an image of reality something which ultimately is only the falsification of reality.' I do not believe that the charge of falsifying reality is warranted. However, the maximal realization of the possibilities of illusionist art, the utmost fidelity in reproducing the visible world, comprises the 'formulation' of an unambiguous relation to reality which ultimately provides a handhold for one — and only one — vision of the world, a completely passive avoidance of commitment.

The historical fate of naturalism is peculiar. I am sure that even today many people will receive with some scepticism, or even determined protestations, my unequivocal classification of impressionism with naturalism — people in whose view impressionism advocates something radically new (and I am not referring to technical details) with respect to naturalism. An increasingly significant portion of the art world, however, including outstanding specialists, has now come to feel that what we call 'modern', the art that first breaks with illusionism (as we have defined it), is not impressionism but rather the paintings precisely of those who have also broken with impressionism, especially Cézanne, Van Gogh, and perhaps Gauguin and Seurat. There is no doubt that for a long time impressionism has been considered the beginning of modern art. If we now know (as significant aestheticists such as Fülep already knew at the start of the century) that this is not true, that impressionism was not a beginning but an end, the end of the epoch of illusionism, the fact remains that in that capacity it genuinely initiated a new art.

The consummation and decomposition of illusionism involves the maximum possible realization of a 'technical' possibility and therewith its exhaustion. But not in the sense of pure technicity. True, in some respects it was no longer possible to generate something 'new' out of illusionist painting; one had to try something else. But neither the need to produce novelty with its aid, nor the need to pass beyond illusionism, arose from the internal technical development of painting. The unequivocal con-summation of illusionist art made virtually tangible at the level of art what could also be felt in a thousand other spheres of nineteenth-century European society: that the bourgeois world view could no longer serve as the framework for a progressive relationship to the world or for any kind of progressive vision. (I would not want to contend for a moment that the new forms and their virtually infinite variety comprise somehow mystically realized incarnations of ideals that negate the bourgeois world. But it follows from the train of my thought that there really is no need for mystical incarnation in order for a new attitude to find expression in the violation of artistic illusionism. After all, artist and beholder together constitute the painting.)

For just this reason, it is impossible to conceptualize modern art as a crisis. Nearly 100 years ago, painting was ruled by 'isms'. Do these reflect the crisis of the bourgeois world-view? Is it possible to conceive of this century as one in which painting is unable to find suitable means of expression? I cannot think of it that way. The crisis of the bourgeois world-view announced itself, not in the breakdown of illusionism, but rather in that the illusionist framework for art, which had been adequate to the bourgeois world-view, became 'exhausted' and could no longer provide possibilities for the realization of artistic ideas.

'Post-illusionism' (meaning both figurative and abstract, and every kind of 'ism' equally) 'formulates', brings to expression, and creates new visions which at least aspire to transcend the framework of the bourgeois world-view and which can no longer tolerate the frames of the bourgeois world. It should be clear to the reader that I not only do not know how but also that I have no desire to explain the concrete 'content', the verbal 'statement' of these visions. But it is certain that this painting demands and creates a new vision of the world. In every manifestation and in every school? Of course not. But why would modern painting, of all things, not (have the right to) bring with it bad, ideological works and tendencies?

I am in complete agreement with Pierre Francastel that the attempt to translate the 'language' of painting into verbal language is a prejudice of modern European existence under the spell of verbalization. But I have to enter into the most forceful debate with the suggestion of his work that the birth of the new, modern, 'post-illusionist' painting simultaneously announces in its own language the birth of a new society. The 'language' of art does not speak of the whole of society. Art expresses the relation that its creator and beholder have to the world — it being understood, of course, that this relation is itself part of the world. If, in our century, painters can no longer paint as did the painters in centuries past, if they have burst the fetters of illusionism as a framework, this 'tells' us no more than that in one way or another the spiritual elite of our age is no longer capable, from incapacity or shame, of accommodating to the framework of the bourgeois world-view.

But we should not blind ourselves: it is really only a question of a spiritual *elite*. In contrast to communal societies where art, including painting, was the business and the 'language' of the whole society, precisely what is characteristic of bourgeois societies is that 'real' art has become the private affair of a small sector. The average individual in the bourgeois world does not live with art; at most he 'consumes' some bad art surrogates. As far as painting is concerned, the majority of these shoddy goods *continues to this day* to be 'illusionist'! Transformation in the way of seeing the world indeed signals, or may signal, transformation of the world. But — as is clear even if we confine our attention to painting — the average person's vision of the world has been little changed.

We should also take note of another thing: it is the most diverse forms of kitsch painting which fashion the visual environment that shapes the vision of the world of the individual growing up in average circumstances and with average capacities, that is, of the child who will some day live a life organized around his own particularity. Children in all parts of the world are taught from texts whose drawings, quite independently of the 'propositional' contents of world-view, instill the bourgeois way of seeing the world.

The transformation of painting does not mean the transformation of the world. Having faith in this presupposes positing an excessively unmediated unity between technique and art. Francastel forgets something when he wages war against regarding painting and art in general as manifestations of ideals. He is right, in so far as the platonizing conception of art really does make it impossible to approach with understanding any art that is alien to our expectations and thus it precludes the lover of Renaissance beauty, for example, from accepting modern art. But he forgets that 'the ideal' has two meanings: not only transcendent ideas suspended above man and history, but also the palpable ideal present in the manifest behaviour of real persons. And if painting has nothing to do with this then it is no more than a mere game or hobby.

In modern painting, of course — at least, in most of its manifestations — there is more playfulness than in the painting of illusionism. This playfulness is responsible for the fact that decorativity and representation again cannot be divided from each other, which is one reason why those who see the mission of painting as residing in some serious 'statement' have often and for long shrunk from the modern. But this playfulness is not a mere game. The object — which is often perhaps really the offspring of the painter's playful creative desire — has a 'will' to beauty and the capacity to offer beauty: to offer it to a new community that is still only an embryo today.

NOTES

1   This study forms part of a longer essay whose first section offers a discussion of the relationship between judgement of taste and aesthetic judgement. The following

conclusion is reached. An aesthetic judgement (e.g. 'this picture is beautiful') is simply a judgement of taste (e.g. 'this picture pleases me') that lays claim to being paradigmatic. Yet, in contrast to the subjective, idiosyncratic judgement of taste, the aesthetic judgement nevertheless disposes of some kind of 'objectivity', although this latter is not something above man and history but instead has its roots in the intersubjectivity and social-historical value preference of definite historical periods and human communities. The separation between judgement of taste and aesthetic judgement is a product of the bourgeois epoch in which a community still endowed with a common, unappealable and (for lack of a historical consciousness) internally unquestionable value-system no longer exists. The individual in the bourgeois epoch strives to develop strictly personal tastes, at the same time that he does his utmost to make his personal tastes paradigmatic, that is acknowledged by others. The antinomies that thus arise are necessarily features of a world where the individual is severed from the umbilical cord of the community.

2   Let me be precise, to avoid misunderstanding. My unequivocal position is that art (including painting) is not cognition (i.e. not the reproduction of something external to it) but rather production, constitution or, as Heidegger says, 'the establishment of a world' (*Aufstellung einer Welt*). It makes no difference in this respect that the reproductive element is always present in production — as a subordinate moment. The work of art *qua* work of art is always a *creatio ex nihilo*, even if some of its elements (subject-matter, theme) were already present before it. After all, once these elements are 'parts' of the work of art, they are no longer what they had been before. I cannot analyse here whether the production—reproduction relationship is really reversed in those domains of human activity that are generally regarded as cognition (including science), nor whether it is true that cognition, in its own fashion, reproduces the 'objective' world. I would remark only that the epoch of illusionism in painting is characterized by the fact that, within it, even art conceives of itself — prior to all philosophical—aesthetic reflections about art — as cognition in the sense used above, as reproduction of the world (that is, the visible world). This cannot be said of painting before or after this epoch, even if it never occurred to contemporaneous metaphysics to call into question the fundamentally reproductive character of cognition. (This is essentially characteristic of the whole of European metaphysics until Heidegger and Wittgenstein.)

3   Today, I can no longer accept the equation of naturalist rationalism and (the) bourgeois ideology. First of all, I do not equate the 'bourgeois' — the individual severed from the umbilical cord of a limited community — with the exploitative capitalist. Nor do I believe that bourgeois society is moving — or even tending to move — towards the dissolution of all forms of community. (See my 'Phänomenologie und bürgerliche Gesellschaft', in Waldenfels, Broekman, Pažanin (eds), *Phänomenologie und Marxismus*, vol. 3, *Socialphilosophie*, Frankfurt, 1978.) Finally, I have come to recognize that if I am to assign value to the achievement of individuality — the great accomplishment of the bourgeois world — then I have to acknowledge that a humanist future cannot mean the replacement of the antinomic structure of the bourgeois world with some kind of eternal communal harmony. (See my 'Marxism and Eastern Europe: a sort of letter to my friends', in my *The State and Socialism: Political Essays*, London, 1981.)

I ought to draw from these positions the consequences for the subject at hand, the relation of painting and world-view. But since the purpose of this volume is to gather together the aesthetic writings of the former Budapest school rather than to reflect the current standpoints of former members of the school, I cannot modify the text. To do so is not absolutely necessary in any case because, in my judgement, the text develops a position on painting which, in a certain sense, anticipates the above indicated shift in my overall standpoint. Taking off from my current views, I would not only not have to adopt a different stand on the dissolution of illusionism in painting, but I could make my train of thought even less ambiguous or contradictory. Today, I no longer need to conceptualize modern painting as the utopian trustee of some kind of communal future that disavows the bourgeois world as a whole. The communal moment is very much present in the 'bourgeois' world. The epochal change that shows up in painting *as well as* in a wide variety of other realms of mental production is not the disavowal of the bourgeois world but rather the admission of its insurmountably antinomic character.

And for me, today, this admission is a claim on the possibility of a humanist future.

7

Don Giovanni

GÉZA FODOR
Translated by Thomas Sail

Kierkegaard writes that sensuality, the sensuously erotic as a principle, as a force, as a realm, was created by Christianity through its exclusion by the spirit, thus defining it as a contrary principle.[1] Mozart's *Don Giovanni* represents the final hours of this state of the world. The opera, in the D minor andante introduction to the overture, begins with the unexpected return of the spirit. This wholly musically conceived beginning is at the same time one of the most fantastic visions of musical literature: a true apparition. The mass of dominant chords, developed with inherent asymmetry, voiced in the tonality of D minor by the entire orchestra, evoke inarticulate monumentality, a sort of massiveness. The intonation is chilling: it is not without justification that Abert likens it to the concept of Medusa's head.[2] But there is a sudden change in the music. The formerly dense and concentrated sound becomes sublimated, transparent, almost ethereal. At the same time, it becomes clearly more articulate. On the one hand, a pregnant and consistently repeated rhythm gains form:

Example 1

on the other, the octave steps of the wind instruments — those gigantic yet weightless steps of the spirit — implement a pure periodicity. Thus the apparition has become even more unreal, and at the same time more concrete. Now a vigorous process of the development of internal dynamics begins: the first violins sketch a melodic line, while the semi-quaver movements of the second violins create a restless pulsation. The energies thus liberated are discharged in threatening sforzatos, and die immediately. Still, the music proceeds unmistakably towards a climax of tension. And indeed two, near-volcanic outbursts bear witness to the manifestation of an irresistible power. Now follows what seems like a slow retreat — a retreat no less awesome than the outbursts. The rhythm we have noted before is taken up on the basses, while the scale passages of the flutes and violins (crescendo in ascent, piano in descent) disturb by their ambiguous gestures of surging and retreating, threatening and withdrawing. At last the imminent danger is past, all emotions turn inward, the grandiose throbbing of the basic rhythm and the gurgling tremolo engulf and absorb all, until the tension practically evaporates in the final beats, the apparition is torn to shreds, becomes hot vapour rising with the sharp staccato of the strings.

Renaissance tragedies often begin with the allegorical figure of Vengeance appearing to announce that the guilty will be punished. It only intones the drama, then stands aside without interfering in the course of the action. Yet it is the one which sets out everything; the audience sees the events through it alone. Here, too, in the slow introduction of the overture, an apparition emerges, then disappears. It signifies and decides something. The spirit disappears, to let the universal drama be seemingly played out again; the departure of Spirit from the world and the breaking loose of sensuality. Yet the audience who have heard this music, feel that this cannot be wholly true. The power manifesting itself in this music in D minor is not one that feels this world no longer to be its own, rather it is a Shakespearean 'perturbed spirit'.

The intonation of the opera is unforgettable, and Hotho is justified in writing: 'This pain-riddled, deep, sepulchral solemnity gave me a warning premonition of Don Giovanni's fate, which he will not avoid.'[3] This, however, is merely the audience's premonition. As the apparition disappears, the world-stage is occupied by the realm of sensuality, in complete ignorance of the forewarning.

The finishing point of the D minor andante, the pedal-point, marks the introduction of the D major molto allegro. There is no transition between the two parts, there is, rather, an abrupt switch, the second part almost stepping on the heels of the first. This second part is a single symphonic movement with a single meaning of its own, all of it the totally direct, unreflecting expression of the energy, life-force, sensuality and *joie de vivre* that sweep everything else away. All inner differentiation, contradiction and resolution, tension and release, all variety, take place within this homogeneous manifestation, being its continuous meta-morphosis, its constantly changing quality of passion and emotion. The D major molto allegro is the *musical* expression of the realm of sensuality.

The two parts of the *Don Giovanni* overture are built upon two fundamentally different construction principles. The first is a succession of musical tesserae, none of its themes is developed. Perceptible continuity is represented only by the consistency of its internal acceleration — a truly unified trend, from the minims of the beginning to the demi-semi-quavers of the end. The basic characteristic of the slow introduction still consists in the duality where the details, arrayed side by side thematically, are transmuted into organisms of mood. This compositional oddity precisely expresses the ambiguity of the first part. No dramatic figure is outlined as the subject; the action proper has not begun. For us, the apparition — like the ghost of Hamlet's father for Horatio, Bernardo and Marcellus — is merely a 'dreaded insight', an 'apparition', a 'portentous figure', an illusion. 'This spirit, dumb to us', so suggestive by his mere appearance, is made to appear to us auditorily through the compositional contradictions of the music.

In contrast, the second part is a complete and contained symphonic movement, realized through consistent thematic work. A world of music that ignores everything external to it, standing alone, expressing internally its multifaceted potentials.

Thus the overture links two worlds that are opposites in every respect — most essentially in the way they are composed. In other words, two opposing poles of a divided world are confronted. This monumental symphonic prologue promises a world-drama. The overture remains open with a C major chord on the fifth degree of F major; the musical curtain rises.

With the first introduction we find ourselves not within a universal drama, but in an *opera buffa*: Leporello voices his indignation over the fate of the servant. The famous 'notte e giorno faticar' theme is a true eighteenth-century *buffa* cliché, yet it identifies with an individual in a unique and symbolic manner. The theme is endowed with so much significance by the exposition that seeks the essential, by pregnant attitude, but chiefly by the characteristic place expressed in the totality of the organic musical development of the figure. With these indignantly rising sequences, Leporello works himself into a true rage. Having satisfied his psychological need — after an effectively sustained B — he pauses in satisfaction, as if enjoying his self-generated anger, and now indulges his mood with vocal flair and abandon: 'voglio far il gentiluomo . . .' What we hear belongs, we are certain, in Leporello's permanent repertoire: rebellious indignation, at its pitch, becomes undisguised admiration, even more importantly, the echo of his master. This is expressed unmistakably by the orchestra (mainly by the violins, the oboes and the bassoons). In this moment the figure of Leporello becomes highly ambiguous: it seems that his grumbling and his admiration are the expressions of the same fact: he is his master's captive, not his servant. And thus he is on a human level. The link which ties Don Giovanni and Leporello is not a status relationship, but a linking of lives.

As soon as the music begins to express this relationship, it brings the framework of the *opera buffa* into question. Both psychologically and stylistically, Mozart allows this dimension to be felt very subtly, yet quite precisely. For a moment, a strange light flashes across the waves of emotion; but only for a moment, for, in the subsequent bars, Leporello's discontent subsides into the commonplace again. The process has come to rest, only to be repeated but in an somewhat different emotional level. Now, instead of self-generated indignation, comes bitter irony. We can sense that this is another favourite theme of Leporello's thoughts. It starts with an air of facile superiority (with a gallant gesture by the orchestra), then the irony, the ambiguous identification, becomes gradually more bitter, before finally arching into overt self-pity: 'ed io far la sentinella'. Here Leporello's bitterness sinks to its low point, and only with a renewed outburst of rage — an ambiguous outburst — is he able to overcome it. This explains the repetition of the previous section. With this reprise, the essence of the figure of Leporello is revealed, not merely in the details but in the total modelling as well: his ambivalent attachment to Don Giovanni. In a certain sense, Leporello is Don Giovanni's *alter ego*. For this reason, his relationship with his master is characterized by a sort of running in circles around himself. His rebellion can never reach the point of the actual parting of the ways, for it turns into admiration at the decisive moment, and finally relapses into capitulation. Then the process starts again. This cycle alone can ever be repeated, with the circle sometimes wider, sometimes narrower, with differing emotional postures. Accordingly, Leporello's scene musically is linear, a succession of thematically discrete sections. There is no development of theme or motif; in principle the chain of internally independent sections could be continued infinitely. Even in their organizing role the ever-recurring episodes reinforce the effect.

Musically, an infinite, circling motion, a ceaseless spinning, was initiated in Leporello's scene. Only by an external event can the action break free of this circle. Such an event is the appearance of Donna Anna and Don Giovanni.

Donna Anna and Don Giovanni's scene stands in sharp contrast to the preceding *buffa* scene, no matter with how rich a meaning Mozart endowed the *buffa* style. The entire scene is overshadowed by the magnificent theme of Donna Anna:

Example 2

The architectonics of the melody imposes proportion and balance, the arch is divided, approximately, according to the Golden Section, into two parts: one unit of staccato rhythm, like a shout, and one of melodic quavers. This melody is the essence of a true heroine. Anna appears at the climax of dramatic tension with tragic presence and assured demeanour. But let us observe how the melody is transmuted in the part of Don Giovanni:

Example 3

Don Giovanni deforms Anna's melody, disturbs its architectonics, its proportions and harmony, breaks its arc. As if the opposite of the creative process were taking place, as if the first still ambiguous, still hesitant, raw draft were 'detaching' itself from the final, crystallized composition. The pure heroism of Anna's melody is reduced to forceful but raw emotionalism. This transformation articulates their relationship, it concentrates the essence of the relationship between Anna and Don Giovanni. Abert had already pointed out the significance of the fact that in contrast to Bertati's *Don Giovanni*, which served as a direct source, here it is not Don Giovanni, but Donna Anna who opens the scene.[4]

It is very important here that, regardless of the preceding events in the opera, that is, in the dramatic relationship between the two, Anna is the aggressive protagonist, and Don Giovanni is totally on the defensive. If Don Giovanni here takes over (and at the same time deforms) Anna's melody, it does not represent his skill of seduction, his *savoir-faire* in dealing with women; on the contrary, it shows his total helplessness, his confused impotence, in the face of Anna's determination. One of the key facts of the opera is embodied in the first musical exchange of Donna Anna and Don Giovanni's scene: namely that Anna shatters Don Giovanni's irresistibility. We may assume that this is the first time this has happened. Thus the drama begins with a decisive turn of fate. In the relationship between Anna and Don Giovanni this turn of events is irrevocable.

Their scene is divided into two parts, and these develop from the dual character of Anna's theme. The first part is dominated by the syncopated, shout-like theme. Here the two protagonists subtly mirror one another: both are aggressors and helpless victims simultaneously. The contradiction in Anna's character and situation becomes manifest. It is an extremely revealing moment when we recognize in the heroine the little girl who nearly bursts into tears at her predicament:

Example 4

Gen - te, ser - vi, al tra - di - to - re!

Clearly, there is a contradiction between Anna as a person and her predicament. Basically, she is a gentle being of pure and simple feelings, in a situation that demands heroism, and she is able to rise to this demand. But an inadequacy exists. Anna's inner drama begins with this contradiction. And Don Giovanni, the aggressor in the libretto, becomes defensive in the music. This is not altered by the fact that fairly early on his part becomes coherent and clearly articulated; but his self-assured tone cannot make us forget that the musical process is determined by Anna. The girl, seeing that no one is coming to her aid, overcomes her momentary weakness and confronts Don Giovanni with even more unshakable resolve. As if, in the second part, the physical struggle were to yield to moral indignation. The theme here is no less passionate, yet is more melodic, and elaborate. Its characteristic quaver pattern here is derived from the second section of Anna's first melody:

Example 5

Co-m'e fu - ria   dis - pe - ra - ta

Don Giovanni follows, imitating Anna's part. This long-drawn-out scene, with its sweeping momentum, contains a unique contradiction. It depicts the clash of two antagonistic temperaments, who totally lack any common meeting-point. These two people indeed, have nothing in common. For Anna, Don Giovanni is totally uninteresting as a man, and a brutal adversary as an opponent. To Don Giovanni, Anna is simply incomprehensible. Thus, in this struggle, the two parties measure up to each other, but are not attuned to each other. Their clash is not a part of a common fate, a common drama, but, in its concreteness, is the potential onset of their separate fates, their separate dramas. This contradiction is precisely expressed by the pseudo-thematic construction of the scene. Although Mozart develops the whole grandiose scene from a single melody, we do not find here the dramatic expansion of themes, according to the principles of the sonata form. Don Giovanni's style is imitation, ambiguous mimicry. It is the mark of Mozart's genius that he chooses to illustrate the total internal otherness of two people by the use of a common theme. Apparently Mozart's aim is a near-symbolic levelling of extremely acute yet exterior conflicts. This is enhanced by the comic voice of Leporello's frightened *buffo* jabbering joining the tragic struggle. The second scene of the opera is also terminated by an extraneous event: the appearance of the Commendatore.

In this next scene — extremely economical — even spare and straight to the point — it is the interrelating of the three basso voices, those of the Commendatore, Don Giovanni and Leporello which is of greatest importance. The scene is intoned by the Commendatore: his declamation is extremely simple and monumental. Kierkegaard was right in stating: 'his earnestness is too profound to be that of a human being; he is spirit before he dies.'[5] In his own way, Don Giovanni continues in the same tone, and although he maintains the crisp style, his response is spontaneously more melodic, unconstrained, even impudent. It is apparent that, in this chivalric conflict he has at last regained his real self, his previous embarrassment — carefully concealed by elegant demeanour — has disappeared. The short dialogue between the Commendatore and Don

Giovanni creates a unique atmosphere. Suddenly, dimensions are enlarged, everything gains extraordinary weight. Even Leporello, who would very much like to slink off, announces his intention with such comic solemnity, mixed with his fear, that he gains in stature. Slowly, everything gains fantastic outlines. Don Giovanni assumes, and resumes, the voice of Leporello. But just as he did previously with the Commendatore's voice, he reinterprets Leporello's. Leporello's melody, which seemed to 'cringe in fear', 'stands erect' in Don Giovanni's voice. The interrelating of the three voices, their attraction and repulsion, is precisely worked out in its finest nuances. Don Giovanni's 'misero', sung *mezza voce*, is echoed in the same rhythm, but forte, and in larger note intervals by the 'battiti' reply of the Commendatore, which again is answered *più voce* by Don Giovanni's 'misero', narrowing the octave intervals of the Commendatore, even his own previous five-note intervals, now to three-note interval steps, that seem to conjure up the image of eyes narrowing in hatred. The three actors in the scene have taken each other's measure with utter precision, the situation tensed to the point of bursting, the equilibrium that had been achieved is ready to explode. A general pause lasting a full bar 'emphasizes' that the situation cannot be sustained.   And now Don Giovanni upsets the situation: 'Misero, attendi, se vuoi morir!'. Abert correctly states that 'these eight bars, together with the pause, are the high point of the entire introduction: the fateful essence of the hero manifests itself with a magnitude equal to the tragic horror which it evokes.'[6] What is so fascinating about the scene is how definitively three people, within the same intonational sphere, can differentiate themselves from one another, how each can demonstrate his own essential self. It is not so much a clash as a measuring-up, each figure delineates his own realm, and action, in relation to the same problem. This, however, does not ease the tension. On the contrary, the uniquely concentrated mood of the scene arises from the irrevocable declaration of the separation of the three intonations.

After the exquisite tension of this scene, the music of the duel comes as a veritable relief, the breaking of a storm as it were. But this, too, is only momentary, the music again turns in on itself.

The scene preceding the duel continues, but in a decisively different atmosphere: that which was 'merely' irrevocable before, now becomes fatally inevitable. The truly fateful significance is carried here by the *sotto voce* voice of Don Giovanni, soaring above the agony of the Commendatore and the aghast *buffo* voice of Leporello. Elsewhere, Hotho has pointed out that Don Giovanni's voice, mocking and radiant with the delight of victory, is unconsciously depressed by horror.[7] Don Giovanni himself unmistakably links two things: Anna's resistance and the Commendatore's misfortune. The allusion in his voice to Anna's melody of outraged rejection is quite explicit:

Example 6

Ah   già   ca - de il scia - gu - ra - to,

(Compare Example 5). It is possible that, on the conscious level, Don Giovanni merely wants to say: Behold the unnecessary but deserved result of the foolishness of both of you. Yet he seems to be saying more than that; his voice betrays a premonition: Don Giovanni's power has been shattered in Donna Anna, and from that moment on all events take on a different hue: everything is rearranged into an alien and incomprehensible relationship for him, which nevertheless undermines the foundations of his existence.

The drama begins with the dual gesture of transcending the border between the individual and metaphysical universe: Don Giovanni enters the stage at the moment of the collapse of his power, when the 'genius of sensuality' is bankrupted in the face of a girl's individuality; he deprives the Commendatore of his individual life, but transfers him into the spirit world. The dual spheres of metaphysical and real-world drama are interlinked. The paradoxical yet grandiose drama in the introduction of *Don Giovanni* arises from this.

Donna Anna returns with Don Ottavio (2. *recitativo* and D minor duets: 'Ma qual mai s'offre'; 'Fuggi, crudele.'). She sees a body lying on the ground: the orchestra expresses the horror of perception. Donna Anna steps closer, recognizes her father: the previous orchestral material, now one fourth higher, depicts the horror of identification. Desperately, she speaks to the wounded man. The first two phrases are sounded in the tone of despair, the third in the voice of love. Here the basic emotional range of Donna Anna becomes manifest. Mozart depicts the emotional agitation of an honest but reserved temperament in the moment of shock; he faithfully records the mellowing and the hardening of the tones, and every slight and repressed expression communicates a tremendous inner struggle. The Commendatore is indeed dead, Anna's irrevocable recognition is recorded by the forte and staccato strokes of the orchestra.

The girl mourns her father with great self-discipline and restraint; the accompaniment — or, more exactly, the interjected wail-like motif of the orchestra — is of an entirely novel character with respect to instrumentation and harmonization. This is the voice of love's suffering, that, for a moment, as Anna bends over her father's body, is able to dissolve in its own sorrowful tenderness. But indeed only for a moment, for the moment of love's self-deceiving hope; then despair returns, ferociously at first, then again mellowed. The unabatable fluctuation of emotions is terminated in a faint, represented with almost biological reality by the orchestra.

Anna nearly falls to the ground, but an imperfect orchestral cadence indicates that Ottavio catches her. Don Ottavio speaks in an incomparably freer, more *cantabile recitativo* style than Donna Anna. Even the practical instructions he gives for the attending of his fiancée sound like tenderness directed towards the girl. These practical tasks do not really occupy his attention, already he turns to the swooning Anna with a compassion that is more like a spontaneous confession of love. But suddenly he is transfixed by the realization, with a forte scale passage: 'il duolo estremo la meschinella uccide'. He must do something: his voice again becomes more practical, terse, but as soon as the body of the Commendatore has been taken away, he returns to his preoccupation with Anna, his love.

The duet itself begins with Donna Anna recovering from her fainting fit, believing, in her momentary confusion, that the murderer is standing before her. Here Anna attacks Ottavio, whom she believes to be Don Giovanni, with one of the most important D minor intonations in Mozart:

Example 7

The rhythmic, as well as the melodic character of the theme are also important:

Example 8

Donna Anna's dramatic, declaiming D minor is dissolved into a lyrical F major *cantabile* by Don Ottavio. At the same time his voice is expressed in a descending scale, which is, in some sense, his musical visiting card, and will appear later, at decisive moments, in many different settings:

Example 9

guar - da   mi un   so - lo   i - stan-te,

This extremely simple melodic line condenses the essence of Ottavio's character: the fully and brilliantly intoned tenor voice, intoned on a G, is the embodiment of openness and frankness, and the serene and pure sentimentality of the evenly-descending melody gives assurance of generous fidelity. Ottavio wants to dispel Anna's hallucination, he wants to be recognized, and in this melodic line he indeed expresses his essential being.

Anna does indeed recognize him, and lets her feelings for Ottavio be known in what is a familiar phrase in eighteenth-century opera:

Example 10

mio   be - ne

The full nature of the relationship between Donna Anna and Don Ottavio unfolds from this short exchange. Their love is mutual, they share the common perspective of their lives. Ottavio's love for Anna is the unconditional love of the sentimental hero, for him nothing else in the world exists, his personality is fulfilled in this devotion. Anna does not know the unconditional nature of sentimental love. Her feelings are attached with equal intensity to two men: to her father and to her betrothed. Filial love and being in love are in total harmony within her, these two emotions coexisted peacefully, one conditional on the other, harmony between these two emotions the natural outcome of the equilibrium of her personality. This harmony is upset by external violence. With the death of her father, a violently felt void is created within Anna's emotions, that cannot be filled by being in love, yet the filling of this void is unconditionally needed for the fulfilment of her love. Thus in this very important respect Anna and Ottavio are totally different people. Ottavio, however, is unable to grasp the full meaning and significance of this fact.

After Anna has recognized her fiancé and has assured him of her love, she returns to the unresolved problem of her life, the problem of her upset inner equilibrium: the loss of her father. Ottavio replies with benevolent impatience:

Example 11

la - scia, o ca - ra,   la   ri-membran-za a - ma - ra...

The rhythm of Anna's previously cited D minor theme reappears in this phrase, indicating that, according to Ottavio's true intentions, his fiancée should let go not merely of the bloody memory, but a whole world of emotions. Ottavio expresses, with the full beauty of his true feelings, that Anna should consider the unresolved problem of her life as closed: 'hai sposo e padre in me'.

Mozart reacts with astonishing sensitivity to one of the great problems of sentimental love: being unconditional, absolute, it is at once humane and inhumane. Ottavio's endeavour is completely humane: he wants not simply to console his fiancée, but generally to free her from her past, to orient her personality towards the future, towards their love. In principle, this is undoubtedly a more mature attitude than that of Anna. Yet, this attitude is, in practice, inhumane towards Anna, not only because Ottavio's demand, within a few minutes of the murder, is impossibly impatient, but moreover, because Ottavio is unable or unwilling to perceive Anna in her full concrete humanity. He sees in her only his sentimental ideal. In the figure of Ottavio, Mozart illustrates sentimental love in its total beauty, and at the same time in its contradictory nature. The conflict of Donna Anna is one of the characteristic personal problems of the eighteenth century, namely the clash of the relationships that one is born into with those that one chooses.

Objectively, from a humanistic point of view a very complex conflict has developed between Donna Anna and Don Ottavio. This conflict, however, will never become overtly phrased musically. Anna herself does not give expression to the conflict, she is still trying to find a way to Ottavio with her problem: she speaks of the loss of her father with greater emphasis, as if asking for help. In return Ottavio restates with even more resolution his previous beautiful yet cruel point of view. This should make it clear to Anna that Ottavio does not accept her attachment to her father. At this point she extricates herself from this sentimental scene with a firm gesture. The duet breaks off. The problems of life that cannot be stated in their true reality, but become manifest in contradictory emotions, will eventually find their problematic form in conventions. In Donna Anna's case restoring her psychic equilibrium in the terminology of chivalric convention, is called vengeance. The duel, which in the introduction assumed the status of a symbolic conflict of powers, here becomes debased to the half-solution of an internal problem that finds no adequate solution.

The duel, vengeance, belong organically to the world of the Commendatore, thus they are self-evident means for Anna. In the *recitativo* which interrupts the duet, she appeals to Ottavio for vengeance in an impersonal voice that will tolerate no opposition. Her fiancé can of course have no objections, but the music of the oath of vengeance reveals his unconquerable, and gradually overwhelming reluctance:

Example 12

Lo giu-ro... lo giu-ro... lo giu-ro agl'oc - chi³ tuo-i, lo giu - ro al no - stro a-mor.

The sharp switch of mood in the music, the internal emphasis in the second part, the softening of emotions, make it clear that for Ottavio the oath of vengeance is only a veiled confession of love. On the other hand, it also shows that because of his unconditional love he must satisfy Anna's demand. The lovers are united in a common predicament, although they remain differently motivated. Indeed, as Hotho states, 'the common torment of this terrible hour pervades the bosom of both.'[8] Vengeance is not an inner concern of either of them. But the murder of the Commendatore creates a conflict in both, for which, in their situation, vengeance is necessarily the minimal solution. Although driven by different motivations, they both feel one way or the other, that they must espouse vengeance, even though it is not the solution to their problems. We have already seen in the introduction that there is a contradiction between Anna's personality and her situation. Her self-appointed heroism by its inner tension is now quite tragic. At the same time Ottavio becomes involved in this contradiction, and since his personality, as well as his whole world-view are quite alien to chivalric etiquette, the obligation of vengeance for him is an even more tragic compulsion. The continuation of the duet arises from this shared tragedy: with extraordinary effort Anna again rises to heroic stature, while Ottavio repeats his oath of vengeance in a voice filled rather with pain, in veiled chromatics, and less ornamentation.

Don Giovanni and Leporello are preparing for a new adventure, but the supposedly unknown lady who enters is none other than Donna Elvira, one of Don Giovanni's abandoned lovers. The personality emerging from her #3. aria in E flat major, expanding to a full tercet ('Ah! chi mi dice mai'), is difficult to assess immediately. The opening of the vocal part is preceded by a comparatively long orchestral introduction, which in itself carries weighty contradictions. The first four bars are conceived as musical contradiction (forte-piano), next appears a now characteristic, exalted formula, a passage beginning with an upbeat and restlessly running down-scale — one that will frequently be cited to express Elvira's pernicious inner trembling. This impulsiveness of an as yet unknown nature reaches its climax in the passionate forte, unisono, staccato twist of the orchestra, followed as a renewed contrast by the compassionate, broadly descending piano motif of the clarinet, bassoon and horn. The vocal part itself is extremely eccentric, characterized by wide intervals, syncopated rhythm and dynamic outbursts. Amidst the agitated, energetic melodies a theme appears which, as shown by F. R. Noske,[9] plays the role of a veritable *leitmotif* in this opera:

Example 13

man-cò   di   fè?

Noske calls this E flat—A—B formula the 'tradimento' (betrayal) motif. Without doubt, Donna Elvira's aria depicts the raging passion, the amorous hatred of the betrayed lover. This, however, is quite ambiguous in an eighteenth-century opera. The discarded woman — the *abandonata* type — was a pitiful and comic role. Mozart does not dispel the ambiguity; in fact, he simplifies it. Every element of the aria is stereotypical, commonplace; combined, they aim at extreme effects. The music constantly approaches the limits of a sort of shop-soiled mannerism, it comes close to debasing its own validity. Yet, a volcanic temperament of such magnitude is manifested in these conventional elements, in the entire musical process, that its shop-soiled character rises to solemn dignity, mannerism is transformed into style, boasting into true greatness, and hysteria assumes tragic proportions. The ambiguity of the eccentric character is further magnified by the musical situation: Elvira's vocal part is joined by the sometimes mocking, sometimes seductive song of Don Giovanni, and Leporello's commentary. The superficially comic situation enhances the comic effect, while Elvira's part remains completely ignorant of it. But this new contradiction can hardly be regarded as comic. The effect mechanism of the aria's composition is complex, and its ultimate secret lies undoubtedly in the eccentricity of Donna Elvira.

Leporello wants both to console and disenchant Elvira by exposing his master. The #4. D major aria ('Madamina! Il catalogo'), the so-called 'catalogue' aria, is one of the keys to the interpersonal relationships in the opera, as Leporello embraces the essence of Don Giovanni, as well as his own relationship to him. Without a doubt it is Kierkegaard who most profoundly understood this aria. According to him the 'catalogue' aria is the epos of Don Giovanni. In Don Giovanni, sensuality appears as principle, and eroticism as seduction. Don Giovanni is a seducer by nature, because his love is sensual, and sensual love is unconditionally unfaithful, for it is not in love with one, but with all. Sensual love exists in the here and now, but the here and now is the composite of an infinite number of moments. Thus again we come to the concept of the seducer. Yet, Don Giovanni's faithlessness is mere repetition. This is undoubtedly one of Kierkegaard's greatest insights regarding the genius of sensuality. This, too, he derives logically; he states decisively that the unequivocal success of Don Giovanni, a seeming asset, is really a deficiency. For Don Giovanni the moment is not filled with content, with richness; for him everything is transitory. For Don Giovanni, to behold and to love are indeed instantaneous, but also disappear with the instant, and so are repeated *ad infinitum*. Thus, sensual love, incarnate in the figure of Don Giovanni, is — employing an expression, not of Kierkegaard, but of Hegel — the 'evil infinity'. Kierkegaard is correct in saying that a poet could not write an epos of 'evil infinity' because he would have to pursue multiplicity, and thus would never be able to complete his work. Kierkegaard's characterization fits particularly the first part of the 'catalogue' aria to perfection. In this aria Mozart made an exception by inverting the traditional slow-fast formula. The first (allegro) part is only seemingly in the typical *buffo* style. If we examine it closely, we cannot fail to notice that Mozart composes the conventional material in such a manner, he organizes it with such sophisticated simplicity, with such superior mastery, with regards to its dynamic, libretto, orchestration, colour, character, and generally its contrast of effects, that it adds up to something totally new in mood and quality — as Abert put it, 'the unsurpassable image of elemental sensual life force'.[10] The music knows no point of rest, everything is in constant motion, the themes literally chase one another.

In the second (*andante con moto*) part of the aria this pursuit is mitigated, the music becomes more descriptive, thus other relationships come to the fore. The minuet, the contours of the melodic line, the individualizing details now present Don Giovanni, the individual; and the manner in which Leporello represents his master reveals his relationship to him. It is probably an exaggeration to call this relationship erotic, as Kierkegaard does. But certainly, Leporello's *alter ego* character unfolds here completely. Thus Kierkegaard is right in saying that Leporello reproduces his master's life not merely as an epic narrator — that is to say, he does not have an objective attitude toward the subject of his narration — on the contrary, 'he is altogether fascinated by the life he describes, he forgets himself in telling about Don Giovanni.'[11] Leporello is a commonplace person, but he possesses a kind of intuitive empathy for the sensuous genius, and his personality, his life, are irresistibly drawn to it; he is inseparably tied to Don Giovanni's life and fate. As a character he is deeply ambiguous, since he tries, with every gesture, simultaneously to satisfy the demands of demonic moral indifference and philistine piety. This is why his character is always comic though, never serene, but clouded by crises.

Zerlina and Masetto, the betrothed village couple, are introduced in the #5. G major chorus ('Giovinette che fate all'amore'). The melody of the folksy 6/8 song is, as Mörike puts it, 'simple-minded and child-like, sparkling with elation throughout'. Its significance lies in its genre-like characterization as well as in its compositional function as the starting and relating point of a new theme. It depicts the couple in their natural state, their conventional normalcy, compared with which their subsequent fate will be in striking contrast. The recurrences and transformations of the intonations surfacing here will throughout be related to this, and through this to the central questions of the entire opera.

Don Giovanni and Leporello appear, and, as Hotho correctly states, 'One look at Zerlina, and Don Giovanni is captivated by the gay naturalness of this charming figure exuding desire.'[12] The attraction, however, is mutual. Zerlina immediately succumbs to the desire radiating from Don Giovanni, by the power of sensuality. Kierkegaard says that Don Giovanni seduces not consciously, according to a set formula, not by words or lies, but purely through the compulsion of sensual desire, the genius of sensuality, that only music can express.[13]

First, Masetto has to be got rid of — by a united effort. Of course, the peasant lad sees what is going on, and expresses his mixed feelings in the #6. F major aria ('Ho capito, Signor, si'). Masetto is the most conventional figure in the opera, and in a double sense. On the one hand, only he is no more than a stock figure in the innumerable plays about Don Giovanni. Mozart does not enlarge his character or make it more complex. This however, is not due to artistic weakness, it is part of the overall plan. On the other, and in a more profound sense, Masetto has no understanding of what is taking place round him. He is an ordinary, everyday figure with no sense of the sensual genius, he sees Mozart's Don Giovanni approximately in the way that Brecht saw Molière's: 'The great seducer must not be imagined as someone who can offer extraordinary artistic performance in the area of eroticism. His success as a seducer is achieved by his dress (and the way he wears it), his tool is his social rank (and the affrontery with which he abuses this rank). His wealth (or his credit) is his tool as well, as is finally, his reputation (or the sense of confidence bred by this notoriety). He has the bearing of a great sexual potentate.'[14] Masetto's relationship with Don Giovanni is also ambiguous; he revolts, yet he knows that his revolt is inherently hopeless. The aria is a masterpiece because its construction is throughout built upon this ambiguity by the constant repetition of the dual gestures of determined start and breakdown, presented in a variety of ways. The contrasts of melodic form, dynamics and orchestration are all expressions of this ever-present comic ambiguity. If in a certain sense Leporello reproduces Don Giovanni at a lower level, then Masetto in turn is a weak version of Leporello. For him, not even this quite pitiful revolt is a truly inner problem: it is merely an external, practical matter. Not for one moment does Don Giovanni become a problem proper of Masetto's personality. This is intimately linked with his total lack of erotic power. He consequently emphasizes Don Giovanni's significance by negative contrast. It is exactly by his difference that Masetto relates indirectly to the central problem of the opera. From this relation arises the hopeless triviality and ever-comic nature of this otherwise honest and decent man who truly loves his fiancée. In the aria, beyond the above mentioned contrasts, this comicality reaches its peak when Masetto — his bitter outburst at Don Giovanni reaching its crescendo — turns to attack Zerlina.

After Leporello finally succeeds in getting rid of Masetto, Zerlina is left alone with Don Giovanni. Their scene, consisting of a *secco recitativo* and the subsequent #7. A major *duettino* ('La ci darem la mano'), concerns the practical development of their relationship established in the moment they first caught sight of each other. Thus, to reiterate, the process of seduction and submission cannot be depicted, since it does not occur in time, it was instantaneous, and the libretto must express this directly. Everything that happens afterwards implies the intuitive recognition of this fact. (In the following, the term 'seduction' will always mean the development, building and organizing of the relationship.) Here we are talking primarily about the overcoming of resistance beyond the basic mutual understanding. Agnes Heller correctly writes: 'Don Giovanni is not simply the man who seduces a multitude of women with his beauty and demeanour. Don Giovanni does not have to overcome individual antagonism. . . . What he has to conquer is feelings of guilt. He induces women to shed their guilt feelings, their feelings of guilt towards transcendence, or to act in spite of it. His enemy is not antipathy, but conscience and the pangs of conscience.'[15] In this, Don Giovanni had always been victorious, until he met Donna Anna, and in this he prevails in the case of Zerlina as well. What is the secret of his exclusive, unfailing conquest? (Let us, for the time being, disregard his failure with Donna Anna.) Kierkegaard is surely right in observing that the object of Don Giovanni's desire is the sensual, and only the sensual.[16] He desires, and this desire acts seductively. Generally, he desires the femininity in every woman; this is where his erotically idealizing power lies. Because of this all differences disappear in relation to this prime desire — femininity itself. Don Giovanni's irresistibility and unconditional conquest result from his constant desire for femininity. Yet he is always able to recognize and captivate it in its own absolute uniqueness. In the *recitativo* part of the scene discussed, Mozart illustrates this process as Don Giovanni, instinctively and with unerring assurance tunes in to Zerlina's inner self.

The text, of course — as in any play about Don Giovanni — presents a tapestry of argument and counter-argument, invitation and evasive reply, but the voices directly illustrate the real process: two people seeking, attuning to, and finding each other. During the entire *recitativo*, Don Giovanni is instinctively seeking the right tone, the tone that is right for

Zerlina, the possible common tone. We are witnesses to an almost artistic creative process, the *recitativo* is one continuous preliminary study for the famous *duettino*. It takes shape slowly, and then the final, the satisfying tone is born. In the last repetition of the *recitativo* Don Giovanni already hints at the captivating melody of the duet:

Example 14

Quel ca-si-net-to è mi- o;

In the phrase 'quel casinetto è mio', the totally disarming opening melody of the duet is already latent:

Example 15

Là ci da-rem la ma-no,   la mi di-rai di   sì,

The pairing is decided by this instinctively found vocal tone, rather than by the promise of marriage.

The intonation of the duet is deceptively simple. Jahn admired in it the simple expression of lightheartedness and joy, the tender feelings inspired by erotic pleasures, gentle and sweet sentiment, heartfelt in the clear sunshine.[17] But Abert emphasizes the erotic surge of this 'siren voice', and points out that even in its simplicity, the intonation is that of a nobleman.[18] Indeed, this is an extraordinarily fastidious yet unreserved simplicity. Absolute directness is without a doubt one of the most important, if not *the* most important characteristics of Don Giovanni.

Don Giovanni lacks in reflection like a natural phenomenon. All his gestures are characterized by the directness of the forces of nature. This is what makes the *duettino* so engrossing even in its simplicity. The crystal-clear, simple melody is accentuated by the finely measured rhythm. Don Giovanni is acting without apparent passion, yet in reality with captivating sensuality. The soaring erotic surge, characterizing, for instance, the vocal line of the count in the #16, duet in *The Marriage of Figaro*, is completely missing from his voice. Yet, the voice of the count is not seductive; it is, at most, frightening as he sings out, unrestrained, without regard to the feelings of the other, his feelings of the moment. The count is unable to grasp Susanna's personality. Consequently, he does not exert a strong, transforming influence. On the other hand, the voice of Don Giovanni expresses exactly what Zerlina desires. In Don Giovanni's personality, this intonation is merely the measured manifestation of demonic sensuality, yet for Zerlina, it is precisely this demonic sensuality that she can relate to.

The ability unerringly to find the exact tone is Don Giovanni's true erotic genius. In words, Zerlina rejects the appeal from her seducer, yet musically she accepts: she assumes the tone, takes over Don Giovanni's melodic line. She feels that she has become captivated, her increasingly ambiguous (erotic and self-conscious) excitement is precisely expressed by the semi-quavers which dominate the end of her reply. Here Zerlina is still in control of herself, she carefully avoids the appearance of involvement, of improper behaviour; the staccato of the orchestral cadence is like a curtsey ending her reply. Viewed from this angle, yet another meaning of Don Giovanni's intonation becomes clear. Giving voice to the tone of demonic sensuality that Zerlina is able to relate to, means that he is leading Zerlina out of her own world by the one route open to her; he raises her above herself. The erotic idealization within the music can be clearly identified; the way Don Giovanni grasps and puts into motion the force which now resides entirely within Zerlina, and which will impel her beyond herself. Zerlina's vocal line, which she has acquired from Don Giovanni, is no longer 'simple-minded and child-like, sparkling with elation throughout', that we heard her sing in the #5. G major chorus. The difference is a matter of quality, not of character. Don Giovanni, of course, senses the change precisely, he is intuitively aware of the quality and content of the moment. The renewed assault is more ardent, more passionate. The energy of the melodic line increases, as does the energy of the tonality: the former A major is replaced by E major. Zerlina's ambiguous excitement also increases, her replies become shorter, more flustered, the demi-semi-quaver movement takes over and the repeated orchestral accompaniment is no longer as measured as before. No longer is it an unornamented staccato but the excited, sensitive demi demi-semi-quaver configuration of the violins. Thus Zerlina is more excited, and at the same time more exciting as well. Don Giovanni can see that this excitement will be heightened by its own dynamism and will lead to total surrender; there is no need to increase the assault, it is enough to maintain his tempo. He repeats his former phrase. Zerlina, on the other hand, would like to formulate her own reply; but the melodic line will not

take shape; it turns into a desperate melodic struggle, as Abert rightly
puts it, 'like a bird caught in a net.'[19] The power of conscience, her
faithfulness to Masetto, are relegated to second place to the erotic
attraction of Don Giovanni.

But Don Giovanni is not satisfied by the mere fact of surrender, which
Zerlina isn't even aware of. He requires total surrender, stated with
unequivocal frankness. His challenge is brilliant in its simplicity:

Example 16

Yearning desire and cool calculation: the voice, pausing for crotchet
intervals with *sforzato* emphasis on the peak point of D, made particularly
acute by the accompaniment, has a feverish and irresistible effect, while it
registers, and almost indulges in, the effect with satisfaction. This phrase
decides the outcome of the struggle finally and irrevocably. Don Giovanni
exploits this irrevocability to the utmost as well. It seems that he is
returning to the opening of the duet. In fact what has happened thus far,
how far their relationship has progressed is revealed in the reprise. Don
Giovanni only starts the *cantilena*: he knows full well that Zerlina will
continue it herself. And indeed so she does. The text is the old one,
evasive and rejecting, yet the melody is increasingly liberated, an infatuated
invitation. But Don Giovanni now wants to hear the overt reply contained
in the innuendo. His melody gradually abandons the original *cantilena*,
and seduction becomes phrased as a question in the melody:

Example 17

la mi di-rai di   sì,

As if Zerlina has become frightened by the sudden directness of the question, she hesitates for a moment. Don Giovanni senses this, and his voice, almost imperceptibly, becomes more forceful, more feverish:

Example 18

par-tiam, ben mio, da quì.

Compared with the earlier variation, the beginning of the phrase is a little more vehement, and this frightens Zerlina even more. Once more she tries to resist Don Giovanni's and her own desire, the 'ma' is voiced resolutely and extended on the highest note now achieved in her melodic line (F sharp). Then her voice falters weakly, the excited demi-semi-quavers signal the nervousness of submission. Don Giovanni senses that the game is nearing its end. His melodic line, previously an appeal, now makes a statement:

Example 19

Vie-ni, mio bel di - let - to:

Vie-ni, mio bel di - let -to:

Before, he sang 'Come with me'; now he sings, 'You already know that you will come with me, come what may.' The desire in the music has been replaced by a statement. And Zerlina's former struggle is repeated, only this time more desperately, more critically and more hopelessly. Zerlina's struggle becomes mere capitulation, the inner struggle has been decided, and cannot be continued, Masetto and the whole world have receded into unmeasurable distance; only Don Giovanni's elemental sensuous attraction is present. Don Giovanni says quite simply:

Example 20

An - diam an - diam!

In this world, inhabited by just the two of them, a world existing beyond the world of humanity, forever and exclusively only one commandment exists: 'Andiam!'.

But Donna Elvira reappears at the very moment when Don Giovanni is about to lead Zerlina into his house. She blocks their way. In the #8. D major aria ('Ah, fuggi il traditor!') Elvira unmasks Don Giovanni in front of the peasant girl, and presents herself as a horrifying example:

> *Da miei tormenti*
> *Impara a creder quel cor,*
> *E nasca il tuo timor*
> *Dal mio periglio!*

It is generally recognized that the style of the aria is archaic, recalling the baroque, or rather the music of Handel. Yet Mozart employs this comically out-of-date mode so consistently, with such seriousness, he imbues it with such volcanic passion, that the effect is moving. What happens is exactly the same as in Elvira's first aria, but this time not on the situational level but purely on the level of musical style. The essence of the aria is exactly the contradiction inherent in the form, the fascinating eccentricity of Donna Elvira. Elvira influences Zerlina not by her revelation. We saw in the previous scene that in the music Don Giovanni turned the peasant girl's head not with lies, not with the promise of marriage, but that Zerlina, the woman, could not resist Don Giovanni's passion, the power of sensuality. The accusation of betrayal does not impinge on the genius of sensuality, and cannot influence one who was swept up by it. The dramas of Zerlina, Don Giovanni and Donna Elvira occur in separate dimensions. Zerlina is not influenced by Elvira's revelation, her accusations, but by the music of the aria, that is to say, by the example of her fate. Zerlina must sense something of the essence, the meaning of Elvira's eccentric message. She comes to suspect not merely the pain of betrayal, of her own inevitable disenchantment, but a tragedy with essentially more profound implications: the unrelieved loneliness, the alienation from the world of humanity, from society, the monomanic obsession. All of this, of course, must be understood not in the light of convention, of lost feminine honour, but in principle. Naturally, it is not implied that Zerlina can see Elvira's problem and her own imminent fate quite this explicitly. What she senses from Elvira's music is that she has encountered a fate that is horrible beyond her comprehension, and this confuses her.

In fact, it would be premature and an exaggeration to speak of disenchantment. Subsequent action will prove this. Zerlina merely becomes confused, but this confusion has existential significance. On the other hand, Donna Elvira knows exactly the secret of her own eccentricity, she can clearly see the problem of her being. She knows all too well that Don Giovanni's love is followed by despair, and the hopeless but obsessive attempt to be rid of despair, the eternal feverishness of love—hate and hope without hope. Elvira knows that having lost Don Giovanni, her life has become totally meaningless, yet this is the only life possible for her. The one desperate way open for her self-realization is continuously to demonstrate the example of her fate.

Yet Donna Elvira's eccentricity has another tone as well. Jahn calls it the 'voice of subdued complaint',[20] a tone that does not reveal her secret with the stirring effect of the extreme gesture, but merely utters it with confessional directness. Still, the melody guards unyieldingly the intellectual incognito, and the unequivocal emotions seek understanding uncertainly and with quiet desperation. When Donna Elvira returns unexpectedly and finds Don Giovanni in the company of Donna Anna and Don Ottavio, this is the tone she strikes. Her *recitativo* that precedes the #9. B major quartet ('Non ti fidar, o misera'), closes with what Noske calls the 'tradimento' motif, while the quartet itself begins on the confessional tone of 'quiet complaint':

Example 21

In the last phrase we again recognize the 'tradimento' motif. Here, the generalization of the motif, the broadening of its area of significance, has taken place within our own hearing, before our own eyes. In the *recitativo* it had still stood for Don Giovanni's betrayal, his deceit, taken in its common meaning: However at the end of Elvira's song, which begs for understanding, it concerns the totality of those unresolvable problems of life, the results of being betrayed. And now a struggle begins to penetrate the core of this motif, and the secret hidden behind it. Don Ottavio and Donna Anna sense that this sorrowful and noble woman has a tragic secret and that it concerns Don Giovanni. Elvira's last phrase continues to echo in the orchestra, where it sounds, disturbingly, around and within them. They cannot be rid of it any more, their voices, touched by compassion and respect, resound in it. This phrase hovers stubbornly over the whole scene — to use Jahn's simile, 'like a motto, hiding the key to the riddle'.[21] Elvira, Anna and Ottavio are desperately trying to articulate a universally significant riddle, to make it their own, to understand, to solve it in this melody. The melody is truly, in the words of Abert, like 'the mourning, in general, of womankind trampled upon by Don Giovanni'.[22] Here it becomes evident that Donna Elvira is actually dangerous to Don Giovanni in a general sense; not merely her aggressiveness, but also her brokenness are the unmasking of the Don Giovanni principle.

Don Giovanni senses this instinctively and unerringly, and he deprecates Elvira's tragedy and the entire situation with shameless superiority. He pursues a seemingly gallant game with the puzzling 'motto' motif:

Example 22

for - se si cal - me - rà,   for - se - si cal - me - rà!

This brutal travesty totally outrages Elvira, and she tries to make herself understood with agitated desperation. Her voice begins to assume its often heard eccentric character, thus endorsing involuntarily Don Giovanni's allegation of insanity. But Anna and Ottavio can no longer be misled, they do not misinterpret Elvira's emotional state. They are moved by the magnitude of 'ignoto tormento', and make a huge effort to understand its secret. Now the problem becomes maximally acute: Anna and Ottavio, almost in a trance, try to identify with Elvira (two incandescent leaps of the sweeping crescendo and tempestuous trioles), while Elvira, in desperation, senses the impossibility of any real understanding (hysterical, scream-like melody). As they get the closest to Donna Elvira, so she becomes farthest removed from them. Donna Anna's voice now resounds with deep compassion, motivated not simply by philanthropy, but by the insight that Elvira's secret bears some unknown relationship to her own fate:

Example 23

che mi di - ce   per quell' in - fe -li - ce

We have heard this almost lost voice before from Donna Anna, when in the introduction, in her struggle with Don Giovanni, she begged for help (see Example 4). Ottavio, too, assumes Anna's chromatic part, never before did he have so much empathy with Elvira, yet he is incapable of establishing a deeper relationship, monomanically he keeps repeating a single empty and emotional phrase. Any sort of real understanding has become impossible, 'no', pronounces everyone, emphatically and single-mindedly. Out of Mozart's painfully magnificent invention, Elvira now expresses her despair in a single, subdued, disturbedly convoluted, formless, perpetually moving, touchingly vocal, melody. This endless melody, composed of mere self-repetition, represents in itself the absurdity of Elvira's life. The struggle to unravel the secret was futile. The hopelessness of establishing a relationship, a mutual understanding, between the normal and the seduced and later abandoned; this is one of the greatest tragedies of the world surrounding Don Giovanni.

Mozart here proves himself the unparalleled master of the technique and effectiveness of musical drama. The quartet of Donna Anna, Donna Elvira, Don Ottavio and Don Giovanni is dramatic in the strict dramaturgical sense of the term. Yet in the course of ostensible dramatic struggle it becomes increasingly clear that the struggle is in fact not physical, but spiritual. The focus of the struggle is the unspeakable, the indefinable. The music, through its own intellectual incognito and emotional unequivocality, is able directly to evoke that which cannot be put into words, cannot be defined, by constant, gesture-like repetition.

Slowly, the drama is enveloped in a mysterious lyrical atmosphere. When this polysemic and arcane atmosphere becomes impenetrable, the antagonists tear themselves away and the clear, objective lines of the dramatic force are redrawn. The dramatic climax is almost at hand, yet the real conflict must remain undefinable, unspeakable, non-objective, thus at the critical moment the drama is turned again into lyricism, into atmosphere. But this atmosphere of undefinable certainty, suspicion and irresolution becomes so dense and unbearable, that everyone — the four stage characters and the audience alike — can sense that the tension and intensity of this atmosphere cannot be sustained; the least unexpected thing, a stray spark, will be sufficient to create an explosion. Even Wagner could not approach this concentration, this intensity of atmospheric dramaticism. Within the entire history of opera no other ill-boding and self-defeating moment exists such as the moment of total pause at the close of the quartet.

Elvira flees in despair, and leaves the stage. In Anna's and Ottavio's consciousness, throughout their senses, a feeling of revulsion is growing, an undefinable malaise, that will not leave them and which they cannot overcome. Don Giovanni does not internalize the atmosphere, but senses its external danger, and wishes to extricate himself from the situation. He offers his services as a nobleman to Donna Anna in an indifferently intoned, conventional *recitativo secco*, then hurriedly takes his leave:

Example 24

a - mi - ci,   ad - di - o.

Noske has noticed the 'tradimento' motif (E flat—A—B) in this leave-taking formula.[23] It is an unintended slip of the tongue, Don Giovanni's spontaneous self-betrayal, the unforeseeable spark that precipitates the inescapable explosion. To Donna Anna the riddle becomes illuminated in the light of an internal explosion of elemental force. More precisely, one of the riddle's implications is exploded: the identity of her father's murderer. The #10. *recitativo* and the D major aria ('Don Ottavio, son morta': 'Or sai chi l'onore') begin with an extremely precise and expressive orchestral contrast in C minor. The vocal line of cellos and basses, swelling out of the deep like a mountainous wave, portray the agitation of Anna's entire being, the revulsion that drives her almost to the point of fainting, is almost physically perceptible. But she is not granted merciful oblivion. The voice of horror erupts in a mighty forte by the entire orchestra. It is important that this upsurge of revulsion, this outburst of horror, is exclusively connected with the identification of the murderer, and is in no sense related to the sensuous or erotic sphere. The identification is final, the perfect cadence after the 'quegli e il carnefice del padre mio' indicates that it is no longer a suspicion but a certainty. Don Ottavio regards Donna Anna's words with awe, what she is saying is so unexpected to him, it sounds so strange, that it seems alien rather than frightening. Ottavio's love renders him receptive to tender feelings only, he is uncomprehending and helpless in the face of Anna's traumatic experience. Anna relates to him the events of the night. Her voice, calm, descriptive at first, becomes more and more agitated. When Ottavio learns that his beloved was also in danger, he too is overpowered by emotions. His whole life is filled with his love, it defines his view of the world, and how he relates to it. He is able to experience only that which is directly related to his love, and he alters reality according to his desires. Thus when Anna relates her own trials, Ottavio can at last truly empathize with her, and he is truly shaken. But as Anna relates the events, she becomes increasingly emotional, as though she is reliving them; at the point when she evokes her cries for help, the voice of horror rises from the orchestra. As if relieved by this, she continues her tale in a calmer tone: no one came to her aid, the unknown assailant embraced her violently, she thought all was lost. Now truly agitated, Ottavio bursts out almost in despair. Perhaps only now does Anna perceive the gravity of the situation, she relates in anguish her desperate struggle and escape. This account also reveals that Donna Anna is totally indifferent to Don Giovanni's sensual power, her desperation is due solely to the manifest inequality of her physical strength, not to the experience of the irresistibility of erotic genius.

Only here, in Donna Anna's aria, does the traditional vengeance aria — a musical form linking musical forms of opposing character — active, aggressive *vs.* passive, anguished — succeed (probably the only time in its entire career in the operatic repertoire), in expressing one person's ontological problem in its own individuality.

As a matter of fact, this vengeance aria constantly contradicts itself. It was mentioned above that Anna wants revenge for the death of her father; the observance of chivalrous conventions is her elementary duty. Now that she knows and has identified the murderer, her conviction is renewed with new intensity. Her sense of violation turns abruptly into a vehement desire for vengeance, and the beginning of the aria — the threatening rumble and violent gesture formulations of the orchestra, the large tone intervals and syncopated rhythm of the vocal lines — with its powerful yet conventional tone expresses precisely her momentary blind passion.

For Donna Anna, however, the murder of the Commendatore has essentially one consequence only: a basic realm of affections and attachments in her life is left without its object, thus the equilibrium of her personality is upset. Anna is left with no less a task than to rebuild and rearrange her life on entirely new foundations. This, however, cannot be accomplished in a moment and this is exactly what Don Ottavio is unable to understand, just as he cannot understand that this process cannot be facilitated from the outside. Undoubtedly, for Donna Anna (and she knows this herself) Ottavio's love represents the direction of her life. Yet, for the moment, this knowledge resolves nothing. Anna must live through the complete collapse of her once established and now disrupted world, and can be helped only indirectly to recognize, on the basis of her own needs, attachments and feelings; what Goethe called the 'true relationship' between them in his famous poem to Charlotte von Stein.

Mozart's procedure here is artistically problematic. The demand inherent in the operatic genre is that the musical drama should bear a consistent relationship to the stage, that in the musical development all its details should find their dramatic counterparts within the play enacted on the stage. In *The Marriage of Figaro* Mozart solved this task with a perfection unique in the history of the opera. However, Donna Anna's aria cannot be rendered adequately on the stage. This poses new problems for the work as a whole. The dimensions of the musical and stage drama become confused. Typically, feminine vengeance does not play a really important role in the Don Giovanni dramas. In fact, the figures of seduced women are always somewhat ambiguous. A seduction, accomplished in disguise and by deceit, is at the same time outrageous and comical in its extraordinary, primitive brutality. Its sole dramatic function is that it inveighs against Don Giovanni; while the consequences for the seduced woman fall beyond the range of dramatic representation. This follows from the self-evident precondition of every Don Giovanni drama: Don Giovanni cannot have a real, human opponent. The format of the characters is depicted accordingly. In principle, this situation obtains in Mozart's opera as well. Musically, Mozart portrays the drama of Donna Anna in this spirit. The ambivalent character of the figure, the compensatory nature of her monumental desire for revenge, reveal her inherent weakness, her incomparability with Don Giovanni. On the stage, however, this ambivalence disappears, ambiguity appears as complexity, and the compensation for personal weakness seems genuinely superior. In its actual realization, Donna Anna's vengeance aria is unconditionally heroic, thus the stage character seems to be larger than the musical figure; thus Anna becomes an equal opponent for Don Giovanni. This impression is not only contrary to the central idea of the work, but soon it will become untenable on the stage as well. A burning desire for revenge that is not realized in deed is, on the stage wholly problematic and, what is more, comical. However, in this opera not even a hint of comedy can be cast over the figure of Donna Anna. Thus there is again a schism between the heroic quality of the aria and Anna's impotence, and this cannot be bridged on the stage. Naturally, these problems are resolved in the music, but the point is that the musical drama of Donna Anna cannot be consistently referred back to the stage. It is in this aria that we must first confront the phenomenon — unknown in *The Marriage of Figaro* — that the congruence of the musical and the stage drama is disrupted, the dimensions of the two become intermingled, with the music slowly disconnecting itself from the grounds of the stage.

This problem is not the same as the fact that Mozart's music incessantly transcends the bounds of the libretto, that the musical action always differs from the dramatic sketch set down in the libretto, that in Mozart's operas the musical representation alone has aesthetic authenticity. All this is true, of course, but — as we have said before — the congruence of the musical and stage representation, the consistent translatability of the music into the stage, is an inherent requirement of the genre. It is unquestionable that in the *Abduction* Mozart has radically transcended the possibilities of the libretto, yet the musical concept can still be realized on stage. *Figaro* is a unique masterpiece precisely because of this. But in *Don Giovanni* this internal principle itself beomes problematic. Not just momentarily, not as an exception in Donna Anna's D major aria.

The representation of Don Ottavio is perhaps even more problematic. Here, however, the congruence of music and stage is disrupted in the opposite direction. The significance of the figure on stage does not come near to its musical significance. We have seen that Ottavio is a sentimental hero, his whole being, his life is filled with the exclusiveness of love. He is able to comprehend and experience only that which is directly related to his love, and he unintentionally alters reality according to his desires. We have seen that this attitude has rather contradictory consequences: on the one hand there is his unconditional devotion, his authenticity as an individual and the future life he can offer Anna; on the other hand, it results in a certain incomprehension and practical inability to act, which creates an unspoken tension between them that perhaps remains subconscious. All of this renders the figure of Ottavio very problematic for the purpose of dramatic presentation. In the previously analysed scene, after the unmasking of Don Giovanni, the problematic side of Ottavio's mentality moves into the foreground, and his figure loses stature dramatically. As we can see, he shows no understanding for Anna's real problems, and as she retells her story every expression of his emotions is restricted either to worrying about the fate of his fiancée, or to relief. Even after Anna's aria, he spells out, in a conventional *recitativo secco*, almost as a polite gesture, his duty-bound desire to exact vengeance. All this, of course, follows equally from Ottavio's character; this, however, is the reason why his character is undramatic. Nevertheless, Ottavio is not placed in an ironic light.

The problem of Don Ottavio's figure unfolds completely in the subsequent #11. G major aria ('Dalla sua pace'). The dramatic difficulties of the aria contain the contradiction between the small stature of the figure of Don Ottavio and his musical greatness. But in the case of Mozart, one cannot judge such a contradiction wholly from a one-sided dramaturgical viewpoint and then acknowledge, incidentally and with a forgiving gesture, the beauty of the music.

The beauty of Ottavio's G major aria is so emphatic, so significant, that it demands closer investigation. At the very beginning of the aria, the G major chord of the strings, and the tenor voice unfolding the inner structure of the chord into melody, sound the doubly meaningful basic ideas of classical music: the homogeneous major chord and the triad, in its total beauty. The entire melody, in which Ottavio effectively defines himself — 'opens out spontaneously with the help of ornamentation and broken chords.'[24]:

Example 25

Dal - la sua pa - ce   la   mia di - pen - de;

In the second half of the opening line, Ottavio's 'signature', the descending scale, also appears (see Example 9). The extent to which this line expresses the essence of the figure is borne out by the fact that it is voiced again in his other, #22. B major aria:

Example 26

e   del bel ci - glio il pian - to   cer - ca - te - di a - sciu - gar,

The positive sound of the major key is coloured by an intimate and delicately dreamy tone; the melody calls forth the next rhyming melodic line. The expression of the first two rhyming lines is completely balanced: it defines the all-embracing, single-minded feeling of devoted love. But here it becomes clear that Ottavio also experiences the trauma. Suddenly, he becomes painfully aware of Anna's grief, the voice of helpless commiseration rises in agony and finally breaks through:

Example 27

quel che le in - cre - sce

Yet here, at its peak, it comes to a halt, it does not give birth to action, the emptiness of the pause engulfs the emotion. Pain turns inward, everything, all life, becomes pointless and empty; if Anna's inner peace is not restored, if she will not find herself in love, it will mean death to Ottavio:

Example 28

mor   te   mi   dà,   mor   -   te,

This is no mere empty phrase, no high-flown assertion. Mozart's music leaves no room for doubt that, according to the logic in Ottavio's life, this consequence is unavoidable. The determined simplicity of the first phrase, and beneath it the emphatic forte of the strings, followed by the unremitting voice of the horns, state an unavoidable and irrevocable conclusion. However, the experience of unavoidability and irrevocability dispel determination, as it inspires horrified despair: underneath the word 'morte', sung in scarcely audible terror, appears, in the ascending chromatic line of the strings, 'a faithful musical image of heart-chilling, slowly ascending terror' in the words of József Újfalussy.[25] The emotional logic of the first part of the aria is completely consistent and authentic on the human level. Mozart is able to summarize in a bare 17 bars the existential potential not only of Don Ottavio, but of the sentimental hero in general, or more exactly, the process of his life becoming absurd. Ottavio is always true to himself, without posturing; he lives and thinks through his fate, in which the possibility to break through back into the world does not exist. Should Ottavio lose Anna's love, he would become totally introspective, and would perish. His being can only find fulfilment in requited love, in the person of Anna. This is told by the second G minor part of the aria. Ottavio realizes that he is only able to relate to Anna in compassion, he can find his life's potential in a total identification with the girl's feelings. This recognition now becomes quite natural to him, the music is brought into equilibrium — into almost too much equilibrium — by the even staccato of the strings and the woodwinds' imitation of a sigh. Ottavio's voice too is filled with soft sentimentality.

But this easing of mood is only momentary, it is compassion's own dynamic that overtakes it and drives it towards increasingly agitated emotion. The deeply descending basses in the orchestra, the string tremolo, the *sforzato* betraying internal turmoil, then the sensitive (descending and ascending) chromatic formulae of the oboes, violins, bassoons and violas portray with precision the realities of anger and mourning. This experience of identification gives to Ottavio's feelings an entirely new orientation and indeed has a cathartic effect on him; certainty — 'e non ho bene, s'ella non l'ha' — is transformed into extraordinary activity: the formerly descending basses begin to soar upwards, the two *sforzatos* and the tremolo of the strings become more emphatic, the music, the internal transformation, reach fever pitch. At this point the formless maelstrom of passions is illuminated by a fantastic, unearthly light, and Ottavio's signature motif emerges, irridescent with an B minor modulation (compare Examples 9 and 26):

Example 29

This motif is the same as that at the beginning of the aria, and at the same time it is different. It expresses the same psychological profile, the same existential content but what at the beginning was a naive ignoring of the world, a spontaneous feeling of identity with oneself, is now the radical delimitation of the world, the final juxtaposition of himself, of his love, to the whole world. Identification with another human being, as the only possibility for existence; the intuitive experiencing of this feeling, gives rise to the intensity and unreal floating quality of the musical expression — almost as a foretaste of Schubert. And indeed, this is somewhat paradoxical as a life potential; there is in it something which is *per se* absurd. As if Ottavio would also surmise this, the emotional logic comes unintentionally into deadly proximity again:

Example 30

The motif of 'morte mi da' is easily recognizable in the last phrase of the voice part, and the renewed heaviness of heart in the surging crescendo of the bass (see Example 28). Thus, unseen, the circle is completed. The second part of the aria is no longer a mechanical reprise. Don Ottavio rethinks the possibilities of his existence by both routes, and comes to the conclusion that Anna's unhappiness means his annihilation. This recognized certainty frees him simultaneously from all terror and the fear of death. The short coda begins with the muted sound of resignation (flute, oboe, bassoon), and ends with the festive music of inner conquest (entire orchestra).

This aria is incomparably more than the 'apotheosis of the sentimental Italian arias of love'; it is not simply a 'tender effusion of love', not simply 'one of Mozart's most beautiful arias of love'. It is a precise and consistent picture by means of the musical drama of a music-dramatic situation, of the ontological problem inherent in it. The essence of the form is the full beauty and imperilled state of the sentimental attitude. Beauty is most directly communicated by melodicity. Don Ottavio lives, above all else, in his melodies. And it is in his melodies that Mozart's melody finds its most personal manifestation in the opera.

This fitting, well-proportioned and balanced structure, homogeneous with regard to line and colour, this formation, reposing within itself like a truly natural phenomenon, is an offspring of *bel canto*. *Bel canto*, justly has been called a world-view by Bence Szabolcsi.[26] The essence of this world-view is beauty itself. But not in an abstract, artistic sense. Beauty expresses the structure of Man.[27] Beauty is the naive, perceptible and yet intellectual expression of the moral harmony and style of the human personality and way of life. Jahn points out that in Mozart the tenor voice of Italian opera has become a 'medium of manly love and tenderness'.[28] In the broader sense, he made the whole of *bel canto* (the beautiful song) into the musical medium of the beautiful person, that is, of the humane essence of human relationships.

Goethe provides a subtle analysis of the linkage between human relationships and beauty in his study of Winckelmann, when discussing friendship in Antiquity. Such a relationship is characterized by

> the passionate fulfilment of beloved obligations, the delight of inseparableness, the devotion towards another person, the life-long, determined dedication, the unconditional following unto death. But even if this deep need for friendship does indeed create and develop its object, only one-sided moral happiness would result for the Antique mind. The external world has little to offer, should, luckily, an object not emerge affording a related, identical need and satisfaction. We are thinking of the need for sensual beauty, and of sensual beauty itself: because the final product of self-enhancing nature is the beautiful being. However, it can create it but infrequently, as too many circumstances oppose its ideas, and even its omnipotence is not able to abide for long in a state of perfection and to make the created beauty permanent, because, strictly speaking, we can say that the beautiful human being is beautiful only for a moment.

The intense significance of Don Ottavio's personality may be expressed by the music artistically whole and harmoniously, in its own extensively limited character. The situation on stage, however, is different. There merely a petty and impotent person appears, who in a critical and dramatic situation, instead of performing worthy deeds, sings at great length though beautifully. The contradiction, however, is much more acute and more universal than Jahn or Abert have perceived it. The problem is not that the figure of Don Ottavio is dramatically problematic, yet musically beautiful. The figure is homogeneous and perfect from the aspect of music-drama. From a music-dramaturgical point of view, Ottavio's aria has no major fault whatever. But the music-drama itself becomes increasingly separated from the operatic stage, as if new dramatic relationships, new interrelations, were being formed in the music, that cannot be expressed on the stage. Compositional value-accents are formed in the musical drama that cannot be translated onto the stage; rather, they can only be distorted. These problems are already posed by Don Ottavio's aria, which we have here discussed, and by Don Giovanni's aria which follows it.

The so-called 'champagne' aria is not the pure unrelated expression of Don Giovanni's essential self to anything else, but rather the bearer of dramatic relationships. First of all it relates to earlier expressions of Don Giovanni's character. Above all else, we have seen that in the second, D major allegro part of the overture the realm of sensuality — that is to say its firstborn, Don Giovanni, as power, not as an individual — is presented in all its musical immediacy. Don Giovanni appeared the second time in Leporello's so-called 'catalogue' aria, in the first part more generalised, in the second part more as an individual, but throughout as a comic figure. Only now does he appear on the stage in his true guise and with full commanding presence. Thus the 'catalogue' aria and the 'champagne' aria have a closely linked underlying message; the ambiguous *alter ego* relationship is manifested in their interaction.

In the second place, Mozart perceives Don Giovanni as an ideal relating to actuality. Mozart represents Don Giovanni's moral indifference as culpable not only towards Donna Anna, the Commendatore, Donna Elvira and Zerlina, but in this esoteric moment as well. In one of the most exposed moments in the aria Don Giovanni reveals himself unconsciously; as Noske had noted, he voices the 'tradimento' motif:

Example 31

This phrase, accompanied *unisono* by flute and violin, with its demonic trill, foreshadows Verdi's great villains, Iago and Paolo Albiani.[30] The aesthetic indifference characterizes Don Giovanni and not Mozart.

And finally, the 'champagne' aria relates to its own immediate precedings as well. Abert, taking the original, Prague, version of the opera as authentic, emphasizes the masterful contrast between Donna Anna's D major aria and Don Giovanni's aria.[31] It seems, however, that with the insertion of Don Ottavio's G major aria a much richer and more meaningful contrast was produced. Here it becomes not merely a matter of contrasting moods, but the direct confrontation of opposing ideals, values as well. Stendhal, in his book on love, has already contrasted the figure of Don Giovanni with Werther, and with Saint-Preux, that is, with the figure of the sentimental hero. Don Giovanni's format is larger, more brilliant, but he is a scoundrel, happy in sin (which, contrary to Stendhal's assumption, is possible). The figure of Don Ottavio is smaller, paler, a figure that is pushed well into the background on the dramatic stage as well as in life, but he is no scoundrel. Yet the depicting of Ottavio's love in Mozart's score is not boring or uninteresting compared with Don Giovanni's. The two figures are unequal not so much with respect to the difference in the power of moral and amoral love. Rather, their inequality has historical significance. Agnes Heller — following Stendhal's argument — puts this very clearly:

> Werther or Saint-Preux are decent, deeply sensitive, even sentimental, loving, considerate burghers, yet incapable of battle, of heroism, of a fight for winning the object of their love. They are natural anti-poles to Don Giovanni, faithful representatives of their age. The honest and nice bourgeois lad, whose soul is far removed from vengeance, who would never draw a pistol against anyone, he has nothing in common with the nobleman's world of hate, he could at most turn it against himself. An honourable citizen and a loving heart, who can easily resign — is this not the figure of Ottavio? Isn't Ottavio the twin brother of Werther and Saint-Preux, the famous sentimental heroes of the Age of Enlightenment? Don Giovanni is the stronger, the more assured, even the greater — but this is the kind of greatness that has no consideration for the Other. The greatness of amoral selfishness. Werther, Saint-Preux, Ottavio are figures of more modest dimensions, but the sort of persons who can be trusted, because they have more consideration for the Other, than for themselves. This is why types like Ottavio are featured neither by Tirso da Molina, or Molière, only by Mozart. This person, created by the Enlightenment, the first, unsure, but pure representative of the new bourgeoisie, promises a safer moral order, not

through his actions, but through his mere existence. It is the figure of Ottavio which transforms the death of the concrete Don Giovanni into the death of Don Giovannism.[32]

Actually, for Mozart the figure of Ottavio is no less poetic than the figure of Don Giovanni, and this fact is of central significance. It touches on the core of the opera as a music-drama. What we have in mind is that musically, in Ottavio's G major aria, for the first time in the course of the action, a determining factor, one that will alter the course of fate, forces itself irresistibly into the foreground, one that until this point was not expressed independently, yet was latent in the action of the music-drama: morality, the this-worldly counter-principle of the 'Don Giovanni syndrome', the sensual genius. We saw that the overture promised a metaphysical world-drama, the struggle between the spiritual and the sensual. Yet Don Giovanni's demonic power is already broken by the resistance of an individual, a moral being, in the first moments of the drama. From here on, the validity and not the power of the moral world-order is represented with increasing artistic emphasis. Thus the problem of destiny in the opera is posed in the context of the relationship between three powers — metaphysical spirit, sensuality and real-world morality — unequal in several senses. This aspect of the music-drama however, is increasingly difficult to relate back to the stage. Moral world-order, because of its static character, cannot be expressed on stage, and thus its validity cannot be manifested in the aesthetic potentials of the operatic stage. Mozart's *Don Giovanni* is, in principle, an authentic work of art only in the medium of music, one that cannot be adequately realized on stage.

Following the 'champagne' aria the focus of the opera again turns to the stage. In the gardens of Don Giovanni's palace, Zerlina is trying to pacify Masetto; she is protesting her innocence. From the #13. F major aria ('Batti, batti, a bel Masetto') it becomes manifest that, in the words of Jahn, 'the fleeting encounter with the seducer had germinated in her soul, which, in developing, changed her relationship with Masetto'.[33] The score reveals that — as Abert rightly points out — Zerlina has learned much from Don Giovanni.[34] Above all, she has learned the bedazzling voice of seduction, the flattering, hypnotic melodiousness of melting lines, soothing thirds and fourths, the technique of employing means and effects. But this technique is no cold, conscious manipulation. If Zerlina handles Masetto in a freer, more self-assured manner, it does not mean that she has learnt the 'trade', but, rather, that, as a woman, she has become increasingly liberated and self-assured. We have seen that Don Giovanni helped her to recognize her own potentialities. Zerlina now realizes these potentialities within the compass of her own life. Thus the aria portrays a dual process: the success of duping Masetto gains value by the increasingly irresistible feeling of inner liberation and fulfilment. For Zerlina, this aria is the proof of true self-realization.

But Zerlina is awakened to the true potentials of her femininity, of being truly herself, only through Don Giovanni. However, prior to this self-realization, she had a different, confusing, alarming Don Giovanni experience originating in Donna Elvira's aria. This warning makes her turn back to her fiancé. Now, though, she enters their relationship as a totally new person. She is more mature, and richer than before. With justice she exults in herself, in her sensual liberation, in the aria. The wonderful thing about Zerlina is just this ability to assimilate this sensual liberation, the realization of her feminine potential; but she is able to enrich it with a relationship that is adapted to her everyday life. With Zerlina, Mozart illustrates those real human needs that partially justify, from the outside, the existence of Don Giovanni. At the same time, he illustrates the limits to the humanistic meaning of Don Giovanni's existence.

Thus Zerlina returns happily to the compass of her own life, having broadened and deepened its potential. But upon hearing Don Giovanni's voice in the distance, she is frightened, not only because of Don Giovanni himself, but because of herself as well. She senses that she will be unable to resist temptation, and suspects that such an affair would bring her unimagined and irreparable harm. She has but one thought: to flee. Masetto, of course, does not understand Zerlina's real motivation at all. He believes that Zerlina's protested innocence was a mere sham, and she is now afraid of the confrontation. Precisely for this he will make no concessions. This is the situation at the beginning of finale #14., the finale of Act I. The first scene of the finale represents the subdued but intense quarrel between Masetto and Zerlina, the clash between the former's intention to unmask her, and the latter's desire to flee. In contrasting Masetto's jealous stubbornness and Zerlina's desperate struggle, Mozart faithfully illustrates the discrepancy between the man's fatal insensitivity and the spiritual refinement, and sensibility of his fiancée. The scene is not merely effective in itself, nor is its importance merely a link in a sequence of scenes on the stage; it is the human inequity it illustrates that thrusts itself with immediate, evocative force towards the centre of the overall scheme.

The next scene brings a sharp contrast to the tone of the finale. With the masked figures of Don Ottavio, Donna Anna and Donna Elvira the atmosphere changes into one of tragedy. The exceptionally simple and short transition by the strings lead into D minor. The compassionate tone of the descending piano motif of the flute, bassoon and oboe is reminiscent of a previously cited turn of phrase in Elvira's #3. aria in E flat major, and evokes a similar spirit. Here too it introduces Elvira's part, beginning with the significant D minor intonation, voiced once before by Anna in a state of unconsciousness (Compare Example 7):

Example 32

Bi - so-gna a-ver co - rag-gio,

Here the intonation signifies that the offended are determined to unmask Don Giovanni. Abert draws our attention to a key element of this scene:

> It is a minor but sophisticated detail that before it condenses into a complete ensemble, Elvira leads, and she draws Don Ottavio along melodically, while Donna Anna follows her own line right away. But she does not do this in the same sense as at the beginning of her aria of revenge; although she has come significantly closer to the real purpose of her life, she still faces the decision with true feminine timidity, she is particularly worried for her fiancé.

This new feeling erupts in Anna's D minor melody with elemental power:

Example 33

Il pas - so è pe - ri - glio - so.

But unable to bear its own weight, the music changes into G minor. Tender love and inhuman anxiety are voiced in Anna's melody:

Example 34

te - mo pel ca - ro   spo - so, pel ca - ro   spo-so,

This passive pain cannot be translated into action, so cannot find release. The dynamics of the feeling tend towards an experience of being totally lost; the voice disintegrates, its notes are isolated. In no more than 26 bars one of the most important turning points in Donna Anna's fate are represented. As soon as she voices vengeance, not as a demand but as an immediate task, she must realize how disproportionate the danger of taking revenge is compared with its significance. She must suddenly experience that vengeance is alien to her, it is not her 'true life purpose'; while on the other hand, she really loves Ottavio. Anna now realizes that she is seriously jeopardising her love by her desire for revenge. With this realization her tragic conflict is emphasized from all angles: Anna is able to love only with her psyche in equilibrium, vengeance is a necessary but not sufficient condition for this equilibrium, yet vengeance might cost the life of her lover. All her endeavours are at cross-purposes. Thus her sense of being lost has real foundations. The most tragic aspect of this turn of events is that when Anna finally recognizes what Ottavio means to her, her situation becomes even graver. With this recognition she has no hope of resolving her existential problem which, from an objective point of view, can afford the only real way out for her. It is as if at this moment Donna Anna is about to be launched with irresistible momentum, towards the ebb of her fate.

However, at this point Mozart interrupts the psychological play with a strong contrast. The sound of a minuet can be heard coming from the palace, Leporello discovers the masqueraders, and his master commands him to invite them to the ball. The invitation, the considering of the invitation, its acceptance, are all fitted into the steps of the minuet. The scene is built on the principle of ambiguity. The smooth and neutral medium of convention carries the most varied shadings. The gaiety of the ball, the careless elegance of Don Giovanni, the suppressed emotions and bewilderment of the masqueraders, the uncouth ceremoniousness of Leporello, and the noble bearing of Don Ottavio are expressed equally by it. This seemingly simple, even flat scene has a continuously fluctuating mood, it goes through constant refraction — 'A masterpiece of musical diplomacy', Jahn could say of this as well.[35]

Leporello leaves the stage, the minuet can no longer be heard, and what follows is another monumental contrast. Before entering the palace, the masqueraders once more confront themselves, their objectives, and ask for heaven's help in achieving them.

It has already been pointed out by Abert that this B major adagio is the centre of the internal action of the finale.[36] Beginning with Hotho, the musicologists have interpreted the 'masque' tercet unanimously as a revenge tercet, although on occasion there is a willingness to acknowledge the differences between the intonations of Don Ottavio, Donna Anna and Donna Elvira. Even the words express a very subtle difference:

> *Anna and Ottavio:*   Protegga il giusto cielo
> Il zelo del mio cor!
> *Elvira:*   Vendichi il giusto cielo
> Il mio tradito amor!

Anna and Ottavio beseech heaven to protect the quest of their hearts; Elvira asks that her betrayed love be avenged. Mozart's music elaborates this difference with subtle psychology. If we listen closely to the parts of Anna and Ottavio, we cannot escape the impression that we are hearing a love duet. Their voices, soaring with transfigured sentimentality, seem to foretell, from the very first moment, the sentimental maturation of *Così Fan Tutte*, and this effect is strikingly heightened by the serenade-like quality of the orchestral accompaniment (mainly in the handling of the wind instruments).[37] The emphasized euphony, the sentimental turns of the melodic line, the intervals and scales that become increasingly unconstrained and give voice to balanced sentiments, the happy flowering of Anna's singing, all give voice to the fact that the mutual expression of love is dissolving all tensions, harmoniously and pleasantly, filling the beings of these two people. Finally, in Anna's voice, a nobly sentimental scale motif is introduced, unmistakably in tune with Ottavio's often-mentioned sentimental 'signature' motif (Compare Examples 9, 26 and 29):

Example 35

il ze - lo del mio cor!

The motif is repeated by the bassoons, then by the oboes, and finally by the clarinets and flutes, becoming gradually more sublimated and significant. This ringing out of the B major adagio hints at certain moments of elevated sentimentality in *Cosi Fan Tutte*, or even *The Magic Flute*, both in its atmosphere as well as its motif.

What had actually happened here? What has caused this unique momentary release, this harmony, experienced with such profound gravity? Just a few minutes before Donna Anna had felt completely lost, she was on the threshold of descending to the low-point of her fate, and soon she will enter the palace of Don Giovanni — a step she well knows that may prove to be fatal. Yet it seems that the music speaks not of leaving the world (as Abert thought), the release of tension, the harmony, are not religious, they do not originate in a transcendental experience. Anna's hopefulness is born again out of intimacy, intimacy realized in a human relationship, in love. In her life this means that she has found her way back into the world. The character of the B major adagio is basically determined by Donna Anna, thus it is the music of the certainty she has found in the world.

Yet, just because of this, its composition is extremely problematic. The problem is similar to that of Ottavio's G major aria, but here it is even more acute. The personal development of Donna Anna is more complicated and proceeds at a slower pace than is demanded by the role she plays within the total concept of the music-drama. It follows from her personality — and, of course, from the aggressive intervention of Don Giovanni — that she can fulfil her life only through a slow, crisis-filled process. Within the total concept of the music-drama, however, there is an increasingly demanding need to confront Don Giovanni with the life of Donna Anna as if it were already fulfilled. The dynamics of the representation of the human realization, and of the validity of life potentials cross one another. From this arises the problematic nature and also the profundity of the B major adagio. We might say that this section is not only the centre of the internal action of the finale, but in a sense the 'esoteric culmination' of the entire opera. As a continuation of the compositional meaning of contrasting Don Ottavio's G major aria with the 'champagne' aria, here the 'human emancipation' of love is portrayed esoterically yet irrevocably, in the interrelationship between Donna Anna and Don Ottavio. Here Don Giovanni, the entire Don Giovanni syndrome, has lost the struggle, in spite of its unquestionable superiority, as far as human authenticity is concerned. If humanly complete love is possible in this world, the mission of Don Giovanni has come to its end.

The change of scene means a new and striking contrast in the musical action. The music leads into the gay riot of the ball in Don Giovanni's palace. The 6/8 metre, the dominant melody, is in the same style as the wedding music of the #5. G major chorus, it is gay and sparkling in every detail, yet here, in the intonation of Don Giovanni, it is not 'child-like and simple-minded', as are Zerlina, Masetto and the peasants, but rather it has elemental force, it is irresistible, sweeping. But on the entry of the three masqueraders, the folksy opening gives way to an aristocratic sequence. The 6/8 time of the E flat major is interrupted, and after an effective pause, the festive, representative tones of the monumental C major *maestoso* in 2/4 time are sounded. Don Giovanni, Leporello, and Don Ottavio, Donna Anna and Donna Elvira (who have accepted the rules of the game as a tactical move) are celebrating liberty with hymnic pathos. This 'viva la liberta' has given rise to much deliberation and convoluted interpretation, while it obviously refers to the freedom afforded by the masque, the incognito — in the words of Abert: *die Maskenfreiheit*[38] — more exactly it refers to licence. Stendhal characterized perfectly the attitude of Don Giovanni towards freedom in the ideological sense:

Don Giovanni casts aside all the obligations he has toward his fellow men. In the big fair of life he is like the dishonest merchant who always buys but never pays. The idea of equality enrages him as does water enrage the rabid; this is why pride of ancestry befits Don Giovanni's character so well. Along with the ideal of equal rights the ideal of justice disintegrates as well, or more correctly, if Don Giovanni is of noble ancestry, these peasant ideas have never approached him; and I believe I justly hold the opinion that the bearer of an historic name is more disposed than any other person towards setting a town on fire when he wishes to cook an egg.

Agnes Heller adds to Stendhal's deliberation the following: 'rebellion without regard to others, individual rebellion is elitist, and as such necessarily carries amorality within itself. Don Giovanni's "Long live Liberty" is the celebration of liberty without equality and fraternity.'[39] It is precisely for this reason that this monumental ballroom toast is not merely an effective episode, but is at the heart of the opera's concept.

With Don Giovanni's invitation to resume dancing a series of scenes starts, constructed with unparalleled dramaturgical *bravura*. On stage with the three consecutively introduced orchestras, three independent yet interrelated stages evolve. Don Ottavio dances with Donna Anna to the minuet of the first orchestra, Don Giovanni with Zerlina to the counter-dance of the second, and Leporello forces Masetto to the German-style dance of the third. Yet, while the different actions take place on the different musical stages, everyone is keeping an eye on everyone else. The actors comment on one another and the events mould each one of them. Such a simple and yet forced interlinking of the most antithetical forces creates an increasing tension that is finally almost unbearable. Don Giovanni is besieging Zerlina more passionately and urgently than before, and the girl knows, even says, that she is lost. At the same time the general tension has become as unbearable, scandal is palpable 'in the air', as it can be felt only in the works of Dostoyevsky. And then, at last, the voice of Zerlina crying for help puts an end to this impossible state of affairs.

What has frightened Zerlina? Obvious and profane answers offer themselves to this naive question. Then, let us ask more crassly: What did she expect anyway? Well, this question is not as crude, and in principle, not as senseless, as it might at first appear. Indeed, Zerlina might have sensed something that she was not prepared for. Every one of Don Giovanni's mistresses will be consumed by a remorseless loneliness, never to find inner peace. Such is the fate of Donna Elvira in Mozart's opera. Elvira's #8. D major aria has already warned Zerlina of such a fate. At most, the girl might have been agitated by the tone, without comprehending its meaning. The warning was sufficient for her to find, even to unfold herself in her own everyday life, distanced from the person of Don Giovanni, from immediate seduction, yet it was not sufficiently comprehensible to shield her against a subsequent siege. The reappearance of Don Giovanni sweeps away even the memory of her previous confusion and Zerlina is unable to resist. Now, however, on the threshold of fulfilment, she must learn from Don Giovanni himself the true nature of erotic genius, of demonic love, and suddenly everything becomes clear to her. Elvira's fate, her warning voice, the demonic nature of Don Giovanni, and her own future become ordered into one intuitive concatenation, and Zerlina's simple, sober, normal being rebels spontaneously at the last moment against the devil, the fate, that so nearly overtakes her. The power of Don Giovanni is again, for the second time in the opera and in real life, broken in the face of the resistance of an individual, a woman.

Zerlina's desperate cry for help has thus interrupted the embarrassed merry-making, the scandal breaks out. The *allegro assai* voices a tremendous outcry. Zerlina escapes, while Don Giovanni embarks on an insolent farce: he declares Leporello to be the seducer from whom he has succeeded in saving Zerlina. Don Giovanni displays the most effective means of the self-assured mannerism that brooks no contradiction; *andante maestoso*, the energetic gestures of the orchestra, the chivalrous tone of the syncopated rhythm of the libretto and finally the threatening trill, this time with the accompaniment of the strings in unison:

Example 36

This trill is rather ambiguous in Don Giovanni's vocal part. On the one hand, it expresses his aristocratic superiority and discrimination, on the other, his uninhibited baseness. It always appears at important, self-revealing moments, thus at the cited instance in the 'champagne' aria (see Example 31), at the beginning of the finale, in a quite similar situation, when confronting Masetto, and further on it will have an important role on two more occasions. Its meaning has always a different nuance, but it never loses its ambiguity: the kind of small, spontaneous gesture that directly reveals the real essence of the individual and, thus in fact betrays him. In the 'champagne' aria it is the audience who must divine its true meaning, at the beginning of the finale it is Masetto, here it is the entire assembly of guests. And they do understand.

Now the moment of unmasking is at hand, Don Ottavio puts an end to the farce. His bearing is unequivocal and determined:

Example 37

Nol spe-ra-te, nol spe-ra-te!   L'em-pio cre-de con tal fro - de

Through its representatives the entire world of humans is standing up to Don Giovanni. And now the attack begins in the allegro. In the dynamic arc (piano—crescendo—forte) of the beginning of the ensemble such an energy is manifested; such an overwhelming force, that Don Giovanni becomes even more confused. The outraged emotions of the opposing camp are churning more and more, and Don Giovanni's confusion becomes complete. At this point, however, something extraordinary happens. The determination to fight is swelling to huge dimensions, it finally becomes overpowering, yet in the process it empties itself, its monumentality is a sham. From the unending series of upward struggling sequences it becomes clear that the expression of power and its effectiveness are inversely related. The exaggerated external gestures of the threat mask an internal impotence. The music contains this contradiction. The outcry reaches its peak:

Example 38

yet it does not overflow into action. Instead, the entire process starts anew. At first Don Giovanni does not understand what is happening. Only very slowly does he comprehend that this overwhelming force is in fact helpless against him. Thus the process is repeated completely a second time, but it does not reach the previous peak. At the corresponding point the opponents' camp becomes enervated:

Example 39

At this moment Don Giovanni can clearly see the internal defeat of his opponents, and he recovers immediately:

Example 40

Luck has made an about turn. Don Giovanni has become master of the situation. He dictates the tempo as well as the vocal material of the last *più stretto* part. The opponent's camp, believing that it is on the offensive, is unwittingly forced into a defensive position, and is now at the mercy of Don Giovanni. In this musical situation the escape of Don Giovanni is not heroic, but a simple, well-timed departure, not without a touch of farce.

This comic situation, of course, affects Don Giovanni first and foremost. There is something demeaning in it, we can say, in the fact that the firstborn of the realm of the sensual must 'take to his heels'. But the comic nature of the situation is even more cruel to the opposing camp. The impotence of superior force, exhausting itself in its own outcry, is unavoidably comic. Yet their attitude remains earnest and justified. The explanation is of course obvious: even the most potent human power is helpless against the demonic. The problem here, however, is the representation, the representability, of this fact. In connection with Donna Anna's #10. D major aria we have already discussed the basic presumption of every Don Giovanni drama, that Don Giovanni can have no real this-worldly opponent, one worthy of his stature. What is more, the entire world of humans cannot be such an opponent. Before Mozart, however, this could be only crudely expressed. The other-worldly intervention was justified not by making the demonic power felt, but by the everyday fallibility of man and the depravity of Don Giovanni. It is not by accident that neither Tirso da Molina nor Molière had their Don Giovanni confront the entire opposing camp at the same time. In drama there are but two ways out of such a situation: either the most primitive comedy of deception or a miracle. Neither fits the general concept of a Don Giovanni drama. In the opera, however, yet another possibility exists for the resolution of such a situation, and it lies in the music: the direct expression of the irresistible force of demonic power against overwhelming human forces. Yet Mozart did not choose this solution. More precisely, Mozart does not express demonic power directly but indirectly, through its results — its paralysing effect on its opponents. Yet in this indirect approach the essential is lost artistically, the representation becomes problematical. For simultaneously Don Giovanni's defeat and confusion is portrayed on the one hand, and on the other, the overwhelming force and impotence of his opponents. This contradiction is expressed by Mozart — just as in Donna Anna's aria — not by means of the composition structure of the music, but by its quality, by the musical process becoming empty, barren. And all this again gives rise to a confusion between the musical and dramatic dimension: the irresistible power of Don Giovanni cannot be directly expressed by the music, and the inner ambivalence of the monumental music of the opponent's camp cannot find dramatic expression. This then gives rise to a hybrid of tragic and comic qualities, that is to say, a homogeneous, an all inclusive tragi-comic atmosphere such as later in the sextet fails to develop. In the final analysis, all problems stem from the fact that the demonic nature of Don Giovanni is not directly represented throughout the drama. Here Don Giovanni is simply a dramatic hero who may differ from the count in *Figaro* as to his stature, but not as to the principle he stands for. Yet this representation — which leads to insurmountable artistic problems — follows from the Don Giovanni principle, the concept of *Don Giovanni* as music-drama.

If we pay close attention to the musical process we see that Don Giovanni becomes flustered not when he takes the measure of the overwhelming force, but much earlier. The threat of the outburst of the opposing forces only increases his confusion. Shaw saw it correctly that Don Giovanni is defeated and confused from the moment that they 'confront him with his villany'. Not that this would shake him morally. Don Giovanni does not recognize morality, thus he cannot transgress its laws. However, by this stage, the unconditional nature of his power has been broken for the third time, and this time unambiguously. In Donna Anna he met total defeat; Zerlina revolted at the last moment; and now all has become concerted and organized into joint action. Don Giovanni is confused by the mere fact of the united revolt of his fellow beings rather than by the potential of this fact.

Here, however, there is a dichotomy in the representation: only the confused individual is represented directly, while the seemingly unchanged reality, the image of the unimpaired devil, can only be perceived indirectly, reflected in the impotence of the opposing force. This apparent depiction of unified artistic viewpoint can be traced back to find a similar theme in the B major adagio: the dramatic event is subordinated to a total concept. But if the purpose has common roots, its methods are diametrically opposed. Donna Anna — that is, the apotheosis of sentimental love — demands sublimated and stylized expression, while the defeat of Don Giovanni — that is, the defeat of the Don Giovanni principle — demands robust, life-like and realistic representation. These two problematical moments of the finale to the first act are inextricably linked together, even in their stylistic contrast, as they are the one-sided expression of the same musical-dramatic fate but viewed from different aspects. In Don Giovanni, the basic demand that is made of every work of art, the crucial aesthetic question, that everything in it should be viewed and represented from the same viewpoint, poses an intractable problem. We have seen that this unity is increasingly disrupted in the relationship between the stage and the music-drama, and in the first finale our attention is called to two moments of disruption within the music-drama. In the case of the B major adagio the directness of the process is lost, and in the instance of the last scenes, it is the directness of the interrelation of the dramatic forces. The real meaning of the process — in this case the interrelation — can be acquired only by retrospective reconstruction, interpretation, the intellectual mediation of the motifs. The musical world-drama places an almost unbearable burden on eighteenth-century opera.

At the beginning of the first act, in the introduction, Leporello imitates Don Giovanni, in the #15. G major duet ('Eh via, buffone); at the start of the second act, Don Giovanni imitates Leporello. This most characteristic and unique pleasure of Don Giovanni for all who are not at the moment being seduced by him, seems the most licentious mockery, an insolent fraud. It may make no sense to ask what the wind does when it is not blowing, yet in the case of Don Giovanni, even though we have likened him to a natural phenomenon, it is reasonable to ask what he does when he is not engaged in seduction. The answer is that in these relationships Don Giovanni is, in most instances, astonishingly vulgar, base and brutal. The musical voice of such interludes is the simple, rolling, *parlando*-like melodiousness of the *opera buffa*. He uses this voice relatively rarely in the first act. But we have seen that in the #9. B major quartet he made insinuations against Donna Elvira in this style, he used this tone with the servants in the finale, and again at the ball amongst the peasants, and finally this is the musical language which voices his confusion. In the second act this style will be used more frequently and, it will be more characteristic, most of all in dialogue with Leporello. At first sight, it signifies no more than that Don Giovanni debases himself stylistically to the level of his servant; he is talking to him in his own language. Actually, the situation is far more complex. Not only is Leporello's relationship with Don Giovanni ambiguous, the opposite is also true. The profound and mutual musical analogy between the figures of Don Giovanni and Leporello becomes obvious for the first time in this duet. For Don Giovanni this relationship is not merely one of the status between master and servant, but the interdependence of their lives. Don Giovanni's persona unequivocally needs this person who is irresistibly drawn to him and bound to him by unbreakable ties. Unconditional ownership, unconditional possession are his universal needs. But in his relationship with Leporello eroticism, the motif of sensual idealization, is completely missing, and consequently his egoistic nature manifests itself here in a vulgar and brutal manner. Towards Leporello, Don Giovanni is not the erotic genius, but brute power which crushes fellow beings and, what is more important, profits from their defencelessness.

Don Giovanni and Leporello now swap clothes. This time Don Giovanni is preparing to seduce Donna Elvira's maid and thinks it will be more plausible to introduce himself as a servant. But, unexpectedly, Donna Elvira appears at the window. The #16. A major tercet ('Ah, taci, ingiusto core') Donna Elvira intones not in her eccentric but in her confessional voice. Utter loneliness is for a moment relieved in natural expression, but this itself constitutes only temporary relief. But that which was expressed finds no relief, once uttered, it keeps rising in her consciousness as a disturbing and disquieting problem. The dynamics of the psychological process transcends relief as soon as it is achieved, and she becomes more and more agitated. When the two-bar theme of the orchestral introduction is repeated, following the vocal part, the values of the notes become abbreviated, as if Elvira's heartbeat were accelerating. The second phrase of the vocal part is, in fact, a more intensively expressed variation of the first; the intimate appeal becomes passionate supplication. Now she identifies the problem: 'è un empio, è un traditore'. Everything stands before her irrevocably, as agitating fact, and the logic of her own feelings and thoughts drive her towards eccentricity again. The two mezzo-fortes of this phrase stand out in stark contrast from the previous piano character, but the emotional figuration of the violins is even more revealing. The contrast of the winds and the strings denotes the ambiguity of Elvira's emotional state, the former express the intimate moments, the latter the impulsive ones. Elvira experiences with full intensity the fact that there is no turning back, that what did occur cannot be rescinded by a sentimental, forgiving gesture. She cannot overcome the Don Giovanni phenomenon and the problem of her life, the vocal part is coloured by near-hysteria, and the ascending chromatic passage that appeared in Don Ottavio's #11. G major aria underlying the word 'morte' (Compare Example 28) is voiced by the orchestra:

Example 41

cresc.

This death motif marks a decisive turning-point. The first finale brought critical changes in the fates not only of Don Giovanni but of all the other actors, Elvira included. The experience of absolute helplessness that she too underwent in facing Don Giovanni places the problem of her life in a new perspective, a new light. Previously, in every feverish moment of her passion, she could identify with herself directly and with total fervour, the realization of the absurdity of her existence did not prevent her from living her life in its every, even though contradictory, form. Now, however, following the experience of absolute helplessness, she is no longer able to do so. From now on, in every moment of her self-consuming life, death lies 'at the bottom of every thought', unconsciously, yet unavoidably. Thus, in the first 13 bars of the tercet, Mozart presents Elvira's entire life problem with extreme conciseness and in a subdued manner, in a more sophisticated and therefore even more unresolvable form, in tune with its dramatic dynamics, nearly in the proximity of death.

At that moment, below, in the street, a dialogue between Leporello and Don Giovanni can be heard: Don Giovanni orders the servant, now in a nobleman's dress, to stand in front of him, and he makes a 'confession of love' from behind his back. Intuitively, Don Giovanni knows Donna Elvira perfectly well. He does not have to find the right tone, he does not have to attune himself gradually to the other, as in the case of Zerlina, he can speak Elvira's musical language perfectly, right away. The musical expression that began with the tercet returns, but now in E major, and higher by a fifth. We already know this A major—E major intensification from the #7. A major *duettino* of Don Giovanni and Zerlina. The increasing energy of the music expresses in both instances the more passionate, more heated assault. But here the temperature of passion is higher from the start, thus the change of tonality also has a heightened effect. In this E major section Mozart illustrates two different effects. He moulds Don Giovanni's part very effectively from the point of view of the audience, while the vocal part depicts Don Giovanni's effect on Donna Elvira. These two effects are not simultaneous. Don Giovanni's seductive song becomes increasingly more elemental, more irresistible. Following in the footsteps of Kierkegaard, we have discussed that beyond Don Giovanni there is no refuge for Elvira, that she can free herself from despair only in his presence, either by trying to overcome it by vocalising her hatred and despair, or by hoping. These emotions are present in the tercet in a more subdued manner, yet perhaps even stronger than before. By the end of the introductory section Elvira has arrived at the lowest point of deadly despair.

It is at this moment that the intonation of the scheming below reaches her ears dully and she recognizes the voice of Don Giovanni. The emotions of hatred and despair immediately overwhelm her, the former emotional violin figure and dynamic fluctuation returns to the orchestra, and her singing becomes even more passionate. But soon she perceives that Don Giovanni is acting seductively. Immediately, all negative emotions evaporate. At this moment a very peculiar musical turn takes place. Donna Elvira intones in the most subjugated voice in the tercet, with the intonation of Leporello's and Don Giovanni's underhand scheming: 'Numi, che strano affetto mi si risveglia in petto.' The artistic motive underlying this has many meanings, all of them very cruel. Above all, it means that the plotting has succeeded, Elvira has fallen into the trap. It also expresses the human dimensions of becoming trapped. For Donna Elvira, the perception of the trap and of immediate, total surrender are the work of the moment. But this surrender is not actualized in the elated fulfilment of hope, the deluge of passionate love, in the storm of emotions. By continuing this same melody, Elvira surrenders with possibly the most vulgar gesture of the opera. Mozart illustrates her love totally without illusions, in its true essence. Now Leporello becomes her musical partner. The same melody expresses Elvira's unfettered emotions and Leporello's astonished mockery. Don Giovanni has achieved his immediate purpose: Elvira has surrendered, she will obey his will like a helpless puppet, the tercet might as well be ended, and Leporello could get rid of Elvira. Yet this is not what occurs. The music is modulated into C major and Don Giovanni begins a maddening *cantilena*:

Example 42

This C major section stands out as if illuminated from the entire scene almost spatially and the music glows — 'space ignites its voice into light'. Never before in this opera has erotic genius spoken with such fire, with such intensity. But why does this occur at this moment, without any dramatic purpose? Don Giovanni's immediate purpose is to make Elvira madly infatuated with him, then to get rid of her to free his way to the maid. As a woman she no longer exists for him, she is no longer the subject of erotic idealization. Yet he handles the affair not in the manner of the *opera buffa*, but elevates it to one of the musical high-points of his life. Here Don Giovanni is ambiguous: this is the only time that demonic sensuality is manifested totally unbridled, and the only time his initiative lacks all erotic intent. Felsenstein's characterization which seems to miss the mark in relation to the 'champagne' aria, is totally apposite for this C major section: 'Hysterical dream, remembrance of what was, what ought to be, and what never can be any more!' That this experience is connected with Elvira has a very deep significance. Not because Elvira is an extraordinary woman. Kierkegaard is justified in rejecting this explanation. More exactly, this deep significance is associated not with the extraordinary nature of Elvira's femininity, but with the out of the ordinary nature of her being. Elvira has 'partaken' of the demonic spirit, having been seduced by Don Giovanni. The demon who, prior to fulfilment, must otherwise measure himself against, tune himself to the object of his desire, can reveal himself, undisguised, in all his unbridled power. But even more important than this association is the fact that the unconditional nature of Don Giovanni's power in this opera can be represented only in retrospect, that is, through Elvira. Don Giovanni can experience the absoluteness of his own being, uninterrupted and undisturbed, only in his relationship with Elvira, the more so since he has nothing to do with her any longer. The C major section of the tercet is Don Giovanni's most irresistibly seductive music in the whole opera, but it is its compositional definitiveness, dramatic purposelessness, its episodic, retrospective character that expresses the central problem of the opera: the end of the Don Giovanni syndrome.

Of course, Donna Elvira suspects none of this, to her the seduction is straightforward. It is because of this that the scene becomes increasingly embarrassing, increasingly repulsive. Hearing Don Giovanni's *cantilena* Elvira is completely sure of herself, and at last she gives full rein to her wounded passions; she believes that her proud resistance will heighten Don Giovanni's love. And Don Giovanni plays along. He begs Elvira's forgiveness with feigned desperation. The utter, and yet unconsciously, inhuman interrelatedness of Donna Elvira, Don Giovanni and Leporello is fated. The relationship between the devil and those flirting with the demonic is a parody bereft of everything that is human. For a moment the possibility of a world wells up where, in empty space, only irresistible, stoic laughter can be heard. Elvira and Leporello are frightened by this possibility. Fortunately, Don Giovanni finally has had enough of this comedy. The music returns to A major, and with it to the beginning of the tercet. This is the moment of introversion, of reflection: Don Giovanni notes with satisfaction that he has achieved his goal; within Elvira all is problematic again; and in Leporello compassion for Elvira is kindled. The vocal parts of the latter two become interlinked, while Don Giovanni is distanced from them. Yet Elvira does not defect, Leporello does not transfer his allegiance, they are both too weak for that. They are merely frightened for a moment. This is why the three voices can meet unwillingly in the intonation of the subversive action. With this Elvira and Leporello reveal their final allegiances, and though aversion is restored, in the end Elvira surrenders to her fate with three melodic gestures. And the death motif is sounded twice, forcefully, by the orchestra. Yet its meaning here is different and more cruel than at the beginning of the tercet: it expresses the perspective of Elvira's surrender, not her self-consumption, not the perspective of pursued and hopeful love, but of love's imagined fulfilment. No matter how Elvira's life will evolve, from now on death will indeed be 'at the bottom of every thought'.

Abert is justified in speaking of the admirable unity of drama and music in the tercet.[40] Yet this perfectly conceived musical action cannot easily be translated into an adequate stage composition. Outwardly, the action is a trivial and vulgar *opera buffa* scene: Don Giovanni sings his song of seduction to Donna Elvira, hiding behind Leporello who is dressed as a nobleman, while the servant, obeying his master's orders, like a puppet on a string, accompanies him with the appropriate gestures of a lover; and in the end the wronged lady is seduced. This scene can only be played out on stage. But the direct comic quality of the stage-play necessarily debases the symbolic and tragi-comic significance of the musical-dramatic process. But even beyond this general difficulty, the feasibility of implementing faithfully on stage the C major section, adhering to its meaning, seems questionable. As discussed earlier, here the music carries almost by itself a quasi-stage effect, demanding emphasis in its presentation. This music, in C major, will not tolerate the presence of Elvira and Leporello; here only Don Giovanni, only the genius of sensuality, exists like a single, high-soaring flame. Yet the logic of the stage presentation, the requirement of playing a scene based to the very end on the characters exchanging roles, contradicts such an exposition of the moment.

Thus Donna Elvira blindly pursues her fate, hurrying into the street, she departs happily in the arms of Leporello dressed as Don Giovanni. And Don Giovanni now serenades her maid. With this serenade a virtually new affair, like that with Zerlina begins. Musically, Mozart summarizes this dramatically decisive fact in the *canzonetta* by avoiding dramaturgical tautology. Don Giovanni's song, due to external events, is merely a 'wasted serenade', but in it a musical-dramatic possibility is hinted at, and at this point in the composition that is all that is necessary and sufficient. The serenade is wasted because Masetto appears, armed, accompanied by some peasants, searching for Don Giovanni to exact his revenge. Don Giovanni is, of course, wearing his servant's clothes and so presents himself as Leporello, and proffers advice on where to find and how to recognize the nobleman. The #18. F major aria ('Metà di voi Quà vadano') is the playing of a role with a multitude of meanings. In the first place it is the counterpiece to the so-called 'catalogue' aria: Don Giovanni is impersonating Leporello, but since he presents his own self as Leporello, he impersonates Leporello as he is impersonating him. More than that, he develops and represents more precisely the two-sided problem in the #15. G major duet that launches the second act; the deep and mutual musical correspondence between master and servant. The equalizing and convergent tendencies expressed there, here diverge, and inequality is prominent. Don Giovanni creates Leporello's and his own caricature with extraordinary comic gusto, yet with such superior virtuosity and playful self-indulgence that only a complete lack of psychological insight explains Masetto's failure to recognize him and, unsuspecting, Masetto allows his fellows to leave, and lets Don Giovanni disarm him. Don Giovanni now simply beats up Masetto and leaves him there.

It is Zerlina who finds her groaning fiancé and she tries to console him. Her #19. aria in C major ('Vedrai, carino') is a summing-up, illustrating the results of personal development. This is particularly apparent when we compare it with her #13. aria in F major, which has many features in common. The atmosphere of both is basically erotic, yet the first is stormily unrestrained, while this one is cosy, intimate. The difference, of course, stems from the diversity of the situations, and diversity of the problems as well. Before, Zerlina had to make amends for her own mistake, now it is that of someone else. But, more importantly, it is a matter of two different stages in Zerlina's development as a total human being. The girl's attitude to love and her concomitant human enrichment that celebrated her liberation in the F major aria, have already settled down. This is not the result of a natural process but the consequence of Zerlina having conclusively ordered her human relationships. For her the 'Don Giovanni affair' is completely closed. All the potential of her femininity, liberated by Don Giovanni, is in her possession, yet now the Don Giovanni phenomenon is utterly hateful to her. She loves Masetto, she feels he is right for her. This C major aria reveals that she is able harmoniously to unfold the entire sensual and emotional wealth of her being in her relationship with him. The first part of the aria creates an intense, homogeneous and balanced erotic atmosphere. This serene eroticism is evoked by the delicate shades of the orchestration, the tender melody, but mainly by the even beat, the rhythm of the entire musical passage. It completely lacks the excitement of the F major aria, an even outpouring of feeling is more deep-rooted, it is intense and genuine. In the second part, due to the wind instrument configurations, the music becomes excited. The effect of the action on stage set down in the instructions (Zerlina places Masetto's hand on her heart), the sensuous impulsiveness, is overt. This is further enhanced by the tonal illustrative effect of the heartbeats, then the passionate, rising arc of her voice with the fermata. Finally, launched by the bursting orchestral postlude (the only forte in the entire aria) the waves of passion close over the heads of the actors. The dynamics, the slow ebbing of the music, does not relieve the tension, but quietly trembling, hints at an approaching fulfilment. In this aria, eroticism is not euphoria but a natural manifestation of life, fusing with love and tenderness. In her previous aria Zerlina had found herself. Here she has found a satisfying human relationship, a normal shared life. If not the most brilliant of arias it is the most meaningful moment of Zerlina's musical-dramatic fate.

Meanwhile Donna Elvira and Leporello find themselves in the vestibule of Donna Anna's house. Leporello is by now feeling very uncomfortable and would like to escape. In the darkness he moves away from Elvira, and the unfortunate woman beseeches him not to leave her:

Example 43

Ah non la-sciar-mi!

This closing formulation of the *recitativo secco* is none other that the 'tradimento' motif. It tells more than the pleading itself. It expresses the fact that at this moment Elvira has sensed her latest betrayal. The tone of the #20. sextet ('Sola, sola in bujo loco') is born of this perception. It is as if a variant of the compassionate motif, twice before associated with Elvira, would sound in the beginning bars. The excited, noble repetition of tones by the first violins joins in at this moment, and from here on apparently, the music merely serves to translate the text into its own language.

> *Sola, sola, in bujo loco,*
> *Palpitar il cor mi sento*
> *E m'assale un tal spavento*
> *Che mi sembra di morir.*

Elvira's melody is filled with apprehension, but without hysteria, or eccentricity, as if the C" to D' seventh of the 'loco' and the emphasis of its first *sforzato* alone would betray her passionate anxiety. To illustrate Elvira's racing heartbeat, the orchestra expresses the pulsing, while the vocal part reveals her breathlessness. Terror engulfs her, and it is not difficult to recognize in the suddenly descending scale of the first violins a version of the violin configuration that had expressed Elvira's agitation many times before.

Finally, when the thought of death is expressed, the 'death' motif is again energetically sounded by the orchestra (compare Examples 28 and 41):

Example 44

Yet the music does not translate the words of the text alone, neither is it a mere mirror of the moments of anxiety, fear and nightmarish visions engendered by a 'dark place', but it does carry a symbolic process. The mere 13 bars that launch the sextet re-phrase the problem of Elvira's fate in a new situation at the instant of perception, suddenly, yet with precision.

It represents the extremely concentrated dramatic turning-point when the accidental, small and insignificant moments in life coalesce into undisruptable concatenation, unalterable and coercive destiny in the light of a sudden internal illumination. Thus Donna Elvira is not simply 'afraid in the dark' — even the term 'tortured by premonitions' is inadequate to express the significance of this musical process. For Elvira, in the logic of her fate, the 'death' motif, annihilation, follows from the perception of the *tradimento* motif, heard as the closing passage of the *recitativo secco* with syllogistic necessity.

The second section of the sextet is in sharp contrast to the first: it is a scene in the tone of the *opera buffa*. Elsewhere on the darkened stage Leporello, stumbling and with comic eagerness, is searching for the exit, but misses it. Now a dazzling contrast ensues. Donna Anna and Don Ottavio appear accompanied by servants bearing torches. The stage, as well as the music are suddenly illuminated. The enharmonic translation of B major into D major constitutes a fantastic light effect. The change is, of course, primarily due to the presence of torches, yet the music expresses more, a deeper meaning. The transposition of the music into D major alters not only the illumination but the character of the scene as well. First, the comic contemptibleness is relieved by noble and festive grandiosity. Following the figure slinking away in the dark, the actors stand forth boldly and appear openly. But this contrast has an even more profound moral meaning. The first section of the sextet taking place in the dark, consisted of an episode involving two people whose life and being were irresistibly drawn toward moral torpidity. Donna Anna and Don Ottavio, however, are morally impeccable, lofty and noble beings. The scene is illuminated not by the flames of the torches alone but by the radiant human purity of Anna and Ottavio as well. Thus in this musical contrast, and beyond its sensual meaning, in its germinal stage and within the confines of bourgeois life, we already find the symbolic and moral significance of the confrontation of light and darkness that will be found again as the principal foundation of *The Magic Flute*.

Ottavio consoles Anna, in a nobly sentimental *cantilena*; his tone is lofty yet sincere, the libretto is reminiscent of Belmont's in the quartet from the *Abduction* ('Welche Wonne, dich zu finden'); and it seems almost inevitable that soon the sentimental variation of Ottavio's 'signature' motif, the descending scale run, is heard (Compare Examples 9, 26, 29, 35 and 37):

Example 45

o - mai del ge - ni - to - re

In Don Ottavio's *cantilena* it is important to note a significant and characteristic feature. As already mentioned, the first finale alters the fate of every character in the opera, so that subsequently the posing of new humane-artistic questions becomes a necessity, and the previous questions are now seen in a different light. But this statement demands some qualification. For Don Ottavio, Donna Anna, Donna Elvira, Masetto and Zerlina alike the sense of absolute helplessness in the face of the devil has been an experience which needs to be assimilated. But for each the degree to which it marks a turning-point in their fate depends on how they approach this task — indeed, whether they are prepared to tackle it at all. We have seen that for Donna Elvira it results in the total precluding of identification with herself, in permanent proximity to death; while Zerlina was motivated to finish once and for all with the entire Don Giovanni phenomenon. In contrast, Masetto failed to grasp the true nature of the events, and continues to view Don Giovanni as no more than a common scoundrel. More interesting still, there is no change in Don Ottavio's attitude, as if the impotence has no personal consequences for him. There is no trace in his voice of downheartedness, depression, confusion, or of having had a generally negative experience. He consoles his betrothed, with the same intimate and untroubled sentimentality as before. He is concerned exclusively with Anna's person; he does not recognise the Don Giovanni experience; for him, the Don Giovanni phenomenon, as such simply does not exist, its effect leaves him utterly unmarked. Don Giovanni and Don Ottavio are two closed worlds; the one knows nothing of the other. The characteristic feature of Ottavio, of all sentimental heroes, of altering reality according to their desires, finds its greatest expression in this fact.

For Donna Anna, however, the events have far more serious consequences. We have seen that in the D minor section of the first finale, where she sees revenge as her immediate duty, she experiences the total hopelessness of her situation: she is able to live and love only when in inner equilibrium, and the necessary but not sufficient condition for her inner equilibrium is revenge. However, revenge threatens her lover and thus the only human relationship remaining to her that can serve to sustain her existence. It is impossible to resolve the problem of her life harmoniously, every step she takes is unavoidably problematic and gives rise to new conflicts. Anna realizes this with a shock, and, overwhelmed by the feeling of being lost, she is precipitated, with apparently unrestrainable velocity towards the low point of her fate. We saw, however, that Mozart, with relative artistic justification, stops this process momentarily in a rather controversial manner (the B major adagio). Subsequently, she enters Don Giovanni's palace with Ottavio and their challenge is overpowered. Yet their defeat is of a totally different character from what Donna Anna could have been prepared for. They leave the palace not after an heroically fought yet lost struggle, but after a hapless scene of overawed impotence, having attempted a stand that they were personally incapable of carrying out. The essential reality of this defeat is experienced only by Donna Anna. In part she must recognize the terrible truth that not only is there no harmonious solution to her life problem but that they are too weak even to find half-solutions, they are unable to take even difficult steps. She now knows that she had worried for her lover unnecessarily, as he survives the danger unharmed, but not because of his strength or good fortune, but because in spite of his brave stance he is so weak that he simply cannot be a worthy opponent of Don Giovanni, since he is unable even to rise to the real danger of his situation. All the problems and conflicts that formerly seemed to be the tragic yet real problems and conflicts of her life, now suddenly seem illusory, unworthy of mention, just as her whole life now seems unreal. On the other hand, Anna — and she alone among all the characters in the opera — experiences with full intensity, in the bankruptcy of her own life, the functional bankruptcy of the human world, of the world of morals, *vis-à-vis* Don Giovanni. Because of this she is radically different from Donna Elvira. Elvira is consumed by the fever of her own passions and, though lonely, she can roam the world incessantly. Anna experiences the impotence of the entire world in her own impotence, but since she is not willing to give up the demands she makes on the world and on herself, she loses the world as well as herself. Their proximity to death is also of a totally different character. Elvira clings to life desperately as if in a panic, while (and she senses this herself) the vortex of death attracts her. All her thoughts are of life, yet 'death lies at the bottom of every thought'. Anna, however, divorces herself from life more and more consciously; she chooses death. Thus for Donna Anna the defeat of the challenge to Don Giovanni is a truly tragic turn of fate, a total human failure. From this point she begins to descend irreversibly and with accelerating speed towards the low point of her fate. And she reaches that low point here, in the sextet.

The light-bearing D major dims to D minor. It is customary to point out, because of the opening melody, that we are hearing the same D minor intonation that has twice before (in the duet between Donna Anna and Don Ottavio, and in the D minor section of the first finale) appeared in the opera (compare Examples 7 and 32):

Example 46

La - scia, al - - men al - la   mia   pe - na

No longer on the offensive, she does not retain a direct trace of the tone of vengeance; she speaks only of inconsolable, unrelievable grief — 'Sola morte, o mio tesoro, Il mio pianto può finir' — since Bach's time the wish for death to bring relief from the torments of life was never so intensely expressed as here, in a bare 12 bars. The passionately tensed arc, with the ecstatic melisma coming just before its peak, this truly musical 'flower of death', is heard twice:

Example 47

so - - - la mor - te,   so - - - la mor- te.

'death alone', and she pronounces it with such unequivocal exclusiveness that she herself must pause for a moment; for what of Ottavio? Anna now forces herself to a final and cruel reckoning. She feels and knows that she loves Ottavio, and him alone, but she feels even more strongly and knows with greater certainty that all the positive qualities of this love, of this relationship, of her whole life are dwarfed by the experience of universal human impoverishment. Anna cannot and does not want to live in a world where her values cannot be practised. Love is merely an abstract and distant potential that does not afford a handhold in this precipitous fall. The love harmony of the B major adagio in the finale of the first act represented only one moment, the gift of the composer rather than of fate.

Yet now she discovers this weak but still viable tie that binds her to the world, and her voice suddenly softens:

Example 48

o   mio   te - so - - ro,

This is the familiar love melody formula of eighteenth-century opera, that was heard when Anna, in her duet at the beginning of the opera, turned to Ottavio ('mio bene': compare Example 10). The tone is no less honest and candid than it was then. However, then it was reassuring, while here it is resigned. Indeed, it is merely a momentary pause on the final road, a warm, loving glance of farewell. Then the passionate impulse towards death resumes. The vocal part struggles upwards with a romantic, almost Wagnerian intensity, as if demanding the end:

Example 49

il   mio   pian - to   può fi - nir,

And now, at the peak, her strength leaves her, her passion is burned out, the pathetic demand is drowned in a bitter cry:

Example 50

il   mio   pian - - - to   può   fi - nir!

This is the third time that this tearful, chromatic melody appears in Donna Anna's part. It was first heard in the introduction, when the little girl crying inside the heroine was revealed ('gente servi': compare Example 4), then in the quartet, when she sensed the similarity between her tragedy and Donna Elvira's (see Example 23). And now, for the third time, when pathos is again drowned in tears, it is not the little girl that is revealed, but the adult human being, suffering *in extremis*. Donna Anna has arrived at the point in her fate where there is only one, by now fatal, final step to be taken; her only other option is to turn back.

The focus changes again. Donna Elvira is searching for Leporello, who, disguised as Don Giovanni, is still trying to escape from her. The two betrothed do not notice them. This short nine-bar scene serves, of course, as a contrast after the music of Donna Anna, yet this contrast is not as vivid as it is ambiguous. The essence of the new musical material is, of course, ambiguity. This is directly expressed by the following theme:

Example 51

The duality of this theme can be compared, with certain reservations, to the famous melody in *Rigoletto*, where the desperate and tortured sobbing of a human being can be heard beneath the forced laughter:

Example 52

In Mozart, however, in contrast to the cruder and directly affective duality of the scene in Verdi's opera, a much more subtle, and at the same time more universal, symbolic, tragi-comic element is present. This atmosphere is established only slowly in the sextet, and envelops the actors as an increasingly unbreachable ambience. We have seen that the sextet was introduced by the truly tragic intonation of Elvira's scene. This, however, was followed in sharp contrast by Leporello's comic scene. The enharmonic turn led out of the contrasting pair of tragic-comic, but only briefly, allowing Anna's music to plummet to its tragic nadir. But we can also see that the music gains symbolic meaning at this point: for here the eighteenth-century opera has grown artistically and harmoniously into a full world-drama. In the scene which follows the tragi-comic element is expressed overtly in the music for the first time. Earlier this mood of meaningful ambiguities has only been given a veiled expression. The ambiguous, dichotomous theme, in which identification and alienation, mercilessness and compassion, irony and pity are unnaturally juxtaposed, is exclusively found in the figure of Donna Elvira. It expresses not her personality, the different facets of her psyche, but her whole situation, the role she fills in the Don Giovanni drama. The music indicates that Elvira is following her unknown fate blindly, helplessly, at the mercy of a superior power that is toying with her. And in this way the musical drama takes place within the framework of the larger world-drama.

Leporello and Donna Elvira are about to exit from the stage when Zerlina and Masetto block their path. This is the moment of 'recognition', the moment when Don Ottavio, Donna Anna, Masetto and Zerlina have at last found 'Don Giovanni'. The moral world again confronts Don Giovanni. Yes, it confronts Don Giovanni himself — without the quotation marks — not only because they all believe that Leporello is Don Giovanni, not even because their mistake is the work of Don Giovanni. In a certain sense the two couples confront the *real* Don Giovanni only now, when Donna Elvira turns to face them. The human world, the world of the betrayed, is itself split in two. Elvira, twice betrayed, brings to the scene the real Don Giovanni, the Don Giovanni problem, not by her mistake, but by her decision, her choice. In the figures of the four menacing, advancing people and of Elvira begging for forgiveness, a moral, a morally indifferent and an amoral world all confront one another. When Anna, Ottavio, Zerlina and Masetto recognize Elvira, shocked surprise runs through the scene. (This 'running through' is expressed by the sequential entry of *sotto voce* parts.) What shocks them is not that Elvira should be a party to such deceit, but the shock of realizing that this is the kind of world where Elvira is capable of such a thing. Only now does the fact that a world without morals exists, become meaningful to them. In the finale of the first act they had already had a direct confrontation with another world, an alien power had rendered them helpless, but none of them could really account for this experience. This fact, this experience, could be accommodated in many different ways, but its essential nature was impossible to determine. They could interpret the effects the devil has had on them in a number of ways, but the secret of this effect was understood by none; they could not explain it. Now, however, Elvira's role raises in all of them the question with which Hamlet confronts his mother: 'What devil was't/That thus hath cozen'd you at hoodman-blind?' and the unspoken, half-formulated question contains the conjecture: Does such a 'devil' exist? Indeed, does the devil exist at all? At first only Zerlina can sense this in its true essence for she is the only member of the moral world who has actually witnessed the genius of sensuality, thus she is the only one who understands the secret, the profound fatality of Elvira's position. The chromaticity, first heard in Anna and Ottavio's parts when, in the quartet, they sensed their common fate with Elvira's (compare Example 23, or Donna Anna's crying intonation in Examples 4 and 50), which is nothing other than the tragic variation of the ambiguous, tragi-comic violin motif, now appears in Zerlina's vocal part:

Example 53

However, the hazy suspicion of the four people does not as yet constitute recognition, their shocked surprise does not yet weaken their resolve. But this is just the 'tragi-comic transgression', the tragi-comic hubris. The music indicates this clearly, the ambiguous violin motif that until now was associated with Elvira's part only, now accompanies all four. And, indeed, the tragi-comic nature of the scene reaches its zenith in what follows: Donna Anna, Don Ottavio, Zerlina and Masetto pronounce the death sentence on Don Giovanni, without the possibility of appeal. Donna Elvira, in utter humiliation, pleads for Don Giovanni's life, and in their midst, awaiting the outcome of the clash, Leporello trembles. Undoubtedly, this is the most horrible scene in the entire opera. All the 'merely' human characters in the opera — the moral and immoral alike — are struggling and suffering, and all of them are betrayed. The common comedy of the situation becomes directly symbolic; the music, the drama and the stage illustrate in their harmonious entirety, with vivid faithfulness the essence of the Don Giovanni syndrome, the not even intentional but 'natural' betrayal of all men. Cruelly, Mozart makes Elvira clash four times with the others. Don Ottavio is ready to kill 'Don Giovanni', when Leporello, in desperation, reveals his true identity. Leporello is truly paralysed by the fear of death, his terror vividly expressed by the descending, chromatic motif of the wind instruments:

Example 54

cresc.

This intonation, repeated six times, seems like the inverse of the oft-quoted death motif (compare Examples 28, 41 and 44). Mozart portrays the moment of recognition again as the 'unstated point'. Donna Elvira, Donna Anna, Don Ottavio, Zerlina and Masetto are effectively stunned — 'Leporello!' As Hotho puts it: 'Wonderment, shame and pain are expressed by this name, and they are set upon by them alternately.'[41] 'Leporello' — in the moment of recognition, as they utter his name, the dynamics are suddenly deflated, the extraordinary internal agitation is expressed only in the rapid bowing of the first violins. Then the excitement explodes. This contrast is repeated one note higher on the scale. Following this extreme expression of total disorientation the ambiguous, tragi-comic violin motif is repeated: Mozart illustrates, by close identification and from a distance, compassionately and pitilessly, regretfully and ironically, that a superior force is playing with the five actors. They stand bemused, they whisper amongst themselves in stunned incomprehension: 'Stupida (stupido) resto! Che mai sarà?' When in the finale of the first act they confronted Don Giovanni they had felt directly the awesome power of the devil, but they were unable to account for it or explain it, they could not even question it. Now, when Donna Elvira turns to face them, the vague outlines of a question begin to take shape in their minds, but before it can be formulated as a conscious question, they are given a crippling answer which they cannot comprehend. As before when the passionate desire for death and bitter cry signified the nadir of Donna Anna's fate, so now this numb lack of comprehension represents the low point in the opera and, at the same time, the paralysing ineffectiveness of the whole human world.

Now, however, an unexpected turn follows: the first, andante part of the sextet is followed by a second, molto allegro part. This begins in true *opera buffa* style. Leporello slowly recovers, at least sufficiently to voice his confusion. And in doing so, he rouses the others out of their inertia, and unleashes their passions; Donna Anna, Don Ottavio, Donna Elvira, Zerlina and Masetto's outrage erupts with elemental force. This, of course, makes Leporello even more desperate and confused. The situation has a bizarre comic quality. Consider the basic intonation itself: Leporello's voice is comical. Then the outburst of the others is very serious, but it is directed against Don Giovanni, not Leporello. Yet the servant does not understand this, he believes their hostility is meant for him. As their rage against Don Giovanni increases, so does Leporello's anxiety for his own fate. This misunderstanding is comic in itself, but because of the context it becomes a tragic — or at least tragi-comic — situation, and as it deepens and intensifies, the stylistic and atmospheric tension also increase. The scene starts within the framework of the *opera buffa*, but by its inherent dynamics it breaks out of these confines, and the resonance of the tensions and ambiguous moods create the scene's unique style and genre. This comes about when they all suddenly perceive the fatal nature of their situation. And this marks the beginning of another turn in the fate of the human world. There is no logical path from numb incomprehension to transcendental, inspirational self-revelation, but there is a subjective path. When Leporello's confused utterance rouses the others out of their psychic inertia, it impels them unconsciously along this path, and having travelled this path in the intensifying storm of their passions, suddenly all previous incomprehension, surmising and mere suspicion are replaced with an overwhelming certainty: they know they are confronting a demonic force.

The experience of facing the unspeakable, the unthinkable, is faithfully expressed by a change in the music, by the sudden change of the style, of atmosphere discussed above: the *opera buffa* is overthrown, the dynamics plummet, the orchestral accompaniment (upon the tone repetition of the cellos and the contrabasses) is reduced to a minimum, and a paradoxical, horrified awe resounds in the *sotto voce* vocal parts:

Example 55

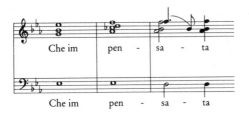

Che im   pen - sa - ta

Che im   pen - sa - ta

as if the shuddering were invoked in its physical reality by the quiet, downward-swooping scales of the violins. Nor is Leporello's fear comical any longer, the chromatic phrase, rising from the depths, recalls the 'death' motif (compare Examples 28, 41 and 44):

Example 56

Mil - le   tor - bi - di   pen - sie - ri

Leporello too is touched by the transcendental experience, and senses for a moment that in Don Giovanni he is threatened by something greater than any immediate danger. When in the finale of the first act his master made a scapegoat of him, or when, together with his master, despairing and beaten, he was surrounded by the opposing camp, Leporello was very frightened. But that fright was purely personal, individual; he was worried about his skin. In the tercet of the second act, however, Leporello has encountered an entirely new experience: he senses that he is not merely involved in dangerous adventures, he is not simply his master's partner in inhumane intrigues, but that he is associated with a power that, for reasons of principle, does not recognize humanity. We have seen that Leporello was already frightened by this in the tercet with Don Giovanni's histrionics, as well as when he heard his own irresponsible laughter; and now, at the sight of even more blatant proof, he is consumed by a real panic. Leporello is undoubtedly still worried above all else for his own skin, yet, following the shock suffered by his opponents, he is increasingly overcome by an 'existential' terror that shakes the foundation of his entire being. Leporello becomes hysterical while the others are merely dumbfounded by the sudden 'insight'. Anna, Ottavio, Elvira, Zerlina and Masetto each keep repeating one note, quietly and in a drawn-out, dreamlike rhythm. Suddenly, a D flat major chord bursts forth from this nightmarish E flat major section; in Abert's words this is the 'sudden outburst of horror'.[42] Now Leporello goes into a state of real shock and cries out desperately to the world, as if it were a final 'recognition': 'in verità'.

But Leporello is not alone. Anna, too, is half-demented, the sound of horror overflows into intense, nearly uncontrolled *coloratura*, beyond the limits of normal expression. Don Giovanni's pursuers, all unable to master their feelings, become completely confused, and the turmoil of confused emotions retards the dramatic development. The beginning theme of the reprise is intoned by Donna Anna and Don Ottavio. In their perturbed consciousness, an energetic variation of Don Ottavio's 'signature-like' scale motif, the momento of a previous, determined but unsuccessful action, develops (compare Example 37, as well as Examples 9, 26, 29, 35 and 45):

Example 57

Mil - le   tor - bi - di   pen - sie - ri

They all adopt this motif, an ominous storm of voices ensues, and Leporello, of course, is frightened once again. The whole process is repeated, beginning with the tragi-comic misunderstanding right through to the anguished horror. But this time they are able to control themselves, the reprise does not lead to renewed confusion as beforehand, but to a grandiose coda. The coda indeed represents elevation: elevation out of the depth into which the human world had fallen at the end of the first andante part of the sextet. The turn of fate, that started when Leporello's utterance roused them from their inertia, reached its crisis at the moment of their 'insight', their intuitive, experiential grasping of the demonic, has now taken a new and final direction. Even though the world of humans may be too weak to combat the devil, it seems strong enough to rebuild its own world out of its ruins, to create a new moral order out of its betrayed and humiliated values. After the earlier experience of paralysis, agitation, hypnosis or confusion, this coda expresses a consolidation, a union of psychic and moral forces unprecedented so far in the opera. The threatening power posed by the offended group in the first finale is dwarfed compared with this totally esoteric uniting of forces. Musically this is expressed principally in the fact that previously the power was manifested by intonation, while here it is manifested by the construction, by the polyphonic organization of the parts. Abert is correct in saying that this style evidences a religious mood. Mozart's musical invention is polysemic. In the eighteenth century the human world can found and build its own humanitarian moral order in the face of Don Giovanni's satanic egoism, consistently, and in the final analysis, only with 'God's help'. Rousseau phrased this problem quite clearly: 'the good man orders his life with regard to all men; the wicked orders for self alone. The latter centres all things on himself; the other measures his radius and remains on the circumference. Thus his place depends on the common centre which is God, and on all the concentric circles which are His creatures. If there is no God, the wicked is right and the good man is nothing but a fool.'[43] It is of great importance that precisely at this point, where the text contains no religious content whatever, Mozart unmistakably illustrates a religious experience. And this is not the reflex-like, conventional prayer of people in trouble, but stems from the most profound religious need. The religious experience that welds all into one lends form to the moral alliance of the 'good', that is people, against the 'evil', or more exactly the morally indifferent devil. At first the alliance is truly united and comprehensive: the first polyphonic section opening the coda contains all the actors' parts. This means no less than the conversion of Donna Elvira and Leporello. Indeed, no matter how ambivalent these two are, no matter how much they are drawn to the demonic power, they cannot transcend their humanity, they cannot themselves become demons. They each accept their humanity in this decisive moment, though on the grounds of different experiences. For Elvira it was the betrayal, for Leporello the imminent danger that proved too much. Elvira had left heaven and chosen the world because of Don Giovanni, and, when he betrayed her, she lost the world as well. Don Giovanni remains for her the only and impossible refuge, she could escape despair only in his presence, either by overwhelming it with her bitter outcry of hatred, or else through hope. In hope she happily believed that Don Giovanni would return to her, since she desired the improbable and wanted to believe it because it was improbable. Thus the essence of Elvira is expressed by happy credulity, for her this was self-realization. But in fact Don Giovanni had again betrayed her, and this time the recognition unmasked not Don Giovanni but Donna Elvira — the absurdity of her being and of her life. The fact is clear as daylight, it is practically blinding, and Elvira is incapable of facing her self-deception any longer. Thus she turns aside, away from her former self, and in one determined move returns to the world and to heaven. In this moment she feels that she has regained her unsullied humanity, and becomes impervious to her own ambivalence. On the other hand from the start, Leporello, as we have seen, wanted to satisfy, with every one of his gestures, the requirements of demonic moral indifference and philistine piety at the same time. This duality surrounded his figure with irresistible though not very lighthearted comicality. His ambivalence gains larger dimensions in the tercet of the second act, when in the uninhibited histrionics of Don Giovanni and his own irresponsible laughter Leporello senses the by now quite natural mocking of everything that is human. This had ensued in the sextet, and through his own action, in so annihilating a manner that he himself had lost his head. Actually it is from the emotional shock suffered by his dreaded enemies that he really understands that in Don Giovanni he is threatened by a danger that is greater than a threat to his life, and incomprehensible within the framework of human existence. And now Leporello takes refuge in and behind the confines of his everyday humanity, like a snail in its shell. He does not want to acknowledge that his life is tied to Don Giovanni's, that he is irresistibly drawn to him. For a moment he feels like a moral person with every right to act on behalf of morality and order. But Mozart's artistic distinction here is also unerring. Leporello has no part in the second polyphonic, a *capella* segment constituting the internal culmination of the movement. The moral greatness granted not just to Donna Anna, Don Ottavio and the simple Zerlina, but even the base Masetto and the errant, self-deluding Donna Elvira, is totally unattainable for him. It may be that Elvira will soon abandon her new conviction, but no subsequent change in the course of her fate can belie the truth of this moment. Leporello, on the other hand, doesn't really comprehend what it is all about. Even with the best of intentions — which he undoubtedly has — he is unable to participate in the restoration of a moral world-order. Still, in the whole of the coda, a new, cathartic experience is born in all the characters, in spite of the differences in the level and intensity of their experiences. If the belief in the primacy of demonic power had paralysed all human energy beforehand, then these people, having in effect taken hold of themselves, now demonstrate with real pathos the validity of their world's moral order.

It has become a commonplace in the academic literature that in the sextet the tragic and comic elements fuse in unequalled perfection. Put more simply we might say that the piece displays through its entire length the various nuances of tragi-comedy. All the way to the coda, the setting of every scene is more or less tragi-comical. This tragi-comic quality expresses what is the most profound problem for the group on the stage of *Don Giovanni*: the human moral order is valid, yet individuals are helpless in the face of Don Giovanni. This is a real and unresolvable contradiction that must somehow be represented artistically and in a complex fashion. We have seen that the first act of the opera illustrates the process of the slow erosion of the unconditionality of Don Giovanni's power, while the validity of the moral order of the world surrounding him gains in stature. This last moment can be faithfully illustrated only in a purely musical mode, and most completely when radically separated from the stage, as, for example, in Don Ottavio's #11. G major aria or in the B major adagio of the first finale. The shifts and fluctuations of emphasis resulting from the concept can be actualized undisturbed only as music-drama, the dramatic interrelating of musical truths and the stage-drama have to be set aside. In the second part of the finale, however, the two worlds have to be confronted directly both in the musical and the dramatic spheres. And since, compositionally, the breaking of Don Giovanni was of real importance to Mozart, he could not place the opposing camp in an overtly tragi-comic light. However, avoiding complex representation exerts its toll, the composition, as we have seen, became heterogeneous. In the second act, following the world-historical precedent of the revolt against Don Giovanni, the intonation of the process of the music-drama is decisively different. Don Giovanni appears more powerful and the world of humanity appears to be more at his mercy than ever. In reality the perspective of Don Giovanni's greatness is consistently retrospective, while the fate of the world of humanity reaches its lowest point, before arching upwards again: Don Giovanni utterly humiliates the moral order, but humanity recreates it. The crisis and turning-point of this process is the subject of the sextet. In the first andante part we see that those characters who in themselves appear tragic, lofty or self-assured are, in reality, no more than Don Giovanni's playthings, and consequently the tragi-comic atmosphere surrounding them increases. In the second molto allegro part, however, the opposite process takes place. The change of tone itself signifies a certain relief. In the first part only the pattern of the situations, the structure of the action, the mechanism of effect are reminiscent of the *opera buffa*; the quality of events and the artistic style are directly symbolic. The symbolic character becomes all-embracing, eventually universal. The second part, on the other hand, takes *opera buffa* 'literally'; with regard to action as well as to style. Leporello's foolish confusion, the emotional outbursts of the confused characters, then Leporello's misunderstanding are tragi-comic not in the symbolic but in the superficial sense, which means that the comic element is greater relative to the preceding part. But, as we have seen, with the moment of 'revelation' a new moral world begins and a new style is born. The transcendental experience of grasping the demonic nature is the way leading out of the sphere of triviality, comicality and tragi-comicality, namely, the style of the *opera buffa*. Even if the characters cannot immediately master this experience, if development is temporarily reversed (reprise!), still the turning-point has been reached. And, indeed, at the second attempt, self-assurance is regained. The coda expresses with uninterrupted pathos the validity of the moral world-order. In Mozart's composition, in the composition of the opera as a whole, the ascension at this point is of decisive significance. There is no better proof of this than that it evolves purely musically, almost without the text; more than this, in spite of the text. We should note that of the 277 bars of music in the sextet, the first part consists of 130 bars, the second of 147; at the same time the first part utilizes 40 lines of text, the second only six, and only to express total confusion:

Leporello and the others:	Mille torbidi pensieri
	Mi s'aggiren per la testa.
Leporello:	Se mi salvo in tal tempesta,
	E un prodigio in verità.
The others:	Che giornata, o stelle, è questa!
	Che impensata novità!

Mozart, in the first part of the sextet develops music-dramatically a sequence of situations that were actually or potentially inherent in the text; in the second part, however, the text is merely reflective, the composer utilizes it merely as sounding material and creates a completely original music-dramatic development through the music. As the breaking of Don Giovanni ensued compositionally, in the finale of the first act, from the concept of the Don Giovanni world-drama, so too in the sextet we see the catharsis of the world of humanity. Value relationships are again re-ordered, human-dramatic problems re-emerge in different relationships, and thus in a new manner. The subsequent structural unity of the opera all the way to the second finale (and now, for the moment, let us disregard the cemetery scene, or provisionally include it with the finale), offers exactly the rephrasing and simultaneously the summation of the problems of life.

Leporello's only thought is to escape from the circle of the offended group. In his #21. G major aria ('Ah, pietà, signori miei') Leporello employs all his powers of persuasion in order to escape. The beginning of the aria indicates that the earlier confused emotionalism of the others made a deep and threatening impression on him:

Example 58

Yet Leporello remembers the clear meaning of the phrase (compare Example 37). He immediately turns it into its opposite, into breathless entreaty:

Example 59

> ah   pie - tà,   pie-tà   di   me,

The energetic variation of Ottavio's signature-like melody here has sunk to its lowest depth in the opera. In this moment Leporello's cowardly whining shows, like a distorting mirror, the understandable, functionally doomed-to-failure attitude of people. At the same time the aria 'puts in its place' Leporello's self-reforming with precision. It becomes clear that this reform is merely the taking of temporary refuge behind philistine mentality. Leporello's first act is to agree with everyone while absolving himself of responsibility. He denounces his master with genuinely heartfelt yet humanly inauthentic moral pathos, he is moved to tears by his own helplessness, and unashamedly makes everyone feel sorry for him. Now unstoppable, vocal explanations follow. We could be forgiven for interpreting this as an outbursting of unabashed histrionics were it not for the frequent seventh jumps, revealing his genuine terror, and were it not that a constantly recurring motif, suggesting stealthy footsteps, indicates that beneath the babbling eagerness lies one tangible thought: escape. Finally, quietly and almost unnoticed, Leporello runs away. Whether he knows it or not, his road can lead him only to Don Giovanni. His ambivalent nature is fatally drawn to him. When he is in revolt against him, whether out of cowardice or because of philistine reservations, he is simply comic. But when he also senses the transcendental danger awaiting him in Don Giovanni, he becomes tragi-comical.

The offended group (Donna Elvira, Don Ottavio, Zerlina and Masetto) are now left by themselves, and Don Ottavio announces that he will seek help from the courts. This is one of the most debated moments of the entire opera, particularly the figure of Don Ottavio. This is what Abert writes:

> That he [Ottavio] wants by all means to hand him [Don Giovanni] over to the courts, has a chilling effect on us, if it does not seem outright comical. Don Giovanni besmirched the honour of his fiancée, and he killed the Commendatore not from ambush but in an honourable duel.

According to the customs of chivalry, authority for punishment is vested not in the civil courts but in the sword of the injured party alone.[44]

This quote represents the common point of view found in the academic literature. It is irresistibly funny when respected twentieth-century scholars unconditionally rise in chorus to defend the validity of the chivalric code, when one of the important functions of the humanism of the modern age has been the critique of these customs, the exposing of their inhumanity. We cannot discuss here the world of the problems associated with the duel, in relation to the ideology and art-history of three centuries. But if we give an overview of the major works on the subject of the Don Giovanni problem from this standpoint, it will be clear that the artistic values attached to duelling and chivalry are all times historical. It is notable that as early as in Tirso da Molina's Don Juan drama, when Prince Ottavio wants to avenge the honour of his betrothed, Isabella, he asks the king's permission to fight Don Juan, and the king denies him. This fact expresses the historical turning point, expressed by Hegel thus: 'the world had settled into public order.'[45] In his lectures on aesthetics Hegel had characterized this state of the world in detail. He pointed out that in it

the moral concept, righteousness, and its reasonable freedom had evolved and became functional already in the form of *lawful* order, so that it is present in externalities as well as in necessity that is by itself motionless — independent of the peculiar individuality and subjectivity of mood and character. . . . Because in the true State the laws, customs, rights . . . are valid in their own *generality* and abstraction as well, and are no longer determined by the accident of individual wishes and particular characteristics . . . substantiality is no longer the *particular* property of one or another *individual*, but is expressed *for and by itself*, on every side, in the smallest detail in a *general and necessary* way. Therefore whatever single individuals are able to accomplish in the area of rightful, moral and lawful action in the interest and the process of the whole, their will and their actualization as well as themselves will still always remain an insignificant matter and mere example compared with the whole. Because their actions always remain the only partial implementation of one individual case, and not its actualization as a generality, in the sense that the action, the case would thus become law or would appear as law. Inversely: it has no significance for individuals as single entities, whether they want it or not, that right and justice should prevail; this is valid according to its existence for an by itself, even though they might not wish it. It is in the interest of the general public that each single individual should be proved to satisfy this and wish it, but the interest of the single individual cannot affect the implementation of the lawful and the moral through the consent of a specific individual — they do not need individual consent — if violated, they are implemented by punishment. Finally, the subordinate position of the singular subject in the developed State is manifested in that each single individual partakes in the whole in a quite defined and always limited manner. . . . For example, punishment for a criminal act is no longer a matter of the heroism and virtue of one and the same subject, but it is segregated into its various phases: the investigation and judging of the facts, the announcement and implementation of the judge's sentence — furthermore, each of the main phases have specially differentiated aspects and the singular individuals actualize only *one* of these. Thus the implementation of the law is not the business of a *single* individual, but is composed of multilateral cooperation and its established order. . . . This exactly is the difference between punishment and revenge. Lawful punishment effectuates the general established law in the face of a criminal act; and it does so according to general forms, through the organs of public authority, the courts and judges whose personal identity is accidental. Revenge can also be just, according to its own self-existence, but it is based on the *subjectivity* of those concerned about the committed deed and visit revenge on the criminal for the injustice committed, on the basis of their own hearts and feelings. . . . Thus, in the orderly State, to mention this as well, the person's external existence is assured, his property is safeguarded, and the person, by and through himself, has authority merely over his own subjective feelings and insight. In a stateless State, however, the security of life and property lies in the individual strength and bravery of the singular subjects; this subject must provide for his own existence and its preservation, and for the preservation of his rights and his belongings.[46]

The subject-matter of Don Giovanni is the irrevocable decline of the heroic age and the genesis of the modern age. At this point in the analysis — in accordance with the composition of the opera — the problem of genesis is of importance to us. First of all, to Mozart, naturally, lawful order does not take the form of 'the moral concept, justice and its rational freedom'. We do not in the least wish to imply that Mozart entertained thoughts on the philosophy of law, but lawful order is undoubtedly an important problem of the life depicted in *Don Giovanni*. The opera does not depict a settled world, but the turning-point when a world without the rule of law gives way to the world of lawful order. Consequently, lawful order is only partly evolved, it proves itself to be partly functional and partly non-functional, it is in part present and in part absent as a 'motionless inevitability'. Don Giovanni is not simply an individual who does not take part in this order, who will not subject himself to it; he is the last symbolic hero of the 'Stateless State', the world without lawful order, not a rebel of the new world, but the consistent representative of the old. At the same time the world surrounding Don Giovanni has indeed changed, and in the new world lawful order is present with 'motionless inevitability', and is valid in its universality. Viewed from this world, Don Giovanni can be perceived only as a criminal of demonic power, and his punishment in this life can be entrusted to God as well as to the law courts, that is, to general authority. The conflict in the *theater mundi* of *Don Giovanni* is primarily the clash of values.

Don Ottavio's #22. B major aria ('Il mio tesoro intanto') consists of two recurring parts, the musical material of which has different moods. The one is intimate and nobly sentimental, the tone we have already heard in the #11. G major aria. The essential identity of the two intonations is confirmed by a motif relationship as well (compare Examples 25 and 26). In both, Ottavio expresses the responsibility he feels for the inner peace of his betrothed, and his anxious love. In the beauty of this richly flowering *cantilena* — a beauty that is significant as a view of the world — the value of romantic love is manifested anew in its full worth.

The martial music of the second part of the aria is in sharp contrast. Ottavio appears in the full consciousness and pathos of the meting out of justice. This is most tellingly expressed by the dynamic and intonational effects of the orchestral material. The vocal line also loses its melodious character: it becomes quite primitive, and achieves its effect mainly in its rhythmic pulse. The more energetic variation of Ottavio's signature-like scale motif reappears (see Example 37):

Example 60

nun - zio vogl'io - tor - nar,

Jahn has already pointed out that the vocal line in the second part of the aria is inferior to that in the first part.[47] In fact the musical quality of the entire second part is problematic. It is, in every detail, conventional and impersonal. Abert also admits that the new feeling is not expressed with as much power of conviction as the former, as he puts it: 'but this indeed fits the man's character splendidly'.[48] Abert does not draw conceptional and aesthetic conclusions from the acclaimed musical value of the #11. G major aria, nor from the mediocre musical quality of the second part of the #22. B major aria. Yet in both instances there is more involved than an authentic 'characterization'. We have already tried to show this in connection with Don Ottavio's first aria. In the second aria, of course, a directly psychological reference is made to the fact that Ottavio's is not a 'bellicose nature', he is not really a person of strength, of grand stature. However, here we are not dealing merely with psychology. Ottavio has no psychic need to punish Don Giovanni. On the one hand, he feels moral outrage, on the other, he is fulfilling his duty as a citizen. And neither needs a show of strength; moral rectitude is sufficient. Vengefulness, however, is completely absent from Ottavio, not only from his psychological make-up, but also from his world-view. In Mozart's opera vengeance belongs to the age of heroes: it is the gesture of the Commendatore and of Don Giovanni. Donna Anna, who experiences the transition from one age to another through her personal fate, relates to vengeance, as we have seen, in a totally ambivalent manner throughout the opera, while Don Ottavio is totally indifferent to it. Ottavio's role in the music-drama is to unmask Don Giovanni and ensure that he is brought to justice; that is, to love Donna Anna in a totally moral manner. Mozart develops his character throughout the opera in this spirit, with the exception of this episode. Ottavio cannot feel the experience of punishment intensely. This seems to be born out by the empty pathos, the inner lack of credibility of the second part of the B major aria. If, however, it is not a matter of lack of invention and artistic inconsistency in the primitive sense, but of conscious effect, then we must confront the same problems as those in Donna Anna's #10. D major aria. On the one hand, Mozart reveals the internal lack of authenticity of a human manifestation directly, through the inauthentic quality of the music; on the other hand, since he phrases this lack of authenticity not through character, but through quality, the original intonation disappears at the sounding of the intonations, and the interpretation creates the illusion of unconditionally authentic pathos. This 'negative' reinforcement of the basic character of the figure creates unresolvable aesthetic problems and tensions in every way. As if the composer had felt this himself, the return passage, leading to the initial musical material of the aria through the *coloratura* and the sentimental chromaticism, rewards us with the joyous experience of natural, liberating self-expression. And more so, since due to the repetition, the aria ends with the material of the second part, so that the reprise is played again briefly but meaningfully in the orchestral postlude. The desire to exact punishment personally is not only foreign to Ottavio's figure and personality, but the figure of a personally punitive Don Ottavio has no place in the concept of the whole opera. No matter what artistic intention underlies the bellicose musical material of the B major aria, the result, the aria itself, is still seriously problematic.

Don Giovanni and Leporello meet each other again in the cemetery of Sevilla, and in a high mood the nobleman recounts his adventures to his servant. But suddenly a ghostly voice is heard whose ten bars are not simply extremely effective, but have great compositional and conceptual significance. Their significance actually lies 'only' in the fact that, at this moment in the opera, this voice is heard at all. This has at least three very important meanings. First of all, it becomes perfectly evident that no matter how much we have become absorbed in the struggle between the world of man and the demon of sensuality, there does exist another power, a third factor, that is also beyond the world of man, that is the denial of all sensuality: the Spirit. Thus the voice of the totally unknown is heard. Yet this totally unknown voice has a wholly familiar ring. The second meaning of the voice is illuminated by the experience of this recognition. We have said in connection with the introduction to the opera that the drama begins with the dual gesture of transcending the confines of the individual and the metaphysical worlds: Don Giovanni enters the stage at the moment when his demonic power is broken, and he deprives the Commendatore of his individual life, delivering him to the world of the spirits, Don Giovanni had unwittingly created his own invincible adversary. Yet he cannot comprehend this even in the moment of confrontation, because sensuality does not recognise the spiritual, thus the voice says nothing to him. Only the audience relates it to the introduction, which is its meaning. What is more, the audience relates the warning even further back, to the overture, thus illuminating that which is utterly unknown to Don Giovanni, namely the fact that the killing of the Commendatore is merely a *casus belli*, his transfiguration merely an implement of the 'perturbed spirit'. The apparition whose appearance and vanishing we witnessed in the slow introduction of the overture, the spirit that appeared and then withdrew, to let the firstborn of the world of the sensual, living his own life, collide with it spontaneously and unknowing, to put himself at its mercy, as if falling into a trap; the spirit that had decided the outcome of the drama before it began, now appears in concrete, dramatic form, to wreak vengeance; not for the death of the Commendatore, not for the honour of women, not for villified humanity, but because the sensuality denied by him is *ipso facto* sinful for him. Thus when the ghostly warning is sounded in the cemetery, the dual circles of the individual, worldly and the metaphysical drama are again linked together, it becomes clear — and this is the third meaning of the sounding of the voice — that *Don Giovanni* is a universal drama in a dual sense. The pivotal events between the heroic age and the modern world take place within the framework of the historic struggle between the spirit and sensuality. Some collapse in this about-turn, some survive it, but in actuality only lawful order can implement it. After the sextet the actors may sum up their fate, but there remains nothing more for them to do. Further action is the business of the courts. Here, however, the Spirit intervenes, in order to bring the metaphysical-historical drama to fulfilment. The Spirit does not implement that which humans are too weak to do, the drama that now begins is not simply the extension of what has taken place so far. Institutionalized public order could handle even a Don Giovanni. But in the meanwhile a drama has been developing and has taken place in another dimension. Thus at the moment the Spirit intervenes, Don Giovanni is objectively already a loser, his power is exhausted. It is part of the essence of the composition and its general concept that the meeting between Don Giovanni and the Spirit takes place at this very moment.

Don Giovanni, however, as we have said before, knows nothing of this, he thinks it's just a prank and so he does not comprehend the voice at all; he thinks the situation is perfectly normal. Leporello, on the other hand, is horribly frightened. Consequently it is he, and not the supposed prankster or the statue who becomes the ready object for Don Giovanni. At this point the relationship that was discussed in connection with the #15. G major duet that starts the second act is fully revealed: in Leporello's view Don Giovanni is not a seductive sensual genius, but a man-breaking force exploiting the helplessness of the other; it follows from the unconditional nature of Don Giovanni's egotism that without eroticism and sensual idealization, it demands maximal exploitation and reduces the other, to a mere implement — to Don Giovanni, Leporello is no more than an object. This is shown with brutal directness in the scene. It is not coincidental that the *opera buffa* intonation reappears. Don Giovanni forces his servant to invite the stone statue to dinner on his behalf. Of course, Leporello objects vehemently, but his master threatens to kill him. The #24. E major duet is born of this situation ('O statua gentilissima'). Thus the style is *opera buffa*, only the seventh jumps in Leporello's part reveal the genuine terror. The musical process throughout the shades of comical, tragi-comical and threatening moods, is proportionate and unbroken. At the first attempt, Leporello is unable to carry out his task. The second attempt is put into even more critical light by the E major—B major transposition. And Leporello withdraws again. Now Don Giovanni's voice rings out in a truly ominous tone ('mori, mori), and the hapless servant senses the imminent threat to his life. At last, at the third attempt, with a final effort, he conveys the invitation in an apparently unrestrained *buffa* voice that nevertheless reveals his inner turmoil. And then the statue nods. The simplicity with which Mozart changes the everyday, cowardly, near-comic voice of fear into the manifestation of almost superhuman terror is admirable. Leporello cannot help but be aware at a closer proximity of the danger, the immeasurable threat, that he had on two occasions before only suspected. Don Giovanni, on the other hand, has not seen the statue nod, he does not understand the change in Leporello's voice, and continues impatiently in the merciless *opera buffa* tone. The servant, nearly transfixed, enacts for him the statue's reply — and it again nods its head. The orchestra echoes the gesture directly. By now Don Giovanni had also witnessed the manifestation. Aghast, he repeats with Leporello the servant's earlier improbable account. The orchestra again recalls the statue's gesture, but this time there is no reply. Simultaneously, the orchestral interrupted cadence, the E major—C major shift signals a definitive turn. This is, absolutely, the moment of enlightenment for Don Giovanni, though certainly not in an intellectual sense. As we have already seen, in the introduction, in the presence of the Commendatore's dead body, a new experience had taken hold of him, and his voice had then revealed a hidden sensation. The unconditionality of his power had been broken by Donna Anna, and from that moment on all events have been ordered into an interrelationship that is alien and incomprehensible for him, although it affects the foundation of his existence. Later on, in the tercet of the second act, the emphatically retrospective presentation of the maximal manifestation of the erotic genius also indicated a premonition of this self-same change in his fate. The crisis-ridden atmosphere of Don Giovanni's life, the unconscious experiencing of the crisis, are most acutely expressed by the E major—C major shift within the tercet. Now, at the sight of the statue nodding its head, Don Giovanni again senses the mysterious connection between the fiascos that have pursued him relentlessly from the outset of the action. It must be emphasized that we are not speaking of a conscious apprehension, but merely of an indefinable instinct that every event is laying siege to the foundation of his being, his existence, his survival. It is due to this feeling that in his reply his own fatal essence is unintentionally expressed. His figure, his voice, suddenly rise far above the framework of the *opera buffa*, and the invitation to dine with him directed at the statue is entered in Don Giovanni's representative, almost heroic style. The statue's answer is affirmative. The E note, which has sounded in the *basso* of the Commendatore and in the voice of the horns, is, in its suppressed emphasis (*sforzato*), like a sober but fearsome final warning. Leporello now understands and experiences the danger he has feared so much, in different places and for different reasons, ever since the tercet. Even Don Giovanni is overcome by a premonition of evil, and for the first time since the introduction anxiety can be heard in his voice. But the scene was too improbable to be truly credible and to be of consequence. Leporello's apocalyptic terror collapses into cowardly fear in a matter of moments, and slowly Don Giovanni's anxiety dissolves as well. Their voices meet in the style of the *opera buffa* again, although more excited and disturbed than before. The duet ends in a driven and depressed state of mind, although still in the character of *opera buffa*. Don Giovanni and Leporello depart in a near flight, towards catastrophe.

We have stated earlier that the structural unity of the opera following the sextet offers a restatement, a summarizing of the problems of existence. The scene of Donna Anna and Don Ottavio, inserted between the cemetery scene and the finale, belongs in essence to this structural unit, while the cemetery scene is connected directly to the finale. This dramaturgical 'cross-stitching' is, however, fully justified. This solution is fortunate not merely from the viewpoint of the effect mechanism, of articulation, but also because it expresses compositionally the preferred significance of Donna Anna's internal drama within the opera. Don Ottavio informs his betrothed that he has done his duty, and Don Giovanni will shortly receive his punishment. Yet Anna is still thinking of her dead father. Ottavio consoles her, he protests his love; but this offends Anna in her grief. The rejection, in turn, hurts Ottavio, who calls her cruel. His reproach shakes Anna, and the #25. *recitativo* and F major aria stem from her state of mind ('Crudele? Ah nò, mio bene!'; 'Non mi dir'). Anna's despair is voiced following definite forte chords: 'crudele!'. Immediately, her voice softens 'Ah nò, mio bene!'. In a mere three bars, another Donna Anna reveals

herself different from the one we first met in her earlier protestation, in
the first part of the sextet. Then Donna Anna was literally 'wilting
towards her grave'. For Ottavio she only had a loving but sorrowful glance
of farewell (see Example 51). But in the second part of the sextet she
undergoes a full catharsis. As we have seen, she has perceived, in the
bankruptcy of her own life, the bankruptcy of the entire human world.
The recognition that they were facing a demonic power, and not an
ordinary individual, did, however, restore her self-esteem to some extent.
From this religious—moral experience she was able to gain the strength
that will restore her faith in humanity, in herself and, not least, in the
human validity of her life-problems. No matter how difficult it may be to
resolve these problems, at least they are the tangible problems of a human
life, not the problems that cannot be expressed in an illusory life. Donna
Anna had regained herself and the world, with all its tormenting conflicts
and intermittently reawakened hopes. Thus for her, there is a way back
from the depth of her fate. In this scene we are not witnessing a forlorn
Anna, but one struggling with the overwhelming conflict of her life. The
outburst and the softening in response to Ottavio's accusation make it
immediately clear that a death-wish no longer holds sway over her, that
her passions are again turned towards human relations. Her hurt agitation,
an appeasing gentleness reveal her love. And now the orchestra plays a
nobly sentimental melody reminiscent of Belmonte's E flat major aria
from *The Abduction*, which will become the main theme of the first part
of the aria:

Example 61

Critics of *Don Giovanni* often ask the question: Does Donna Anna really
love her fiancé? This melody stands as an answer in itself. Mozart's true
love-melody is the central musical idea within the first, *larghetto* part of
the *recitativo* and the aria. It sets the basic mood of the scene and reveals
the true state of Anna's emotions. Yet her love is not unclouded, it is
marked by mourning, the unresolvable problem of her emotional ties to
her father. We have seen that, with the death of her father, one of Anna's
fundamental emotional anchors was left without its object, thus the inner

harmony of her personality was upset. In order to restore it she must build and rearrange her whole life on new foundations. She relives within herself the entire collapse of her former, disrupted life. In the meantime, she is continually surrounded by Ottavio's love, which assures her, as she knows, of the only genuine orientation for her life. Yet she is unable to grasp it. As she is losing her world, herself, so she is losing her love as well. (The B major adagio in the first finale is a lonely episode in this linear fall.) But when she regains her world and herself, her love is rekindled. It seems that Ottavio's love was not without effect after all, even though it did not directly help his loved one. This new loving tone is, however, unimaginable without Ottavio's emotional and musical world. If in the past the voice of love has occasionally broken through the voice of mourning, now the voice of mourning can still occasionally break through the voice of love. The first section of the first part of the aria sings unequivocally of the feeling of love. Beginning with the quoted introductory melody, the emotional mood of the music is unchallenged, and in the end the vocal part blooms with as much happiness as in the B major adagio of the first finale:

Example 62

Anna's voice, however, is becoming increasingly sorrowful and filled with pain in the second section, after the introduction of the second theme. She feels, she knows, that she has not yet completely assimilated the events, that she has not yet regained her inner equilibrium, thus she is not yet able to love Ottavio in a manner befitting them and their relationship. As if afraid to hurt her fiancé with her sadness, she returns to the liberating musical mood of love, but she cannot defy the true feelings of her heart: her voice becomes increasingly sorrowful, so that the music of love itself darkens, and Anna never gets as far as the second theme. The feeling of sorrow, the tragic tension remain unresolved, and musically the first part of the aria remains unresolved too.

Here, however, a strange twist takes place. In the second *allegretto moderato* part of the aria, the voice of hope, of faith in imminent happiness, is heard, quietly at first but with increasingly irresistible power. The release in the voice, the enthused and passionate music are expressing something we might call, using Thomas Mann's expression, *Der Wille zum Glück* (the will to happiness). The demand for and the promise of the fulfilment of love speaks from this music. Not, of course, in the manner of Zerlina, not in direct erotic fulfilment, but in a human relationship, that Anna now realises will be the real foundation of her life.

The opera's finale begins with Don Giovanni's last supper. Kierkegaard's interpretation of this scene goes straight to the heart of the matter:

> As far as the banquet scene is concerned, this may indeed be regarded as a lyric moment, and the feast's intoxicating liqueurs, the foaming wine, the festal strains of distant music, everything combines to intensify Don Juan's mood, as his own festivity casts an enhanced illumination over the whole enjoyment, an enjoyment so powerful in its effect that even Leporello is transfigured in this opulent moment which marks the last smile of gladness, the last farewell to pleasure. On the other hand, it is more a situation than a sheerly lyrical moment. This, naturally, is not because there is eating and drinking in the scene, for that in itself is very inadequate regarded as a situation. Pursued by the whole world, the victorious Don Giovanni has now no refuge other than a small, secluded room. It is at the highest point of life's seesaw that once again, for lack of lusty companionship, he excites every lust of life in his own breast. If *Don Giovanni* were a drama, then this inner unrest in the situation would need to be made as brief as possible. On the other hand, it is right in opera that the situation should be prolonged, glorified by every possible exuberance, which only sounds the wilder, because for the spectators it reverberates from the abyss over which Don Giovanni is poised.[49]

Donna Elvira bursts into this opulent, final, and hence far more intensified mood. She claims that she has come to convert Don Giovanni, but her boundless passion arouses the suspicion that she wants to recover him for herself, not for morality. Soon it becomes clear that the basic turn of her vocal part hides the now familiar *tradimento* motif:[50]

Example 63

And then, with sudden passion, blossoms the melody:

Example 64

While in the libretto Donna Elvira is saying she feels pity, mercy, regret, the music is saying 'I love you'. And this erotic love, stripped of all moral content, indeed, morally totally indifferent, is even more blatantly exposed a few moments later when, while condemning his sinful lifestyle, the word 'life' flourishes unintended with the previous turn:

Example 65

In this scene we can see that Donna Elvira lacks sincerity. She wants to make everyone — including herself! — believe that she is acting in the name of morality, when in fact she is spurred on by the same passion she displayed at the beginning of the opera, when she first appeared on the stage. The internal compromise that she made following the sextet, illustrated by the #23. *recitativo* and E flat major aria, can now be seen in her acute yet not admitted, painfully shameful crisis.

Don Giovanni reacts to Elvira's behaviour in the only way possible: with total lack of comprehension. It is not cynicism when he tells her he does not understand what it is she wants of him, what she wishes him to do, that he is astonished, and finally that makes him kneel before her as she kneels before him. Objectively, this gesture is quite as humiliating as the comedy of the tercet. But then Elvira did not recognise it as mockery, because she was longing for the improbable. Now, of course, she can see the mockery and she wildly reproaches Don Giovanni. He, however, does not, cannot, understand her reproach, as, subjectively, he did not intend to mock Elvira, but merely to express his lack of understanding. At this moment, more than anywhere else in the opera, the moral indifference of his character is most clearly expressed. For Don Giovanni, the significance of Elvira's behaviour is simply incomprehensible. Nevertheless, although the unfortunate woman's words make no sense to him, he knows the tone perfectly and he immediately attunes to it.

In discussing this scene, Abert correctly points out the affinity between Donna Elvira and Don Giovanni: 'Nowhere in the opera does their inner affinity, with its elemental nature, come to the surface so clearly; it is as if a piece of his own being had risen against him once more.'[51] It is precisely due to this fact, of course, that Don Giovanni fails totally to understand Elvira, while, at the same time their inner affinity exposes Donna Elvira as a woman who cannot keep faith with herself, and we see her in an increasingly unfavourable light. Don Giovanni's degrading invitation to Donna Elvira that she should join him at the table fulfils Donna Elvira's hapless fate precisely in its spontaneously vulgar, unreflectingly humiliating, truly natural essence. No matter how horrible, for Don Giovanni this is the only possible response to her conduct. Donna Elvira has no foundations from which to convert Don Giovanni. For essentially she too is amoral, the missionary role is mere self-deception, the device of last resort for the reconquest of her lost love; every note of her voice is fired by sensuous passion. Thus it is wholly fitting that Don Giovanni's final serenade to life should develop from her music:

> *Vivan le femmine!*
> *Viva il buon vino!*
> *Sostegno e gloria*
> *D'umanita!*

The toast takes us into the intonational world of the *Gassenhauer*, the street song. This lyric moment refers to a decadent variation of the 'champagne' aria, it is its cruder reproduction. The energy and intensity of the expression are not diminished, but its character is coarser and more primitive. The decadence of Don Giovanni's life is evident not only in his relationship with Leporello, but in its universal sense as well. The brutality expressed in Don Giovanni's toast to life is so great that both Donna Elvira and Leporello turn against Don Giovanni in disgust. This is the third time that they revolt against him after some critical moments in the tercet, their vocal parts linking in the *tradimento* motif:[52]

Example 66

Don Giovanni's toast now becomes increasingly unrestrained, and Donna Elvira's situation increasingly untenable, as she becomes more and more the object of his mockery.

Elvira's proud and Leporello's vulgar outrage are, in this moment, far more pitiful than touching. Don Giovanni remains true to himself, he is doing no more than living his life consistently, without reflection. And they, who have been flirting with the devil, who were irresistibly attracted to his lifestyle, now turn their back on him consciously, repudiate him, because they are unable to go along with him. Don Giovanni has indeed betrayed them, but they are least justified in reproaching him. Don Giovanni's humiliating treatment of her justly fulfils Elvira's fate. The unhappy woman is eventually unable to endure the humiliation and flees in despair. Her horrified scream is heard from outside. Don Giovanni sends Leporello to see what has happened. The servant too cries out in terror. The orchestra hovers on the threshold of D minor tonality. But with a sudden twist it avoids this key, and a final, ominous, *buffa* episode between master and servant follows in F major.

Leporello reports that the statue is standing outside. Don Giovanni, of course, does not believe him, but he can no longer talk to Leporello, who is hiding under the table in panic. Now the statue of the Commendatore enters. Mörike writes: 'Now follows the lengthy, terrifying dialogue that carries even the most sober soul to the utter limits of human imagination or even beyond it, until we seem to see and hear that which cannot be grasped by our senses, and something at the depth of our souls, we feel, keeps flinging us from one extreme to the other.' The theme we are already familiar with from the slow introduction to the overture sounds in the orchestra. The identification is now accomplished: the Spirit, the absolute denial of sensuality, is confronting the firstborn of the realm of sensuality, the erotic genius.

In the first andante part of the scene the two metaphysical forces circle one another, as if sizing each other up from every angle. Their voices are worthy of each other. Mörike aptly characterizes the essence of the scene: 'The immortal voice of the dead Commendatore, unaccustomed to human speech, reluctantly speaks once more.' But in Don Giovanni's voice too we hear a dignity, force and final soberness resonating unheard before from him throughout the course of the opera. The feeling emanated from the voice of the Spirit is completely alien to this world, and Mozart expresses it with inordinate acuteness at this point. When the Spirit rejects the proffered worldly nourishment, its vocal part ranges over all twelve chromatic notes in eight bars:

Example 67

In the musical world of Viennese classicism this effect is extremely bizarre. Mörike is quite right when he writes: 'with what extraordinary horror does his voice creep up and down, irregularly, over the rungs of a ladder woven out of air.' Mozart also weaves the voice of Leporello into the scene, with the *buffo* bass of the servant sometimes rumbling below the ghastly dialogue, sometimes interrupting it. This, however, is a totally strange, one might say apocalyptic *buffo* style. We have earlier heard this voice in the tercet, the sextet and the duet of the cemetery scene. Now Leporello experiences in all its burgeoning intensity the danger he has feared so much.

Don Giovanni, on the other hand, knows no fear at all. His voice soars with quiet dignity, with determination; it soars with a near romantic intensity previously unheard in the opera. It is as if the scene is reproducing the Commendatore—Don Giovanni—Leporello scene of the introduction but on a higher plane. Indeed, the metaphysical struggle is also continued in the historic tone of chivalry. The duel between spirit and sensuality is not depicted here with the abstraction of morality. These are no abstractions but real life-forces, and have been known as such for centuries. The stone statue and Don Giovanni are not mere abstract principles but living symbols. The situation is slowly becoming simplified, the subject of the conflict narrows to the invitation and its acceptance. Both vocal parts are honed down to their essence. The voice of the Spirit is a terse declamation, while Don Giovanni is emphatically cavalier in style. In the end, Don Giovanni's chivalrous, historical voice resounds in all its splendour:

Example 68

Ho fer   mo il co - re in pet - to,   non ho ti - mor;   ver - rò!

This section is the farewell to the heroic age. In like manner, the same intonation will be heard a century later from the lips of Sir John Falstaff, a comic, anachronistic knight bidding farewell to the age of heroes:

Example 69

Al - lor - scom-pa-ri   rà   la ve - ra   vi - ri - li - tà   dal mon-do.

The conflict reaches its climax. Its tempo quickens (*più stretto*), the rejoinders become shorter. Unmistakably, the ascending passages of the cellos and basses evoke the duel in the introduction, completing the metaphysical circle of the Don Giovanni drama. The scene is now simply that of Don Giovanni and the Spirit mutually denying one another. Neither does more than complete his course, express his own essence in a wholly consistent manner. It is the clash between a 'yes' and a 'no', and they make sense only in the context of their relationship. By themselves neither can lay claim to objective truth. The Spirit thrusts Don Giovanni into hell, but in doing so it too no longer has a place in the world. Both disappear in the final catastrophe. With the resolution of the metaphysical drama the conflict between sensuality and spirit has lost its meaning. The realms of sensuality and of the spirit are annihilated simultaneously, so that a unified human world-order can rise to take the place of a divided world.

Like a light breeze that blows away irritating smoke, the infernal A minor is now abruptly relieved by a liberating G major. The world of men, the characters in the opera and the law officers appear. The certainty of success resounds in the voices of Donna Elvira, Don Ottavio, Zerlina and Masetto, as if saying: 'Now show your power!' In defending the unconditionally victorious civic order Donna Anna is also liberated, she can breathe freely again. At this point the text only hopes for the delivery of justice ('Solo mirandolo Stretto in catene, Alle mie pene Calma darò'), but the music already speaks of true consolation, of finding oneself. The softened melodics of the orchestral accompaniment which gently rocks the simple vocal part, is none other than the major variation of Donna Anna's G minor melody when she was worrying about Ottavio in the first finale (see Example 34):

Example 70

This reference accurately expresses the fact that in the defence of lawful order Donna Anna is at last able to bid farewell with relief, to a whole world, to her own past and to that of humanity. This is the first time in the history of the opera that 'intimacy protected by authority' appears with a positive accent, even if its nature is restricted.

Leporello recounts his master's end and the actors once again are confronted with transcendence, and shudder in the face of the unspeakable ('Ah, certo è l'ombra Che l'incontrò'). This last mystical experience constitutes a personal turning point only for Donna Anna, her vocal part again leads into a painful yet liberating chromatic passage, like crying (see Examples 4 and 23):

Example 71

The ending of this *allegro assai* section, in fact, is an answer to the ending of the first part of the sextet. They have now received the final answer to the question that then had weighed so heavily on their consciousness. We are, of course, not speaking of conscious questions and answers. Fact has answered fact, power replied to power. Previously they have experienced the upsetting of their equilibrium, now they experience its restoration. It is in this moment that the Don Giovanni-drama becomes a part of the past for them. Donna Anna, who is now stepping into a new and fulfilling life, takes her leave with some regrets. But these are not directed towards Don Giovanni, but to her father, whom she has now lost for ever. The resolution of a problem is, in some sense, always a loss.

Don Ottavio can no longer see any obstacles to the fulfilment of their love, but Donna Anna wants to observe a year of strict mourning. The critics of *Don Giovanni* who, in analysing the music, generally dismiss the text lightly and consciously, usually refer to this as the decisive argument to prove the superficiality of the relationship between Donna Anna and Don Ottavio. However, here, if anywhere, the music and the text have conflicting messages. This G major *larghetto* is one of the most beautiful, most brilliant love *cantilenas* in Mozart. The music knows nothing of a year of mourning, nor of mourning at all; it knows of no delay, it is fulfilment itself. The melodics of the unbroken, intertwined tenor and soprano voices, sometimes following each other, sometimes melting into one another, are like a distillate of the beautiful music of Don Ottavio and Donna Anna, the musical summarizing of their true relationship. Indeed, 'this is the voice of a world beyond Don Giovanni'. The emphasis here is on this past; on a world lacking the greatness and heroism of Don Giovanni, yet one which can be complete and human in itself. This G major *larghetto* is the pure, unequivocal variation of the B major adagio in the finale to the first act, only now, after Don Giovanni has been destroyed it is authentic and free of problems from a dramaturgical point of view as well. It proves that real love does exist, can be achieved even after the demise of sensual genius.

Only for Donna Elvira is love dead. Nothing exists for her. When we last see her, at the beginning of the finale, her existence has become humanly absurd. Her fate is not tragic; essentially, she collapsed at one point and she is no longer able to accept her fate. Her decision to enter a convent is not a conventional gesture, but is symbolic in the deepest sense. The rest of her life will be spent brooding, tossed between moral and religious ecstasy and the memory of carnal love. No one has ever left Mozart's stage so bereft of hope. But the composer has no pity for her, he denies her even the glory of personally expressed pathos. Donna Elvira has let herself down and after her dramatic fiasco she is reduced in the hierarchy of character as well, and her entering the convent is announced by Zerlina and Masetto in *opera buffa* style.

The fate of the peasant couple has finally reached a haven; and Leporello is free to find a new and better master.

Now only the D major presto follows, summing up the opera's moral. And contrary to nearly all of the literature on the subject of *Don Giovanni*, we are convinced, from analysing the music, that Mozart is depicting the 'festive hour of the everyday' without distancing himself, in an unconditionally affirmative manner.

The final presto part of the finale to *Don Giovanni* is the 'festive hour of the everyday'. As a continuation of the second part, or the coda to the sextet, the moral order, the lawful order, here becomes once and for all omnipotent, and not only as an institution, for it is authenticated within the individuals. The new bourgeois world demonstrates its validity for the first time in full consciousness. If the voices of the actors are shaken, this is not for compassion for the fallen devil, but due to the knowledge that order has been born of catastrophe, out of the collapse and imperilment of the world. They have all been participants in a tragic yet uplifting experience. Dynamic contrasts, the monotony of the melody, then the slow opening-up of the melodics illustrate accurately the touching yet increasingly joyful celebration. An almost timeless moment of hymnic enthusiasm is apparent in the four bars where, over the third and fourth chords of winds and strings, resting on the B pedal-point, the passage of the violins descends. Mozart voices the transcendental experience of being moved by the affirmation of justice for the second time after *The Abduction*:

Example 72

But after this high point of transfiguration the memory of tragedy wells up once more, and the vocal parts of Donna Anna, Don Ottavio, Donna Elvira and Zerlina express the experience of crying, of mourning, descending chromatically for 12 bars (see Examples 4, 23, 52, 71):

Example 73

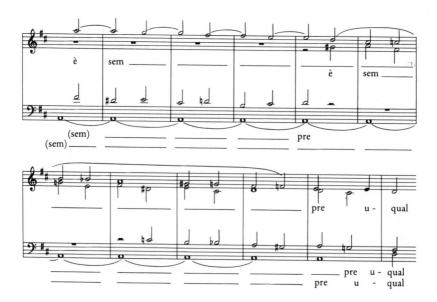

At this moment they all express the knowledge that their world has collapsed and another has taken its place, even though the collapse has nearly destroyed them as well. There is no one who has not been hurt or given wounds in the process. Everyone has something to mourn and bewail, something to remember for a moment with pain, before greeting a more humane world with a much more unrestrained joy, even though they will not really feel at home in it. And we must not forget the playful violin-figure that is nearly always present in moments of happiness as of mourning as well:

Example 74

This is a small but very revealing sign of a new feeling for life that sounds through every crisis in this final presto, and is heard with worshipful seriousness in the vocal parts only.

Don Giovanni is a unique masterpiece in the repertoire of both drama and opera, the sole encompassing historical masterpiece of the eighteenth century. As such, it necessarily annihilates the genre that serves as its foundation, the contemporary opera, out of whose potentialities it creates a totally unique form that is barely able to withstand its own internal tensions. It is no accident that its unique significance becomes evident for the first time when the relationship of modern life and drama enters into consciousness. We are thinking of the famous exchange of letters on this subject between Goethe and Schiller. On one occasion, Schiller wrote to Goethe:

> I was always hopeful that a nobler form of tragedy would evolve from the opera, as it once evolved from the chorals of the ancestral Bacchus-festival. Opera is free of all servile imitations of nature; this way the ideal could steal onto the stage. With the power of music and the freer, more harmonic excitation of sensuality, opera prepares the temperament for accepting the nobler sentiments. Here free play becomes manifest even in pathos, because it is accompanied by music; and the element of wonder, that is here tolerated, can render us indifferent toward the mere subject.[53]

Goethe, with equally profound understanding of the problem and for the works of Mozart, replied:

> You could have seen your hope regarding opera totally fulfilled recently in *Don Giovanni*, pity, however, that this opera is a completely isolated phenomenon, and with the death of Mozart all hopes for something similar have come to nothing.[54]

NOTES

1 Kierkegaard, *Either/Or*, vol. I (Princeton University Press, Princeton, N.J.), pp. 59—60.
2 Abert, *W. A. Mozart*, vol. II (VEB Breitkopf & Härtel Musikverlag, Leipzig, 1956), p. 386.
3 Hotho, *Vorstudien für Leben und Kunst* (Stuttgart und Tübingen, 1835), p. 92.
4 Abert, *Mozart*, p. 395.
5 Kierkegaard, *Either/Or*, p. 123.
6 Abert, *Mozart*, p. 396.
7 Hotho, *Vorstudien*, p. 96.
8 Hotho, *Vorstudien*, p. 98.
9 F. R. Noske, *Musical Affinities and Dramatic Structure* (Studia Musicologica XII, Akadémiai Kiadó, 1970), pp. 196—202.
10 Abert, *Mozart*, p. 405.
11 Kierkegaard, *Either/Or*, p. 132.
12 Hotho, *Vorstudien*, p. 103.
13 Kierkegaard, *Either/Or*, p. 100.
14 B. Brecht, *Stücke*, XII (Aufbau-Verlag, Berlin, 1962), p. 181.
15 Agnes Heller, *A kierkegaardi esztétika és a zene. Érték és történelem.* [*Kierkegaardian Aesthetics and Music. Value and history*] (Magvető, 1969, pp. 351—2.
16 Kierkegaard, *Either/Or*, p. 97.
17 Jahn, *W. A. Mozart*, vol. II (Druck und Verlag von Breitkopf und Härtel, Leipzig, 1867), pp. 362—3.
18 Abert, *Mozart*.
19 Ibid., p. 410.
20 Jahn, *Mozart*, p. 367.
21 Ibid., p. 358.
22 Abert, *Mozart*, p. 412.
23 Noske, *Musical Affinities*, p. 201.
24 Bence Szabolcsi, *A melódia története* [*The History of Melody*] (Zeneműkiadó, 1957), p. 170.
25 József Újfalussy, *A valóság zenei képe* [*The Musical Image of Reality*] (Zeneműkiadó, 1962), p. 88.
26 Bence Szabolcsi, *Mozart* (Dick Manó kiadása, Budapest, 1921), p. 49.

27 G. Lukács, *Az esztétikum sajátossága*, vol. I [The Specificity of Aesthetics] (Akadémiai Kiadó, 1965), pp. 280—1.
    G. Lukács, *Goethe: Faust és Puskin helye a világirodalomban* (A Világirodalom I.c. tanulmánykötetben) [Goethe's *Faust* and Pushkin's place in world literature, in *World Literature*, vol. I] (Gondolat, 1969).
28 Jahn, *Mozart,* p. 670.
29 Noske, *Musical Affinities*, p. 197.
30 Péter Várnai, *Adalékok Verdi operáinak negativ tipizációjához*. [*Additions to the Negative Typecasting in Verdi's operas*] (Magyar Zene, 1966/5).
31 Abert, *Mozart*, p. 414.
32 Heller, *Kierkegaardian Aesthetics*, pp. 356—7.
33 Jahn, *Mozart*, p. 364.
34 Abert, *Mozart*, p. 416.
35 Jahn, *Mozart*, p. 264.
36 Abert, *Mozart*, p. 421.
37 It was Bence Szabolcsi who, in his lectures at the Academy of Music called attention to the obvious relationship of this part to the serenade music of Mozart and of this era in general.
38 Abert, *Mozart*, p. 424.
39 Heller, *Kierkegaardian Aesthetics*, p. 357.
40 Abert, *Mozart*, p. 429.
41 Hotho, *Vorstudien*, p. 129.
42 Abert, *Mozart*, p. 440.
43 J.-J. Rousseau, *Émile*, trs. B. Foxley (London, Dent, 1965), p. 315.
44 Abert, *Mozart*, p. 442.
45 Hegel, *Előadások a világtörténet filozófiájáról* [*Lectures on the Philosophy of World History*] (Akadémiai Kiadó, 1966), p. 688.
46 Hegel, *Esztétikai előadások* I [*Lectures on Aesthetics*, vol. I] (Akadémiai Kiadó, 1952), pp. 186—9.
47 Jahn, *Mozart*, p. 381.
48 Abert, *Mozart*, p. 444.
49 Kierkegaard, *Either/Or*, p. 132.
50 Noske, *Musical Affinities*, p. 197.
51 Abert, *Mozart*.
52 Noske, *Musical Affinities*, p. 198.
53 Schiller to Goethe 29 December 1797. *Der Briefwechsel zwischen Schiller und Goethe*, I. (Insel Verlag, 3 ausgabe), p. 460.
54 Goethe's reply to Schiller 30 December 1797. *The Correspondence between Goethe and Schiller* (Gondolat, 1963), pp. 276—7.

Contributors

Ferenc Fehér was, until 1986, lecturer in politics at La Trobe University, Melbourne, Australia. He is now senior lecturer in humanities at the New School for Social Research in New York. He was a student of Georg Lukács, a literary critic and a political dissident in Budapest till 1977. He is the author of *Dostoevsky and the Crisis of Individual* (1972), *Hungary, 1956 Revisited* (1982, with A. Heller) and *Dictatorship Over Needs* (1983, with A. Heller and G. Markus) and editor of *Political Legitimation in Communist Countries* (1982, with T. H. Rigby) and *Khrushchev and the Communist World* (1983, with R. F. Miller). He is widely published on aesthetic and political theory in several languages.

Géza Fodor, a former student of Georg Lukács, teaches theory of music at the Budapest Academy of Music. He is a well-known Hungarian opera critic and the author of *Music and Drama*. The latter includes his book on Mozart's operas, a chapter of which is published here.

Agnes Heller was, until 1986, reader in sociology at La Trobe University, Melbourne, Australia. She is now Professor of Philosophy at the New School for Social Research in New York. She was the best known student of Georg Lukács and until 1977 was active in Hungary as a philosopher and a political dissident. She is the author of *A Theory of Needs in Marx* (1977), *Renaissance Man* (1978), *A Theory of Feelings* (1978), *A Theory of History* (1981), *Hungary, 1956 Revisited* (with F. Fehér), *A Radical Philosophy* (1984), *Dictatorship Over Needs* (1983, with F. Fehér and G. Markus), *Everyday Life* (1984) and *The Power of Shame* (1985).

Mihály Vajda, a leading political dissident in Hungary for 15 years, and a former student of Georg Lukács, is now a politically unemployed language teacher and translator in his native country. He is the author of two books on Husserl's philosophy, and *Fascism and Mass Movement* (1978) and

The State and Socialism (1981). He is widely published on modern philosophy and political theory in several languages.

Sándor Radnóti, a former student of Georg Lukács, is a politically unemployed translator in Hungary and a well-known dissident. He is widely published on the theory of literature, arts and aesthetics in several languages.

Gáspár M. Tamás, a philosopher and a political dissident first in Rumania and later in Hungary, is at present a politically unemployed translator in Budapest and a well-known activist of the dissident movement. He is widely published on the philosophy of culture and on political theory, and is the author of *The Eye and the Hand* (in French).

Index

Abert, H. 150, 154, 157, 164, 168, 170,
  174, 184, 186, 187, 189, 191, 192,
  193, 204, 218, 219, 224, 227, 228,
  237
Absolute Spirit 63−4
  institutionalization of 63−5, 74−6,
  104
action painting 130
Adorno, Theodor 7, 14, 61, 67, 68, 69,
  70, 90, 99, 114
  'dialectic of enlightenment' 67−9
  elitism of 69−70
  and 'end of art' 67, 69
  Introduction to a Sociology of Music 70
  lyric poetry and music 7
  and rationality 67−70
  theory of music 67−70
  and Vienna School of New Music 14,
  68, 69
Aeschylus 106, 110, 112, 114
aesthetics; aesthetic theory 1−22, 71−3,
  119, 138
  of Adorno 7, 67−70
  in bourgeois (modern) period 10−13,
  15, 17
  deductive 13−14, 17, 18, 21−2
  emergence as independent sphere 1−4
  inductive 14−15, 17, 18, 21−2
  judgement 138
  of Lukács 7−8, 69
  and philosophy 1−4, 8
  and philosophy of history 2, 5−8, 11,
  13, 18, 20, 69
  realist and anti-realist 120
  and totality 21−2

and *Weltanschauung* 6−7, 10, 13, 14,
  19−22
  see also art; art criticism
African plastic art 13
Apollinaire 88
Arcimbaldi 11
Aristophanes 105, 112
Aristotle 5, 9, 10, 16, 42, 82, 103, 109
  Poetics 5
art 1−22, 63−5, 74−6, 104
  and bourgeois (modern) epoch 8−13
  Byzantine 122
  and commodity production 4
  criticism 14, 18, 21−2
  and decoration 121−5, 126, 141
  detachment from life 3−4, 80−1, 90
  distribution 62−3, 64, 73
  emancipation of 77, 84, 90, 91, 92, 93,
  97
  'end of art' 60−1, 63, 67, 70, 74
  experimental 69−70
  high 83, 86, 89, 93
  'high' and 'low' 61, 70, 81, 83−4, 85,
  88−9, 92, 99−100
  institutionalization 61, 62, 63, 64, 65
  low 82, 86, 88
  merger with life 66−7, 101
  modern 60, 70, 84, 86, 87, 88, 94
  'object content' 10, 12−13, 19−20
  as objectivation 63, 65
  ornament 128
  and pre-capitalist epoch 8−13, 15, 17,
  19
  production (creation) 5, 62−3, 64, 73
  'reality content' 10, 12−13, 19−20

reception 5, 20, 62−3, 64, 65, 73, 79,
    87, 89, 90, 91, 93, 95, 96, 98
representational 126, 127, 128
and self-creativity 73
and 'species values' 3−4, 6
and style 62, 63
universal concepts of 77, 78, 81, 82, 84,
    85, 87−8, 89, 92, 93, 94, 95, 96,
    100
'will to art' 79, 98
see also aesthetics, art works,
    autonomous art, culture
art works 78, 79, 81, 86−7, 89, 90
as form 81
historicity of 4, 5
artistic value 92
Austen, Jane 39
autonomous art 67, 78, 87, 93, 94, 96,
    101
avant-garde 60, 61, 62, 63, 85, 86, 89
see also modernism

Bach, Johann Sebastian 68, 211
Balázs, Bela 8
Balzac, Honoré de 8, 29, 31, 33, 41
Barthes, Roland 98
Bartók, Béla 15, 69, 95
Baudelaire, Charles 88
Benjamin, Walter 10, 20, 21, 72, 88, 99,
    101
Bertati; *Don Giovanni* 154
Bloch, Ernst 90
Braque, G. 62
Brecht, Bertolt 100−1, 114, 166
Bürger, Peter 61, 62, 63, 64, 65, 66, 67,
    70

Cervantes, Miguel de 28, 43, 59
Don Quixote 24, 28
Cézanne, Paul 135, 145
Chamfort 109
Cimabue 138
cultural egalitarianism 67, 72−3
Culture
high 2, 82, 96, 100−1
'high and low' 70−3, 83, 97
homogenization of 72−3
low 82, 87, 93, 96, 97, 98, 100−1
mass 71, 77−99
mediations in 73
mythologies of 98

Dadaism 62, 66
Dante 94
Davidov, J. 99
Defoe, Daniel 29, 30−1, 43
Robinson Crusoe 29, 30, 31, 38
Dickens, Charles 36, 48
Dostoevsky, F. 8, 66, 194
Duchamp, Marcel 65

Eco, Umberto 89−91
Engels, Friedrich 51, 58
epic 7, 23−59
bourgeois 33, 38, 39, 43, 46, 47, 48, 50,
    51, 58
characters of 50−1, 53
and destiny 48, 49−50, 53, 56
and education 47
heroes 28−9, 32, 33, 43, 44, 48, 49,
    54, 56
and 'human essence' 24, 25, 26
and the individual 44−5, 50−1
and the novel 24, 26, 27, 28, 30, 32, 33,
    34, 42−5, 47−50
and organic community 25, 30, 34−5,
    37, 41, 43, 47, 51, 55, 58
poetry 23, 30, 42, 53, 58
thematic representation 32, 33, 34−5,
    37, 43, 49−50
and time 55−7
unity of man and world 24, 46
and values 41, 42−3, 57
Euripides 9, 103−17
Alcestis 115, 117
Andromache 110
Electra 110
Hecuba 110
Medea 111
The Trojan Women 111
Eyck, Jan van 143

Felsenstein, W. 203
Feuerbach, Ludwig 8, 51, 57
Fichte, J. G. 101
Fiedler, Konrad 14, 144
Fielding, Henry 8, 39, 43
Amelia 43
Tom Jones 47, 56
Flaubert, Gustave 8
L'Éducation Sentimentale 24, 55
Francastel, Pierre 146, 147

France, Anatole 66
Fülep, Lajos 136, 145

Gadamer, Hans-Georg 82, 97
Gauguin, Paul 72, 145
Gautier, Théophile 14
genius 17—18
Giorgione 11
Godard, Jean-Luc 100
Goethe, Johann Wolfgang von 9, 20, 23,
    25, 35, 39, 42, 56, 67, 90, 94, 178,
    184, 245, 246
  Wilhelm Meister 47
Goldmann, Lucien 39, 40, 41, 42, 44, 52,
    59
Goldsmith, Oliver 35, 36, 39, 79
Gombrich, E. H. 120, 127, 128, 132, 136
  Art and Illusion 120, 127
Gorgonzola 11
Greece, ancient 6, 26, 106, 110
  art 45, 58, 133
  epic 26
  tragedy 26, 106, 112
Gris, Juan 62

Habermas, Jürgen 34
Handel, G. F. 172
Hauser, Arnold 65
Hegel, G. W. F. 2, 5, 6, 7, 23, 24, 25, 30,
    32, 33, 36, 41, 43, 44, 50, 63—4, 69,
    101, 108, 164, 225
  Aesthetics 6, 108
  Phenomenology of Mind 31
Heidegger, Martin 40, 59, 148
Heller, Agnes 59, 143, 167, 186, 193
Hindemith, Paul 95
Homer 11, 12, 13, 23
  Odyssey 51
Hotho 151, 157, 162, 165, 191, 216
Huxley, Aldous; *Brave New World* 65

Jacobins 34, 173
Jahn 168, 174, 184, 187, 190, 227

Kafka, Franz 11, 34
Kandinsky, Wassily 95, 123
Kant, Immanuel 2, 5, 14, 17, 18, 19, 71,
    94, 101
Karátson, Gabor 130, 136, 142—3
Keller, Gottfried; *Der grüne Heinrich* 47,
    56

Kierkegaard, Søren 5, 8, 66, 150, 156,
    164, 165, 166, 167, 201, 203, 235
kitsch 89—91
Klee, Paul 95
Kleist, H. 117
Kokoschka, Oskar 95
Kristeva, Julia 66

Leibniz, Gottfried von 68
Leonardo da Vinci 91, 144
Lessing, G. E. 7, 11, 20, 107
literaturi; modern 66
Lorenzetti, Ambrogio 124
Lowenthal, Leo 80, 83, 98
Lukács, Georg 5, 7, 8, 11, 19, 20, 23, 24,
    25, 28, 32, 33, 42, 44, 48, 55, 56, 59,
    66, 69, 93, 94, 121, 122, 123, 125,
    127, 128, 136, 142
  *Aesthetics (The Specificity of the
    Aesthetic)* 48, 93, 107, 124
  The History of Modern Drama 19
  The Theory of the Novel 23, 24, 26, 28,
    29, 31, 32, 44, 46, 55
lyric poetry 7

Mahler, G. 68
Mallarmé, Stéphane 66
Mandeville, Bernard 43
Mann, Thomas 235
  Doctor Faustus 68
  Joseph and his Brothers 47
Marcuse, Herbert 95, 99
  An Essay on Liberation 101
Martini, Simone 124, 129
Marx, Karl 2, 4, 5, 24, 25, 27, 30, 34, 40,
    43, 44, 45, 49, 53, 57, 99
  Economic—Philosophical Manuscripts
    53
  Grundrisse 30
  Theories of Surplus Value 99
  Zur Judenfrage 34
May, Karl 90
Mayakovsky, Vladimir 88
Michelangelo 11, 144
modernity; modernism 65, 70, 85
Molière 166, 186, 197
  Le Misanthrope 11
Mondrian, Piet 120, 123
Mörike 165, 238, 239

Mozart, W. A. 153—243
   bel canto 184
   and modern age 225—7, 243, 245
   musical and stage drama 178—9, 198,
      204, 221
   representation of Don Giovanni 197—8

Nietzsche, F. 100, 101, 103, 104, 105,
      106, 107, 128
   The Birth of Tragedy 103, 104
   The Twilight of the Gods 105
Norris, Frank 23
Noske, F. R. 163, 173, 176
Novalis 8, 99
novel 23—59
   and alienation 23, 39, 44
   ambivalence of 26—8, 32, 36, 43, 57
   and authenticity 40
   Bildungsroman 47, 56
   and bourgeois society 23, 26—8
   and capitalism 24—7
   critics of 25
   and defetishization 48
   duality of self and world 28, 29
   and emancipation 26—32, 36, 41
   as epic 23, 24, 26, 27, 28, 30, 33, 38,
      39
   and everyday life 37—9
   and the family 35—6
   fatality and chance 51—6
   and fetishism 27, 33, 42, 52—4, 58
   formlessness of 26
   and the fortuitous individual 46—51
   genealogical 36
   heroes of 28—9, 32—3, 35—7, 43—6,
      54—5
   historical 33
   and individuality 44—5, 46—8, 50—1,
      57
   and market 40, 42, 52—4
   'problematic individual' 44, 46
   and production 33
   and public sphere 34—7, 50
   and reification 28—31, 33, 43, 55
   and representation 30, 32, 33, 41, 44
   and self-creation 31, 33
   and self-education 47—9
   and sentimentality 42
   and society 26—9, 33—5, 44, 57—8
   superiority 30—1
   and time 55—7

   and totality 24—7
   'transcendental homelessness' 24—7
   universality of 40
   and values 32, 39, 41—4, 56, 57

Paduano, Claudio 117
painting
   illusionist; illusionism 101, 120, 121,
      125, 126, 131, 134, 137, 138—9,
      140, 141, 142, 143, 144, 145, 146,
      147
   impressionism 127, 134
   modern 131, 145, 147
   post-illusionism 146
   and relation to visible world 119—21,
      124, 125—6, 127
   and representation 121—38, 141, 147
   signification and representation 127—8
   stylistic changes in 129, 132
Picasso, Pablo 62, 120
Plato 11, 105, 111
Plotinus 1
post-modernity, postmodernism 92
   theories of 60—1, 66, 67, 69, 70, 74

Racine, Jean 11
Radnóti, Sandor 71
Ranke, Leopold von 26
Raphael 9
Raphael, Max 136, 137
rationalization 61, 68
   of art 61
   of music 68—9
   see also art, institutionalization of
religion 63—4
Rembrandt 123, 124, 144
Renaissance 133, 134
Richardson, Samuel 35, 36
Rilke, Rainer Maria 4, 96
Rousseau, Jean-Jacques 2, 11, 35, 219
   La Nouvelle Héloïse 2

Schelling, F. W. J. 5, 78, 81, 101
Schiller, J. F. 20, 23, 25, 56, 81, 85, 245
Schlegel, Friedrich 8, 66, 78, 81, 83, 101
Schoenberg, Arnold 69, 95
Schopenhauer, Arthur 104
Schubert, Franz 183
sculpture 129
Seurat, Georges 145
Shakespeare, William 108, 114

Shaw, George Bernard 198
Socrates 104, 105, 106, 112
sophists 104, 110, 112
Sophocles 9, 112
Spinoza, Baruch 52
Stendhal 186, 193
Sterne, Laurence 8
Stravinsky, Igor 68, 69, 95
Swift, Jonathan 43, 59
Szabolcsi, Bence 184

Tarkovsky; *Rublyov* 84
taste 87, 139
    community of 87—8
    and idea of form 87
    judgement of 15—16, 138, 140
Tieck, Ludwig 99
Tintoretto 120, 144
Tinyanov 86
Tirso da Molina 186, 197, 225
Tolstoy, Leo 23, 39
    War and Peace 39

tragedy 106, 107, 113, 115
    modern 108

Újfalussy, József 181

Van Gogh, Vincent 135, 145
Vasari 9—10
Verdi, Giuseppe 185
    Rigoletto 213
Vernant, J.-P. 112
Vico, Gianbattista 13
Virgil 13

Wagner, Richard 68, 104, 176
Weber, Max 16, 43, 61, 65, 67, 68, 69
    theory of music 67—8
    The Sociology of Music 67
Weil, Simone 104
Wilder, Thornton 52
Winckelmann, Johann Joachim 9, 107,
    184